Insights 2

A Content-based Approach to Academic Preparation

Jan Frodesen
University of California, Santa Barbara

Christine Holten
University of California, Los Angeles

Linda Jensen
University of California, Los Angeles

Lyn Repath-Martos
University of California, Los Angeles

Donna Brinton, Project Coordinator
University of California, Los Angeles

 LONGMAN

Insights 2: A Content-based Approach to Academic Preparation

Pearson Education, 10 Bank Street, White Plains, NY 10606

Editorial Director: Joanne Dresner
Senior Acquisitions Editor: Janet Aitchison
Development Editor: Kathleen M. Smith
Production Editor: Liza Pleva
Text design: Christine Gehring Wolf
Cover design: Pinho Graphics
Composition: Publication Services
Photo and text credits appear on pages 203–205.

Library of Congress Cataloging-in-Publication Data

Frodesen, Jan, [Date.]
    Insights 2 : a content-based ESL text for academic preparation /
Jan Frodesen . . . [et al.] ; Donna Brinton, project coordinator.
        p.   cm.
    ISBN 0-201-89857-8
    1. English language—Textbooks for foreign speakers. 2. English
language—Composition and exercises. I. Brinton, Donna.
II. Title.
PE1128.J48   1997
428.2'4--dc21   96-46288
                                                        CIP

17 18 19 20   V012   15 14 13 12 11

Dedication

We dedicate this book to the content area professors who renewed our faith in the possibility of excellent university teaching: Carolee Caffrey (biology), Kerry Ferris (sociology), Steven Spiegel (political science), and Robert Hurt (astronomy).

Contents

Acknowledgments

This project was envisioned and conceived under the close scrutiny of Joanne Dresner, Editorial Director at Addison Wesley Longman. It was nurtured throughout its process by Allen Ascher, Senior Acquisitions Editor, with assistance in the later stages by Janet Aitchison, Acquisitions Editor, and had all its rough edges smoothed over by Kathy Smith, formerly of Addison Wesley Longman, who saw us through the development stage, spending hours of her time editing our prose and gently suggesting changes that greatly improved the pedagogical quality of the finished product. Finally, it was polished in the production stages by Liza Pleva. Under Liza's supervision, the manuscript took shape and began to resemble a real book rather than a collection of manuscript pages. Additional help was provided by Janet Battiste, Development Editor, by Amy Durfy, Senior Administrative Assistant, and by Polli Heyden, who assisted us with permissions. To all the above individuals, we express our extreme appreciation and admiration for their professionalism.

More than to anyone else, perhaps, we are indebted to Professors Carolee Caffrey, Kerry Ferris, Steven Speigel, and Robert Hurt for so kindly allowing us to invade their classrooms, tape their lectures, borrow their reference materials, and use their course readings and assignments as the cornerstones of this project. Without their support, consent, and enthusiasm for our project, this book would not exist.

For their indispensable services (such as videotaping and editing, tape transcription, library runs, artwork, photocopying, proofreading, editing, etc.), we are truly indebted to the following work study assistants in the UCLA Department of TESL and Applied Linguistics: Joseph Choi, Zalika Davis, Eric Franklin, Rahel Getachew, Beth Gregory, Jerry Ching-Jen Huang, James Jauregui, Edward Kim, Clinton Lee, Greg Lyon, Margarita Mkrtchyan, Elysabeth Nguyen, Nicholas Nguyen, Susan Reese, Ruth Rivera, Soo Bin Shin, James Suh, Jimmy Trinh, Mike Wang, Ha Cuc Emma Truong, Vu-Uyen Nguyen, Sasha Mosely, Kevin Tucker, Veronica Peet, Anna McKay, Julie Lin, Amy Barranco, Eunice Quezon, Vy Nguyen, Catherine Trinidad, Shannon Cisch, Maura Newberry, Darius Degher, Fumitaka Hayashi, Joy Jacob, and Sung Park.

Additional thanks are due to Todd Darling of On-Time Off-Line for his assistance in editing the videotape and to Sandy Wallace and Mila August at UCLA for providing administrative assistance and for tolerating the chaos that often ensued as we scrambled to meet deadlines.

We are also grateful to those who piloted our materials or otherwise gave us feedback: Foong Ha Yap, Susan Strauss, Kathy Howard, and Jo Hilder at UCLA and Judy Gough, Agnes Kang, Steven Lasswell, and Randy Rightmire at UCSB. These individuals pointed out many problems in the manuscript that we had overlooked in our initial development of the materials and served as the inspiration for numerous activities that were incorporated into the final product. Needless to say, any remaining flaws are due to oversights or shortcomings on our part.

Finally, we express our sincere gratitude to our families and friends for their patience and support, and we wish to acknowledge Professors Marianne Celce-Murcia and Dorothy Danielson for being our mentors and encouraging us to reach our full professional potential.

Introduction

OVERVIEW

Insights 2 is designed to equip ESL students with the ability to cope with the English language demands of academia. The text is focused primarily on the academic skills of reading, writing, listening, and speaking, with an emphasis on writing. We have integrated these skills with short grammar and vocabulary activities, all in a content-based approach. A basic premise of the text is that, in order to effectively approach any college writing task, students must be prepared to synthesize material from multiple authentic sources, gleaning information from lectures and written and visual sources. For the best result, students must use all four skills of reading, writing, listening, and speaking to produce a written assignment.

  Insights 2 is targeted at matriculated ESL students, specifically, those enrolled in community college or university courses that are prerequisite to the freshman composition requirement. It is also appropriate for the final level of intensive language programs, where students are being prepared to enter English-medium colleges and universities.

RATIONALE

Many ESL students enrolled in U.S. colleges enter higher education with a fairly high degree of general English language proficiency. Studies have shown, however, that this proficiency is not sufficient for dealing with the complex demands of the university. These students must gain a proficiency in the register of academic English (Cummins, 1979; Collier, 1987). The goal of this text is to provide students with academic language skills that will enable them to succeed in their courses across the curriculum.

  Much insight into English for Academic Purposes (EAP) curricular issues is provided by the body of literature that describes the academic language needs of these students (Kroll, 1979; Ostler, 1980; Johns, 1981; Bridgeman & Carlson, 1984; Horowitz, 1986; Santos, 1988; Spack, 1988; Fulwiler & Young, 1990). Among the recommendations made are the following:

1. Authentic materials and tasks gathered from across the disciplines should form the core of the EAP curriculum. Tasks should provide students with the tools for synthesizing information from multiple sources, for reading critically, and for efficiently processing academic information. Similarly, the development of learning strategies and metacognitive/metalinguistic skills should be introduced and reinforced.

2. Personal or writer-based writing, although it may lead to more reader-based texts, should not be the end goal of the academic writing curriculum. Emphasis should be placed instead on the research paper, summary writing, and analytical writing (including essay-exam writing).

3. The EAP curriculum should avoid "one-shot" assignments and instead require students to follow a more sequenced approach (involving notetaking, summarizing, journal writing, multiple drafts of writing assignments, etc.) as preliminary steps toward a more polished product.

4. Listening in an academic context requires the development of the same comprehension and critical analytical skills as those required for successful academic reading and writing.

5. Students should be encouraged to be active researchers or ethnographers of the academic discourse communities in which they are engaged.

APPROACH

Insights 2 has grown out of the authors' long-term experience with matriculated ESL students and represents our effort to construct a meaningful and motivating content-based curriculum that addresses their academic language needs. Materials from various disciplines (in the form of authentic university reading assignments and lectures) form the cornerstone of the teaching materials. Each unit simulates the process that ESL students actually experience in their university courses as they attend lectures, do assigned course readings, participate in discussion, and elucidate ideas in written form (e.g., midterm exams, final exams, and term papers). Thus, each unit weaves together listening, speaking, reading, and writing about one high-interest topic from a university discipline.

The materials acknowledge the need for university students to command a high level of accuracy and fluency in their oral and written output. Therefore, grammar and vocabulary development are given an integral and integrated place. The treatment of grammar and lexicon in these materials always derives from and occurs in a rich and authentic discourse context. The materials encourage students to generate, analyze, and revise text to practice reading and writing certain discourse-governed and grammatically based structures within the context of larger discourse.

AUDIENCE AND PURPOSE

Insights 2 addresses the needs of community college and university students who are enrolled in courses that are prerequisite to freshman composition. These students need instruction that focuses on oral language development, attention to grammatical accuracy and vocabulary enrichment, and experience in reading and producing a variety of academic text types. The units consist of videotaped lecture segments, accompanying academic readings, and related literary passages. In the related language and writing tasks, the focus is on schema building for listening and reading comprehension purposes, academic and rhetorical strategy development, and refinement of vocabulary and grammar skills needed to comprehend, discuss, and write about the unit content.

UNIT ORGANIZATION

1. *Insights 2* consists of four units drawn from the physical, life, and social sciences. These discipline-specific units are further subdivided into three chapters, each of which treats the same high-interest topic from a variety of perspectives.

2. Each of the four units contains three chapters—Introduction, Exploration, and Expansion.

   - *Introduction*   The first chapter of the unit serves as a general introduction to the topic to be explored. The readings and lecture segments are accessible to those with little or no prior knowledge of the topic, and they aim to generate interest and enhance understanding of the issues.

   - *Exploration*   The second chapter of each unit introduces students to the primary academic source materials (i.e., academic readings and lectures). The related tasks promote critical understanding and require students to synthesize material from a variety of sources.

   - *Expansion*   In the third chapter of each unit, the readings and lectures take a larger view of the academic concepts. Tasks in this chapter require students to connect the knowledge gained from the previous chapters to human life and concerns as represented in the literature readings. The final writing assignment requires students to synthesize and evaluate the issues of the unit and to present their point of view in an academic essay.

3. All lecture segments are authentic and were videotaped in actual university classes. The videotaped materials are supplemented by the authentic reading materials assigned for this course and other topically related readings (including literature). Many of the unit's tasks replicate those used in the actual content classes.

4. Special features contained in *Insights 2* include Academic Strategies, Targeting Vocabulary, and Targeting Grammar. These features, located throughout the chapters, help students expand their range of metacognitive strategies, enlarge their general academic and field-specific vocabulary, edit for common language errors, and employ more sophisticated grammatical structures in their oral and written output. All issues pertaining to language are systematically addressed from a discourse perspective.

5. The chapters contain multiple "writing to learn" opportunities, including journal and reading-response assignments along with academically based writing assignments. These academically based writing assignments represent typical genres found in the university. All of these assignments take a process approach and are set up so that students have multiple opportunities to draft and polish their ideas and language.

CHAPTER ORGANIZATION

The three thematically interwoven chapters contained in each discipline-specific unit are further subdivided into the following sections: Exploring the Concepts, Working with Sources, and Integrating Perspectives.

1. **Exploring the Concepts** This section encourages students to apply their background knowledge as they approach the new concepts and, therefore, promotes interest in the content. The activities provide a foundation for the academic material that follows in Working with Sources. Subsections that may be included are

   - *Exploring through Visual Images* Visuals from everyday life (e.g., drawings, photographs, cartoons) activate the students' understanding of the content to which they will be exposed.

   - *Exploring Background Knowledge* Students' prior knowledge about the topic is tapped through a variety of activities such as brainstorming and values clarification.

   - *Exploring through Writing* Students are encouraged to share initial reactions to the content via journal entries or quickwrites.

   - *Exploring through Discussion* Students share personal experiences and opinions and apply concepts to real-life situations.

2. **Working with Sources** Students encounter introductory or core readings and videotaped lecture segments that present the basic issues or concepts. Subsections that may be included are

   - *Understanding through Visual Images* Visuals such as photos, charts, and graphs from popular sources and academic textbooks allow students to preview the issues contained in the listening and reading tasks that follow.

   - *Understanding through Listening* The lecture segment expands students' information about the academic content. Graphic organizers are utilized to aid students in recognizing the important ideas and the structure of the lecture. The related tasks encourage critical analysis, guiding students in their notetaking and listening comprehension.

   - *Understanding through Reading* The reading presents students with information that is either directly linked to the listening or that expands on the topic. Students are guided toward a fuller understanding of the text through tasks that encourage text processing.

- *Understanding through Literature*   A literature excerpt or short piece that relates to the academic reading and listening segments allows students to explore the topic from a literary perspective, fostering critical application of the unit's issues.

3. ***Integrating Perspectives***   In this section the concept or issue is examined in greater depth, either by offering an additional perspective or by asking students to apply the concepts learned to a new situation. Students demonstrate their understanding by applying, analyzing, or evaluating the concepts of the unit. Subsections that may be included are

   - *Applying the Concepts*   This activity promotes synthesis or application of the information from Working with Sources, often through the use of graphic organizers or visuals.

   - *Analyzing through Visual Images*   Students react critically to visual images such as cartoons or illustrations, drawing on their understanding of the topic.

   - *Analyzing through Discussion*   Through discussion (e.g., ranking or problem-solving tasks), students enhance their understanding of the reading and videotaped lecture material to which they have been exposed.

   - *Evaluating through Literature*   Students read and react to a piece of unadapted literature (e.g., a short story, an extract from a longer work of fiction) and critically apply one of the frameworks or theories from the unit to this work.

   - *Evaluating through Writing*   This writing task allows students to synthesize the main ideas from the sources, employing their expanded knowledge of grammar and vocabulary. Within each unit, the writing tasks progress from personal to academic. Each unit culminates in a writing assignment for which students are provided clear guidelines and instructions to enhance their academic writing skills.

REFERENCES

Bridgeman, B., & Carlson, S. (1984). *Survey of academic writing tasks required of graduate and undergraduate foreign students.* TOEFL Research Report No. 15. Princeton, NJ: Educational Testing Service.

Collier, V. P. (1987). Age and rate of acquisition of second language for academic purposes. *TESOL Quarterly, 21*(4), 617–641.

Cummins, J. (1979). Linguistic interdependence and the educational development of bilingual children. *Review of Educational Research, 49*(2), 222–251.

Fulwiler, T., & Young, A. (Eds.) (1990). *Programs that work: Models and methods for writing across the curriculum.* Portsmouth, NH: Boynton/Cook Heinemann.

Horowitz, D. M. (1986). What professors actually require: Academic tasks for the ESL classroom. *TESOL Quarterly, 20*(3), 445-462.

Johns, A. M. (1981). Necessary English: A faculty survey. *TESOL Quarterly, 15*(1), 51–57.

Kroll, B. (1979). A survey of the writing needs of foreign and American college freshmen. *ELT Journal, 33*(3), 219–226.

Ostler, S. (1980). A survey of academic needs for advanced ESL. *TESOL Quarterly, 14*(4), 489–502.

Santos, T. (1988). Professors' reactions to the academic writing of non-native speaking students. *TESOL Quarterly, 22*(1), 69–90.

Spack, R. (1988). Initiating ESL students into the academic discourse community: How far should we go? *TESOL Quarterly, 22*(1), 29–51.

Insights from Biology

Introduction:

Innate and Learned Animal Behavior

In the past, biologists often categorized animal behavior as either genetic or learned. Today, however, most animal behaviors are seen as a combination of these two forces. This unit explores the extent to which various animal behaviors are influenced by genetics and molded by the environment.

Exploring the Concepts

Exploring through Visual Images

The illustrations on the next page show animal behavior—some behaviors are influenced by genes, others are learned.

Task 1: For each illustration, discuss with a partner the type of behavior, its probable origin (genetic or learned), and its function(s). Then fill in the grid. In the fourth column, list any unanswered questions you have about the behavior. The first one has been done for you.

Garden Spider Spinning a Web

Male Frigate Bird Courting a Mate

Squirrel Opening a Peanut Shell

Cheetah Marking Its Territory

Type of Behavior	Origin	Function(s)	Your Questions
1. spider spinning a web	genetic	to catch insects and other prey; to provide a home for the spider	Can the spider spin webs from birth? Does it make the same type of web every time? Are all web patterns the same, or do they differ from spider to spider?
2.			
3.			
4.			

Exploring Background Knowledge

Task 2: Read the following two passages, which explain *genetically programmed* and *learned* behavior. In groups or with a partner, make a list of other examples of each type of behavior in human beings and animals.

Genetically Programmed Behavior

Spider webs are objects of beauty and marvels of engineering. The construction of a classic web used to capture prey requires complex behavior. For example, a garden spider, as immortalized in the children's story *Charlotte's Web* by E. B. White, spins a new web every day in the early morning hours before dawn. From an initial attachment point, she strings a horizontal thread. From the middle of that thread she drops a vertical thread to a lower attachment point. Pulling it taut creates a Y, the center of which will be the hub of the finished web. The spider adds a few more radial supports and a few surrounding "framing" threads. Then she fills in all the radial spokes according to a set of rules. Finally, she lays down a spiral of sticky threads with regular spacing and attachment points to the radial spokes. This remarkable feat of construction takes only half an hour, but it requires thousands of specific movements performed in just the right sequence. Where is the blueprint for Charlotte's web? How does she acquire the construction skills needed to build it?

The blueprint is coded in the genes and built into the spider's nervous system as a motor "program," or score. Learning plays no role in the expression of that complex blueprint. Newly hatched spiders disperse to new locations and usually spin their webs without ever having experienced a web built by an adult of their species. Nevertheless, they build perfect webs the first time; each of the thousands of movements happens in just the right sequence. It is remarkable that the genetic code and the simple nervous system of a spider can contain and express behavior as complex as spinning an orb web.

Source: William K. Purves, Gordon H. Orians, and H. Craig Heller (1995). *Life: The science of biology* (4th ed., p. 1029). Sunderland, MA: Sinauer Associates.

Learned Behavior

Learning appears to be an essential component in determining some animal behaviors. Among at least some animal species, the capacity to learn specific kinds of information may be especially pronounced during certain early stages of development. This form of learning, which seems to be time dependent, is called imprinting.

For example, some birds are able to walk a few hours after hatching and will traipse after their mother as she moves away from the nest. The young birds must learn something when they walk after an object, because they form an attachment to their guide and hurry after it whenever it moves off. However, if young chicks or goslings are not offered any object to follow within a couple of days after hatching, they lose their readiness to imprint. Thus it appears that the young animals are primed during a short sensitive period early in life to form a learned attachment to a moving object, normally their mother.

Source: Cecie Starr and Ralph Taggart (1989). *Biology: The unity and diversity of life* (5th ed., pp. 811–812). Belmont, CA: Wadsworth.

Working with Sources

UNDERSTANDING THROUGH VISUAL IMAGES

COMMITTED reprinted by permission of United Feature Syndicate, Inc.

TASK 3: This cartoon shows a young male lion cub about to learn from the example of his father. In groups, discuss the humor of the cartoon.

TASK 4: The cartoon portrays a clear division between appropriate behavior for male and female lions. Write a journal entry stating your opinion about whether gender-appropriate roles (in animals or in humans) are largely learned or innate. Share your journal entry with a partner.

UNDERSTANDING THROUGH READING

The following text makes a distinction between behavior that is learned and behavior that is genetically programmed. It further explains how scientists determine whether a behavior is genetically determined or learned.

TASK 5: Skim the text to locate the section that explains the procedure used by scientists. Then read the excerpt and write a two-sentence summary of the procedure.

GENETICALLY DETERMINED BEHAVIOR

William K. Purves, Gordon H. Orians, and H. Craig Heller

[1]   A behavior that is genetically determined rather than learned is also called a **fixed action pattern**. Such behavior is highly stereotypic, that is, performed the same way every time. It is also species-specific; there is very little variation in the way different individuals of the same species perform the behavior. The behavior is expressed differently, however, in even closely related species. For example, different species of spiders spin webs of different designs.

[2]   Fixed action patterns require no learning or prior experience for their expression, and they are generally not modified by learning. Another spider example illustrates this point. Spiders spin other structures in addition to webs for capturing prey. Most spiders lay their eggs in a cocoon that they form by spinning a base plate, building up the walls (inside of which they lay the eggs), and spinning a lid to close the cocoon. Although this behavior requires thousands of individual movements, it is performed exactly the same way every time and is not modified by experience. If the spider is moved to a new location after she finishes the base plate, she will continue to spin the sides of the cocoon, lay her eggs (which fall out the bottom), and

spin the lid. If she is placed on her previously completed base plate the next time she is ready to begin a cocoon, she will spin a new base plate over the old one as if it were not there. If she is nutritionally deprived and runs out of silk in the middle of spinning a cocoon, she will complete all the thousands of movements in a pantomime of cocoon building. Once started, the cocoon-building motor score runs from beginning to end, and it can be started only at the beginning.

[3]   Fixed action patterns are good material for studying the mechanisms of animal behavior. We can study their genetics and the sequence of events whereby gene expression eventually results in a behavior; the influence of hormones on the development and expression of the behavior; and the detailed neurophysiology that underlies the behavior. First, however, we must demonstrate that a given behavior *is* genetically determined. One powerful way of proving genetic determination is to deprive the animal of any opportunity to learn the behavior in question, then see if that behavior is expressed.

Deprivation Experiments

[4]   In a deprivation experiment, an animal is reared so that it is deprived of all experience relevant to the behavior under study. For example, a tree squirrel was reared in isolation, on a liquid diet, and in a cage

without soil or other particulate matter. When the young squirrel was given a nut, it put the nut in its mouth and ran around the cage. Eventually it oriented toward a corner of the cage and made stereotypic digging movements, placed the nut in the corner, went through the motions of refilling the imaginary hole, and ended by tamping the nonexistent soil with its nose. The squirrel had never handled a food object and had never experienced soil, yet the fixed action patterns involved in burying its nut were fully expressed.

[5]   Deprivation experiments occur naturally. Many species, especially insects living in seasonal environments, have life cycles of one year and the generations do not overlap: The adults lay eggs and die before the eggs hatch or the young mature into adults. Learning from adults of the parental generation is impossible in such species, so the complex behavior necessary for survival and reproductive success must be genetically programmed. Web spinning by spiders is an example of complex behavior in species that may have no opportunity to learn from other members of their species.

Fixed Action Patterns versus Learned Behavior

[6]   The ability to learn and to modify behavior as a result of experience is often highly adaptive. Most of human behavior is the result of learning. Why then are so many behavior patterns in so many species genetically determined and not modifiable? We've already considered one answer to that question. If role models and opportunities to learn are not available, there is no alternative to programmed behavior. Fixed action patterns also can be adaptive when mistakes are costly or dangerous. Mating with a member of the wrong species is a costly mistake; the function of much of courtship behavior is to guarantee correct species recognition. In an environment in which incorrect as well as correct models exist, learning the wrong pattern

of courtship behavior is possible. Fixed action patterns governing mating behavior can prevent such mistakes.

[7]   Many behavior patterns are intricate interactions of genetically programmed elements and elements modified by experience. One example that has been the subject of elegant experiments is bird song. For most species, such as the white-crowned sparrow, learning is an essential step in the acquisition of song. If the eggs of white-crowned sparrows are hatched in an incubator and the young male birds are reared in isolation from the song of their species, their adult songs will be an unusual assemblage of sounds. This species cannot express its species-specific song without hearing that song as a nestling.

[8]   Studies of what birds can learn and when they can learn, however, reveal strong genetic limits to the modifiability of their behavior through experience. In the case of a white-crowned sparrow, it must hear its species' song within a narrow **critical period** during its development. Once this critical period has passed, the bird cannot learn to sing its species-specific song regardless of how many role models it experiences. What a bird can learn during its critical period is also severely limited, as revealed by experiments on hand-reared chaffinches that were played various tape recordings of bird songs during their critical periods. If exposed to the songs of other species, the chaffinches did not learn them. They also did not learn a chaffinch song played backward or with the elements scrambled. Even if they heard a chaffinch song played in pure tones, they did not form a template. If they heard a normal chaffinch song along with all these other sounds, however, they developed templates and learned to sing the proper song the following spring. Thus the chaffinch is genetically programmed to recognize the appropriate song to learn and when to learn it.

Source: (1995). *Life: The science of biology* (4th ed., pp. 1030–1034). Sunderland, MA: Sinauer Associates.

TASK 6: The examples of animal behavior from the reading are listed here. Explain what each example shows about the origins of animal behavior. The first one has been done for you.

1. Infant squirrels raised in a cage who had never experienced soil or nuts nonetheless demonstrated digging and burying behavior.

   Explanation: <u>Digging and burying behavior is innate in squirrels. In other words,</u>

   <u>this behavior is not learned but is genetically programmed.</u>

2. Spiders continue to perform the complex motions of cocoon spinning even when interrupted (e.g., when they are transplanted from their cocoon base or when they run out of silk).

   Explanation: _____

   _____

3. Many species of insects have a life cycle of one year and thus the generations do not overlap, yet the young manifest the same behavior as the parent generation.

   Explanation: _____

   _____

4. The song patterns of young male white-crowned sparrows hatched in an incubator do not resemble those of their parents but are an unusual assemblage of sounds.

   Explanation: _____

   _____

5. Chaffinches who were exposed during their critical period to recordings of bird songs of other species did not learn to sing those songs.

   Explanation: _____

   _____

Targeting Grammar: Timeless Conditionals

One type of conditional sentence in English is the *timeless conditional*. Timeless conditionals are used to express the idea that if a certain condition holds true, the result will usually or always be the same. These conditional sentences consist of two clauses:

1. the subordinate clause (containing a verb in the present tense)
2. the main clause (containing a verb in the present or future tense)

The subordinate clause is introduced by the subordinating word *if*. Notice that the word *if* in this type of conditional sentence means *when* or *whenever*.

CONDITION: SUBORDINATE CLAUSE (Present Tense Verb)	RESULTING BEHAVIOR: MAIN CLAUSE (Present or Future Tense Verb)
If the spider **is moved** to a new location after she finishes the base plate,	she **will continue** to spin the sides of the cocoon, **lay** her eggs (which fall out the bottom), and **spin** the lid.
If young chaffinches **are deprived** of hearing chaffinch songs and **are exposed** to the songs of other species,	they **do** not **learn** them.

TASK 7: The following sentences represent ideas taken from the reading. The first half of each incomplete sentence presents conditions that always lead to a certain behavior. Complete the missing half of the sentence, paying attention to the correct use of verb tense (i.e., present tense in the subordinate clause and present or future tense in the main clause). The first one has been done for you.

1. If a spider begins to spin a cocoon and is moved from her original base plate, _____

   <u>she will continue to spin the cocoon.</u> _____

2. If the spider runs out of silk while spinning a cocoon, _____

   _____

3. If a role model or an opportunity to learn is not available, _____

   _____

4. If scientists play a chaffinch song in pure tones to chaffinches who have been deprived of chaffinch songs since birth, _____

   _____

5. However, if these chaffinches hear a normal chaffinch song, _____

   _____

TASK 8: Rewrite each of the situations as a timeless conditional sentence. The first one has been done for you.

1. Mother goats that do not nuzzle or lick their newborns within five to ten minutes after birth do not recognize the infant as their own.

   <u>If mother goats do not nuzzle or lick their newborns within five to ten minutes</u>

   <u>after birth, they do not recognize the infants as their own.</u>

2. Kangaroo rats who hear the sound of a rattlesnake can avoid the rattlesnake bite by jumping backwards.

   _____

   _____

3. Adult male robins who see a tuft of red feathers on the breast of another male robin make aggressive displays of behavior and even attack an intruder.

   _____

   _____

4. Herring gull chicks peck at a red dot on their parent's beak when it returns to the nest, causing the adult to regurgitate food for the chicks.

   _____

   _____

UNDERSTANDING THROUGH LISTENING

VIDEO

> **Lecture:** Proximate and Ultimate Causes of Animal Behavior
> **Segment 1:** Learned versus Innate Behavior in Australian Birds
>
> **Professor:** Carolee Caffrey
> **Course:** Biology 2: Principles of Modern Biology

In this first segment of the lecture, Professor Caffrey uses the example of two Australian birds, the galah and the pink cockatoo, to discuss the intricate interplay between genes and the environment.

Targeting Vocabulary: Key Terms

TASK 9: All the words listed here are used to discuss animal behavior that is either *genetically programmed* or *learned*. Put a G in the blank next to those words that you would expect to find in a reading about genetically programmed behavior; put an L in the blank next to those words that you would expect to find in a reading about learned behavior.

_G_ coded

____ not modifiable

____ determined

____ imprinted

____ innate

____ altered

____ closed behavior

____ fixed

____ adaptive

____ modifiable

____ programmed

____ hard-wired

____ instinct

____ open behavior

ACADEMIC STRATEGY:

FINDING AND NOTING IMPORTANT IDEAS FROM EXAMPLES IN LECTURES

Because many of the concepts presented in lectures are abstract, professors routinely use examples, either brief or extended, to make the information accessible to students. However, taking notes on such examples can be challenging.

METHOD
To take notes on examples in a lecture, ask yourself the following questions. You might ask many of the same questions to highlight information in a text.

- What part of the example should I write down? In how much detail?
- What parts of the example are relevant? What parts are not?
- Does the example illustrate a generalization that the professor has made already, or is it leading to a generalization that the professor is about to make?
- Does the professor directly state the generalization, or must I infer it?
- If the example is one of several, are these examples illustrating the same point, or is each making a different point?

PUTTING IT TO WORK

For example, in the segment of the lecture you are about to watch, Professor Caffrey uses the extended example of baby galahs who are reared by pink cockatoo parents. Some parts of the example are simply background information—*facts about all bird contact calls*—that does not pertain to the main point Caffrey is making. Other parts—*galahs reared by pink cockatoos give cockatoo-like contact calls*—relate directly to the central concept of the lecture that genes and the environment interact to create animal behavior. For example, Caffrey gives general background information about all bird contact calls before she discusses the fact that galahs reared by pink cockatoos give cockatoo-like contact calls. A good notetaker would probably not take down the general information on contact calls but would note the information about the kind of contact calls given by cross-fostered galahs because it illustrates the interaction of genes and the environment.

MAKING DECISIONS

A good notetaker doesn't just "take dictation" from the professor. Rather, he or she constantly sifts all the information to figure out the larger generalizations or framework the lecturer is creating. Based on this strategy, the notetaker makes decisions about what is or is not relevant information.

TASK 10: In her lecture, Professor Caffrey gives an example of how genes and the environment interact to influence the behavior of galah babies raised by cockatoos. Before watching, preview the following sentences taken from the lecture. Put a √ next to the **six** sentences that you believe represent the most important information about this topic.

_____ The pink cockatoo is larger.

_____ And these cross-fostered galahs fly like cockatoos.

_____ At any rate, these cross-fostered galahs produce cockatoo contact calls, but galah alarm calls.

_____ Both species nest in holes or cavities in trees.

_____ Cockatoos, the more aggressive bird, end up incubating the nest, even if there are a couple of galah eggs there.

_____ They are like parrots.

_____ Females lay one egg a day for about four days.

_____ Galah kids beg for food using galah begging calls.

_____ Okay, these guys, they are big birds.

_____ Sometimes a female galah and a female pink cockatoo end up laying eggs in the same cavity.

_____ Sometimes cross-fostered galahs make a mistake when flying; instead of flying with slow wing beats, like a cockatoo, they fly fast like a galah and speed up ahead of their group.

_____ They live in the same eucalyptus woodlands in Australia.

TASK 11: Watch the lecture as many times as necessary. Then identify whether the behavior of the nestling galahs is *galah* (i.e., genetically programmed) or *cockatoo* (i.e., imprinted) by circling the appropriate term. Decide whether the behavior is *innate* or *learned* and circle the appropriate term.

BEHAVIOR	GALAH OR COCKATOO?	INNATE OR LEARNED?
begging calls	galah cockatoo	innate learned
alarm calls	galah cockatoo	innate learned
contact calls	galah cockatoo	innate learned
flight patterns	galah cockatoo	innate learned
food preferences	galah cockatoo	innate learned

TASK 12: Watch the lecture again and write down two general ideas that Professor Caffrey wants you to take away from the lecture about innate and learned behavior in these Australian birds. Compare your generalizations with those of a partner.

1. _____

_____

2. _____

_____

⊚ Targeting Grammar: Expressing Possession and Relation in *Of*-phrases

Prepositional phrases beginning with *of* are very common in academic English; *of* is, after all, the most common preposition in English.

Many *of*-phrases fit into one of two categories: possession and relation.

PHRASES THAT EXPRESS POSSESSION (SOMETHING BELONGS TO OR IS AN INTEGRAL PART OF SOMETHING ELSE)

    the territorial marking of a lion   the beak of the parent bird

    the nervous system of the spider   the sides of the cocoon

Some possessive *of*-phrases may also be expressed in possessive, or -'s, form:

    the territorial marking of a lion ⇒ a lion's territorial marking

    the nervous system of a spider ⇒ the spider's nervous system

PHRASES THAT EXPRESS RELATION (OTHER RELATIONSHIPS)

EXAMPLES	TYPE OF RELATION
an individual of the same species	member of a group
a section of the beach	part of a whole
marvels of engineering	descriptive

In general, it is not acceptable to rewrite *of*-phrases expressing relations with an -*'s* phrase before the noun:

Unacceptable: the same species' individual
                               the beach's section

TASK 13: Underline the *of*-phrases and write the type for each (*possession* or *relation*) on the line provided. If the *of*-phrase can be rewritten as an -*'s* phrase before a noun, rewrite it. The first two have been done for you.

1. The construction <u>of a classic web used to capture prey</u> requires complex behavior.

   <u>Relation   (cannot be rewritten as -'s phrase)</u>

2. The attachment <u>of birds</u> to their mothers occurs early.

   <u>Possession   Birds' attachment to their mothers . . .</u>

3. Mating with a member of the wrong species is a costly mistake.

   _____

4. Kangaroo rats avoid the bite of a rattlesnake by jumping backwards.

   _____

5. The territorial sense of wild animals is very strong.

   _____

6. The remarkable thing about the world of insects is that their mysteries are performed in broad daylight before our eyes.

   _____

7. Observations of young squirrels reveal that migrating from home is a gradual process.

   _____

UNDERSTANDING THROUGH LITERATURE

For seven years, Mark and Delia Owens observed the animal life of the Kalahari Desert in the southern African nation of Botswana. The following excerpt from their book *Cry of the Kalahari* recounts the territorial marking behavior of two brown hyenas, Star and Shadow.

TASK 14: As you read the following passage, look for examples of innate, or genetically programmed, behavior in the actions of Star and Shadow.

STAR

Mark Owens and Delia Owens

[1]   The few scanty reports on brown hyenas described them as scavengers, real loners that ate only carrion or occasionally hunted small mammals. At first we thought this description was probably accurate: Star followed that feeding pattern and was always alone. But soon we began seeing some extraordinary behavior that made us question whether browns were indeed solitary creatures.

[2]   Any information about how many of them live in a group, whether or not they defend a communal territory, and why they associate together is important for the conservation of hyenas. But there is another reason to investigate their social life: Man is also a social carnivore and by understanding the evolution and nature of societies of other predators, we can better understand our own sense of territoriality, our need for identity as part of a group, and our aggressive tendencies as competitors.

[3]   Later that night, following Star when she left the carcass, we noticed that she did not wander aimlessly over the range, but traveled on the distinct pathways she had used on previous nights. Some of them joined or crossed well-used game trails, such as Leopard Trail, a major route for gemsbok, kudu, giraffe, jackals, and leopards moving north-south along a string of temporary water holes at the foot of West Dune. Usually, however, the hyenas' paths were visible only as faintly divided grass or lightly compacted sand.

[4]   Star paused at a grass clump, smelling a small, dark blob at nose level on one of the stems. Then, in a most bizarre display, she stepped over the grass, raised her tail, and everted a special rectal pouch. By swiveling her hindquarters to feel for the stalk, she directed the two-lobed pouch to the stem and "pasted" a drop of white substance that looked remarkably like Elmer's Glue. After she had lowered her tail, she retracted the pouch and walked on. We took a sniff of the paste; it had a pungent, musty odor. Just above the white drop, a smaller rust-colored secretion was also smeared on the grass.

[5]   During the following weeks we saw other hyenas traveling the same trails that Star used, always alone, and often stopping to smell the paste that Star and others had left on the grass-stalks. Before moving on, they would add their own chemical signature to the stem, so that in spots where paths crossed, a grass clump could have as many as thirteen scent marks, very much like a sign post at a highway intersection.

[6]   Late one night we were following a very timid female, about Star's size, that we had named Shadow. She was walking south along the riverbed on one of the hyena paths and pausing every hundred yards or so to smell a scent mark and then paste over it. She crossed South Pan through Tree Island and entered the thick bush, where we lost her. It was one o'clock in the morning, so we stopped for coffee on the edge of the riverbed before looking for another hyena. We were sitting on top of the Land Rover in the moonlight sipping from our Thermos cups, when Star came along. She crossed the first hyena's path and stood smelling Shadow's fresh paste mark for nearly a minute, her long hairs bristling. Then she changed course and followed quickly after her.

[7]   We managed to keep Star in sight until we could see Shadow walking back toward Star in the moonlight, the two dark forms moving silently through the tall, silvery grass. We stopped, Mark flicked on the spotlight, and the most unusual behavior we had ever seen between two animals began to unfold.

[8]   Star approached and Shadow crouched down until her belly was flat to the ground. She drew her lips up tightly and opened her mouth wide, showing her teeth in an exaggerated grin. Her long ears stuck out from her head like a floppy hat, and her tail curled tightly over her back. Squealing like a rusty gate hinge, she began crawling around Star, who also turned, but in the opposite direction. Each time Shadow passed beneath Star's nose, she paused to let her smell the scent glands beneath her tail. The hyenas pirouetted around and around, like ballerinas on a dimly lit stage.

[9]   The strange greeting continued for several minutes, even after Star tried to walk on down the trail. Each time she began to move away, Shadow hurried to lie in front of her, inviting Star to take another sniff under her tail. Like an aristocratic lady dismissing her attendant, Star finally stood with her nose held high, refusing to further indulge Shadow. Eventually she walked away, and Shadow departed in a different direction.

Source: (1984). *Cry of the Kalahari* (pp. 74–75). Boston: Houghton Mifflin.

TASK 15: Make a list of the innate, or genetically programmed, behavior that Star and Shadow exhibit. Compare your list with a partner's list.

Targeting Vocabulary: Guessing Meaning through Context

Even for native speakers, academic texts contain many unknown words or words whose meanings are difficult to define precisely. Good academic readers do not look up every unknown word in a passage. Rather, they make intelligent guesses about the meanings, based on certain clues within the sentence or the wider paragraph context.

Here are some tips for making better guesses about the meanings of words you don't know.

1. Often, the words immediately surrounding the unknown word help to establish its meaning.

   The few scanty reports on brown hyenas described them as scavengers, real loners that ate only carrion or occasionally *hunted small* **mammals.** (We can guess that a *mammal* is a small animal that is hunted.)

2. Sometimes the sentence itself contains a definition or restatement (often in an appositive construction following a comma).

   The few scanty reports on brown hyenas described them as **scavengers,** real loners that *ate* only *carrion* or occasionally hunted small mammals. (We can guess the meaning by noting that these animals eat carrion [dead meat].)

3. Often, you must use the entire paragraph to establish meaning from context.

   The few scanty reports on brown hyenas described them as scavengers, real **loners** that ate only carrion or occasionally hunted small mammals. At first we thought this description was probably accurate: Star followed that feeding pattern and was always *alone.* But soon we began seeing some extraordinary behavior that made us question whether browns were indeed *solitary* creatures. (We find clues to the meaning by noting the adjectives *alone* and *solitary.*)

Sometimes you cannot determine a word's meaning through context. In such cases, stop to look up the meaning if (1) it is essential to your understanding of the passage or (2) you have encountered the word before and are curious to know its exact meaning.

TASK 16: Write your "guess" about the meaning of each word in bold by looking at the italicized clues in the sentence. Do not look up the meaning of the words in a dictionary.

1. Any information about how many of them live in a *group,* whether or not they defend a **communal** territory, and why they associate *together* is important for the conservation of hyenas.

   Meaning: _____

2. Later that night, following Star when she left the carcass, we noticed that she did *not wander* **aimlessly** over the range, *but* traveled on the *distinct pathways* she had used on previous nights.

   Meaning: _____

3. Some of them joined or crossed well-used *game* trails, such as Leopard Trail, a major route for **gemsbok, kudu,** *giraffe,* **jackals,** and *leopards* moving north-south along a string of temporary water holes at the foot of West Dune.

   Meaning: _____

4. We took a *sniff* of the paste; it had a **pungent,** *musty odor.*

   Meaning: _____

5. Just above the *white drop,* a smaller *rust-colored* **secretion** was also *smeared* on the grass.

   Meaning: _____

TASK 17: Circle any words in the sentence that provide a clue to the meaning of the word in bold. Then write your "guess" about the meaning. Do not look up the meaning of the words in a dictionary.

1. She crossed the first hyena's path and stood smelling Shadow's fresh paste mark for nearly a minute, her long hairs **bristling.**

   Meaning: _____

2. We stopped, Mark **flicked on** the spotlight, and the most unusual behavior we had ever seen between two animals began to unfold.

   Meaning: _____

3. **Squealing** like a rusty gate hinge, she began crawling around Star, who also turned, but in the opposite direction.

   Meaning: _____

4. Star approached and Shadow **crouched down** until her belly was flat to the ground.

   Meaning: _____

5. The hyenas **pirouetted** around and around, like ballerinas on a dimly lit stage.

   Meaning: _____

Integrating Perspectives

APPLYING THE CONCEPTS

On an animal-collecting expedition in the province of Jujuy in Argentina, the naturalist Gerald Durrell made a purchase for his private zoo—a rare species of wild cat called a Geoffroy's cat. When he was unable to get the two-week-old wild cat to eat, he hit upon the idea of buying a domestic tabby cat and putting the two cats together. In the passage that follows, Durrell tells what happened.

TASK 18: This passage is filled with examples of learned behavior. Read the passage to find them.

Jujuy

Eventually I chose a fat, placid female tabby which was approximately the same size and age as my wild cat, and carried it back in triumph to the garage. Here I spent an hour constructing a rough cage, while the tabby kitten purred vigorously and rubbed itself round my legs, occasionally tripping me up. When the cage was ready, I put the tabby kitten in first, and left it for an hour or so to settle down.

Most wild animals have a very strong sense of territory. In the wild state, they have their own particular bit of forest or grassland which they consider their own preserve, and will defend it against any other member of their own species (or other animals sometimes) that tries to enter it. When you put wild animals into cages the cages become, as far as they are concerned, their territory. So, if you introduce another animal into the same cage, the first inmate will in all probability defend it vigorously, and you may easily have a fight to the death on your hands. So you generally have to employ low cunning. Suppose, for example, you have a large vigorous creature who is obviously quite capable of looking after itself, and it has been in a cage for a period of a few weeks. Then you get a second animal of the same species, and you want to confine them together, for the sake of convenience. Introduce the new specimen into the old one's cage, and the old one may well kill it. So the best thing to do is to build an entirely new cage, and into this you introduce the weaker of the two animals. When it has settled down, you then put the stronger one in with it. The stronger one will, of course, still remain the dominant animal, and may even bully the weaker one, but as far as he is concerned he had been introduced into someone else's territory, and this takes the edge off his potential viciousness. It's a sort of Lifemanship that any collector has to practice at one time or another.

In this case I was sure that the baby Geoffroy's was quite capable of killing the domestic kitten, if I introduced the kitten to *it*, instead of the other way around. So, once the tabby had settled down, I seized the Geoffroy's and pushed it, snarling and raving, into the cage and stood back to see what would happen. The tabby was delighted. It came forward to the angry Geoffroy's and started to rub itself against its neck, purring loudly. The Geoffroy's, taken aback by its greeting as I had hoped, merely spat rather rudely, and retreated into a corner. The tabby, having made the first overtures of friendship, sat down, purring loudly, and proceeded to wash itself with a self-satisfied air. I covered the front of the cage with a piece of sacking and left them to settle down, for I was sure now that the Geoffroy's would do the tabby no real harm.

That evening, when I lifted the sacking, I found them lying side by side, and the Geoffroy's, instead of spitting at me as it had done up until now, contented itself with merely lifting its lip in a warning manner. I carefully inserted a large bowl of milk into the cage, and a plate containing the finely-chopped meat and raw egg, which I wanted the Geoffroy's to eat. This was the crucial test, for I was hoping that the tabby would fall upon this delicious fare and, by example, encourage the Geoffroy's to eat. Sure enough, the tabby, purring like an ancient outboard engine, flung itself at the bowl of milk, took a long drink and then settled down to the meat and egg. I had retreated to a place where I could see without being seen, and I watched the Geoffroy's carefully. To begin with it took no interest at all, lying there with half-closed eyes. But eventually the noise the tabby was making over the egg and meat—it was rather a messy feeder—attracted its attention. It rose cautiously and approached the plate, while I held my breath. Delicately it sniffed round the edge of the plate, while the tabby lifted a face that was dripping with raw egg and gave a mew of encouragement, slightly muffled by the portion of meat it had in its mouth. The Geoffroy's stood pondering for a moment, and then, to my delight, sank down by the plate and started to eat. In spite of the fact that it must have been extremely hungry it ate daintily, lapping a little raw egg and then picking up a morsel of meat which it chewed thoroughly before swallowing. I watched them until, between them, they had cleaned both plates, then I replenished them with more milk, egg and meat, and went to bed well satisfied. The next morning both plates were spotless, and the Geoffroy's and the tabby were locked in each other's arms, fast asleep, their stomachs bulging like two little hairy balloons. They did not wake up until midday, and then they both looked distinctly debauched. But when they saw me approaching with the plates of food, they both displayed considerable interest, and I knew that my battle with the Geoffroy's was won.

Source: G. Durrell (1961). *The whispering land* (pp. 124–131). London: Penguin Books.

TASK 19: Though the tabby and the Geoffroy's are both cats, they displayed quite different behavior. In the chart, use your own words to fill in the missing information about the cats' contrasting behavior.

THE GEOFFROY'S CAT	THE TABBY CAT
The Geoffroy's snarled and raved when it was first placed in the cage with the tabby.	
	The tabby purred loudly and began to wash itself.
	On seeing the milk and meat and raw egg, the tabby purred furiously and began to eat and drink.
The Geoffroy's approached the plate and sniffed its edge cautiously.	
	The tabby was a messy feeder.
The next morning the Geoffroy's was still asleep, and its stomach looked like a fat balloon.	

TASK 20: With a partner, discuss what the differences between the Geoffroy's and the tabby reveal about innate and learned behaviors in cats.

Evaluating through Writing

Task 21: In your groups or with a partner, select one of the animal behaviors below. Design a deprivation experiment that would allow you to determine whether the given behavior is primarily learned or innate. On separate paper, write a paragraph describing your experiment. The first one has been done for you.

1. Mother goats that do not nuzzle or lick their newborns within five to ten minutes after birth do not recognize the infant as their own.

   In the experiment, I would take a mother goat with a newborn kid and remove the kid from the mother. I would then bottle feed the kid and keep it separated from its mother for a period of three days. At the end of that period, I would return the kid to the goat herd (consisting of its mother, other female goats, and other kids), and I would observe whether the kid went to its mother and if the mother recognized the kid as her own.

2. Kangaroo rats who hear the sound of a rattlesnake can avoid the rattlesnake bite by jumping backwards.

3. Adult male robins who see a tuft of red feathers on the breast of another male robin make aggressive displays of behavior and even attack an intruder.

4. Herring gull chicks peck at a red dot on their parent's beak when it returns to the nest, causing the adult to regurgitate food for the chicks.

EXPLORATION:
PROXIMATE AND ULTIMATE CAUSES OF ANIMAL BEHAVIOR

To completely understand animal behavior, biologists must set it in a larger context. They examine the proximate causes (the immediate causes of a behavior) and the ultimate causes (longer-reaching causes that affect the survival of the entire species). This chapter presents a framework for analyzing both the proximate and ultimate explanations for any animal activity.

Exploring the Concepts

EXPLORING THROUGH VISUAL IMAGES

"Self-help" books, or books that give suggestions for improving oneself or solving a personal problem, have become very popular in the last twenty years. The cartoonist here pokes fun at this trend by showing animals reading self-help books to learn ways to enhance their chances of survival.

In the animal self-help section.

TASK 1: Think of an animal or insect with a distinctive behavior or physical feature (e.g., a spider, a turtle, a rhinoceros, a bear, a praying mantis). With a partner or in a small group, formulate one piece of helpful advice on survival that a humorous self-help book would give this animal. An example has been done for you.

male peacocks - To attract peahens, your tail feathers need to be distinctive and in prime condition; be prepared to fan them at the first sight of an attractive female.

EXPLORING BACKGROUND KNOWLEDGE

TASK 2: One of the basic theories in biology is Charles Darwin's concept of natural selection, or "survival of the fittest." Fill in the WHAT? and WHY? in the diagram and discuss with a partner everything you know about what kinds of changes in physical appearance or behavior occur in animals and why these changes occur. Share this information with your classmates. An example is given for HOW?

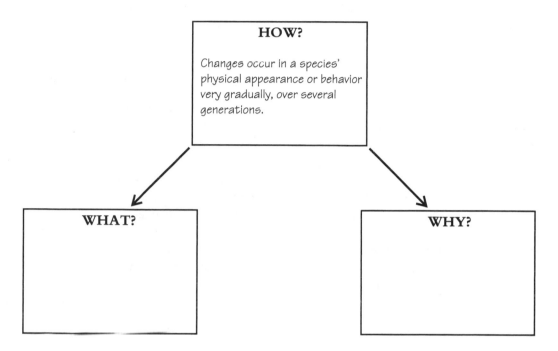

HOW?

Changes occur in a species' physical appearance or behavior very gradually, over several generations.

WHAT?

WHY?

EXPLORING THROUGH DISCUSSION

TASK 3: Discuss the progression of humans from their origins as four-legged animals to two-legged creatures that walk upright. What advantages are there to this behavioral adaptation? Can you think of any disadvantages? With a partner, fill in the chart. An example has been done for you.

ADVANTAGES	DISADVANTAGES
Arms and hands move independently from legs and feet.	More weight is distributed onto the feet.

EXPLORING THROUGH WRITING

Biologists explore the two categories of *proximate* and *ultimate* causes to arrive at two complementary explanations for any animal behavior.

TASK 4: Review this chart to discover the differences between the two types of explanations for animal behavior. Apply the questions in the chart to the example of humans beginning to walk upright. Write a journal entry in which you give the proximate and ultimate causes of this behavioral adaptation. Share your writing with classmates.

PROXIMATE CAUSES OF ANIMAL BEHAVIOR	ULTIMATE CAUSES OF ANIMAL BEHAVIOR
• What is the causal relationship between the animal's genes and its behavior? • Is the trait to some extent inherited from the animal's parents? • What responses in the body trigger the behavior, and how are the body's chemicals and hormones involved in the response? • How are the animal's nervous and muscular systems integrated to enable it to perform the behavior?	• What is the purpose or function of the behavior? • How does the behavior assist the individual in overcoming obstacles to survival and reproduction? • How has the behavior evolved, and how has it changed over evolutionary time? • What was the original step in the historical process that led to the existence of the current behavior?
These questions are designed to investigate how an individual manages to carry out an activity. They ask how mechanisms within an animal operate to enable it to behave in a certain way.	These questions help determine why the animal has evolved the proximate mechanisms that allow it to perform an activity.

Adapted from: John Alcock (1993). *Animal behavior: An evolutionary approach* (pp. 1–3). Sunderland, MA: Sinauer Associates.

Working with Sources

UNDERSTANDING THROUGH LISTENING 1

VIDEO

Lecture: Proximate and Ultimate Causes of Animal Behavior
Segment 2: Sexual Receptivity in Lions

Professor: Carolee Caffrey
Course: Biology 2: Principles of Modern Biology

In Segment 2 of her lecture, Professor Caffrey reinforces the distinction between proximate and ultimate causes of animal behavior. She gives an example of a reproductive behavior exhibited by female lions in the same pride, all of whom become sexually receptive at the same time.

In their lectures, professors use predictable words and phrases to signal the important information. Paying attention to these cues is a valuable guide to taking and organizing lecture notes.

The following are some of the most common ways in which cues function:

- *Marking openings of main topics:* Often the professor will give a clear verbal indication of the beginning of a new topic. Sometimes, these openings take the form of questions that the instructor will answer.

  "I'm going to introduce the topic of X."
  "By talking first about X . . ."
  "How does X work?"
  "What causes X to happen?"

- *Marking closings of main topics:* Professors also tend to clearly signal the end of a topic or subtopic.

  "Okay, that's the explanation for . . ."
  "So, that is how X and Y interact . . ."

- *Returning to a previous topic:* Lecturers often use verbal signals to indicate a return to a previous topic following a digression (e.g., an extended example, an anecdote, an off-topic comment).

  "So, just to restate . . ."
  "Back to X . . ."
  "Anyway, to return to what we were talking about earlier . . ."

- *Designating the overall structure of the information:* Professors guide students in outlining the information being presented. For example, they often tell the students in advance how many categories or theories or examples they will discuss.

  "It basically boils down to **two** categories."
  "There are **several** different ways of answering that question."

- *Signaling important points:* When lecturers want to ensure that students have heard and written down a given point, they often repeat that information or signal its importance in some other way.

  "I'll say this again."
  "So again, let me repeat . . ."
  "What I want you to understand is . . ."
  "Now I'm going to give you a new word."

- *Introducing examples*

  "The first example involves . . ."
  "I'm going to give you examples to help you understand the concept."
  "I'm going to give you another example."

- *Making reference to relevant course readings*

  "That's what Chapter _____ concentrates on."

- *Signaling when to stop taking notes:* Some lecturers tell students when to just sit back and listen.

  "You don't have to write down all these words."
  "You don't have to write all this down because you already know it."

TASK 5: Watch the lecture and take notes on the most important information. Use a separate piece of paper.

TASK 6: Compare the notes you took in Task 5 with a partner's notes. Did you include all the important information? Go back to your notes and revise them to include any important points that you missed.

TASK 7: Look at the following sentences from Professor Caffrey's lecture. In the right-hand column, indicate the type of signal that each sentence represents. Refer to the Academic Strategy on page 21 to help guide your decision. Watch the lecture again if necessary. The first one has been done for you.

LECTURE INFORMATION	TYPE OF SIGNAL
1. I am going to give you a couple more examples about behavior.	Introducing examples
2. Just to introduce them, I'm showing you a cool picture of lions.	
3. Anyway, they eat zebras and gazelles and they defend those territories that have a supply of zebra and gazelle on them.	
4. Okay, so that's the way the system works.	
5. Here are three interesting observations about lion behavior and their explanations at both the proximate and ultimate level.	
6. So that's the interesting observation, that all females in a pride are going into estrus at about the same time.	
7. So what is the function of everybody cycling at the same time?	

Targeting Vocabulary: Informal versus Formal Language

A common claim made about academic language is that it is formal rather than informal. In fact, lecturers often use informal language very effectively to communicate academic concepts and definitions. Look at the following sentences to see how Professor Caffrey mixes formal language and informal equivalents to communicate her point.

Within a pride, all the females are **related**. They are all **sisters, moms and daughters, aunts and nieces, and even grandmas and granddaughters.**

Male lions leave their **natal** pride; they actually leave the pride they were **born into.**

TASK 8: Match the formal expression with its informal equivalent. Write the letter of the corresponding informal expression in the column provided. The first one has been done for you.

	FORMAL EXPRESSIONS	INFORMAL EXPRESSIONS
_g_	1. copulate	a. babies/kids
_____	2. something is finished/at an end	b. booted out
_____	3. interesting	c. your period
_____	4. litter/offspring	d. broadcast out/send to the outside
_____	5. female cycle	e. cool
_____	6. forcibly removed	f. go into heat
_____	7. emit	g. have sex
_____	8. come into estrus	h. that's it/it's over

UNDERSTANDING THROUGH LITERATURE

In the following passage, the naturalist Annie Dillard communicates her fascination with insects and their aggressive behavior as she describes a female praying mantis laying her egg case.

TASK 9: As you read the following description, highlight or underline the passages that describe what the female praying mantis does to her mate.

PILGRIM AT TINKER CREEK

Annie Dillard

[1]   I was ambling across this hill that day when I noticed a speck of pure white. The hill is eroded; the slope is a rutted wreck of red clay broken by grassy hillocks and low wild roses whose roots clasp a pittance of topsoil. I leaned to examine the white thing and saw a mass of bubbles like spittle. Then I saw something dark like an engorged leech rummaging over the spittle, and then I saw the praying mantis.

[2]   She was upside down, clinging to a horizontal stem of wild rose by her feet, which pointed to heaven. Her head was deep in dried grass. Her abdomen was swollen like a smashed finger; it tapered to a fleshy tip out of which bubbled a wet, whipped froth. I couldn't believe my eyes. I lay on the hill this way and that, my knees in thorns and my cheeks in clay, trying to see as well as I could. I poked near the female's head with a grass; she was clearly undisturbed, so I settled my nose an inch from that pulsing abdomen. It puffed like a concertina, it throbbed like a bellows; it roved, pumping, over the glistening, clabbered surface of the egg case, testing and patting, thrusting and smoothing. It seemed to act so independently that I forgot the panting brown stick at the other end. The bubble creature seemed to have two eyes, a frantic little brain, and two busy, soft hands. It looked like a hideous, harried mother slicking up a fat daughter for a beauty pageant, touching her up, slobbering over her, patting and hemming and brushing and stroking.

[3]   The male was nowhere in sight. The female had probably eaten him. Fabre says that, at least in captivity, the female will mate with and devour up to seven males, whether she has laid her egg cases or not. The mating rites of mantises are well known: a chemical produced in the head of the male insect says, in effect, "No, don't go near her, you fool, she'll eat you alive." At the same time a chemical in his abdomen says, "Yes, by all means, now and forever yes."

[4]   While the male is making up what passes for his mind, the female tips the balance in her favor by eating his head. He mounts her. Fabre describes the mating, which sometimes lasts six hours, as follows: "The male, absorbed in the performance of his vital functions, holds the female in a tight embrace. But the wretch has no head; he has no neck; he has hardly a body. The other, with her muzzle turned over her shoulder, continues very placidly to gnaw what remains of the gentle swain.

And, all the time, that masculine stump, holding on firmly, goes on with the business! . . . I have seen it done with my own eyes and have not yet recovered from my astonishment."

[5]   I watched the egg-laying for over an hour. When I returned the next day, the mantis was gone. The white foam had hardened and browned to a dirty suds; then, and on subsequent days, I had trouble pinpointing the case, which was only an inch or so off the ground. I checked on it every week all winter long.

Source: (1994). *The Annie Dillard reader* (pp. 311–312, 316–317). New York: Harper Perennial.

TASK 10: Why does the female praying mantis eat her mate? Use Professor Caffrey's explanations of the proximate and ultimate causes of behavior to explain this. Compare your ideas with a classmate's.

 Targeting Grammar: Complete versus Reduced Relative Clauses

WHAT ARE RELATIVE CLAUSES?
Relative clauses modify nouns or noun phrases and function as adjectives in a sentence. They consist of

1. a relative pronoun *(who, which, that, whom, whose,* preposition + *which)*
2. a subject and a predicate

They directly follow the nouns or noun phrases they modify. They can appear after the first noun in the sentence or after any subsequent noun.

TWO TYPES OF RELATIVE CLAUSES
1. A *complete relative clause* includes the relative pronoun followed by the modifying clause.

   The female mantis clung to the horizontal stem of wild rose, **which pointed to heaven.**
   (complete relative clause)

2. A *reduced relative clause* does not include the relative pronoun—it is deleted. Depending on the type of reduced relative clause, sometimes other parts of the modifying clause are also deleted.

   The male, ~~who is~~ **absorbed in the performance,** holds the female in a tight embrace.
   (reduced relative clause)

CONDITIONS FOR REDUCING RELATIVE CLAUSES
Reduced relative clauses occur when the relative pronoun meets one of three conditions:

CONDITIONS	RULES	EXAMPLES
1. the object in the relative clause	Delete the relative pronoun.	The eggs ~~that~~ the female mantis had laid were hidden in an egg case.
2. the subject of a relative clause with the auxiliary *be*	Delete the relative pronoun and the *be* auxiliary.	I saw something dark like an engorged leech ~~that was~~ rummaging over the spittle.
3. the subject of a relative clause with the verb *have* or *have not*	Delete the relative pronoun and substitute *with* or *without* for *have* or *have not.*	The female, ~~who has~~ **with** her muzzle turned over her shoulder, continues very placidly to gnaw what remains of her partner.

CONDITIONS FOR NOT REDUCING RELATIVE CLAUSES

Reduced relative clauses cannot occur when the relative pronoun meets one of three conditions:

CONDITIONS	EXAMPLES
1. the object of a preposition	It tapered to a fleshy tip **out of which** bubbled a wet, whipped froth.
2. the subject of a relative clause with a main verb that is not *be*	I saw something dark like an engorged leech **that rummaged** over the spittle.
3. the possessive *whose*	The hill is eroded; the slope is a rutted wreck of red clay broken by grassy hillocks and low wild roses **whose roots** clasp a pittance of topsoil.

TASK 11: The following sentences contain complete relative clauses. Underline the relative clause. Put an R in front of the relative clauses that can be reduced and NR in front of those that cannot be reduced. Rewrite those that can be reduced. The first one has been done for you.

___R___ 1. It looked like a hideous mother <u>who was slicking up a fat daughter for a beauty pageant</u>.

       <u>It looked like a hideous mother slicking up a fat daughter for a beauty pageant.</u>

_____ 2. The mantis, whose abdomen was swollen, was upside down on a wild rose stem.

_____ 3. On her walk, the author came across a dark object that was puffing and throbbing like a bellows.

_____ 4. The egg casing, which starts out as a white foam, subsequently hardens to brown.

_____ 5. A chemical that is produced in the abdomen of the male triggers the mating rite.

_____ 6. These egg casings remain in the place in which the female originally lays them all winter long.

_____ 7. The egg casing that the mantis was arranging was like a white froth.

UNDERSTANDING THROUGH LISTENING 2

VIDEO

Lecture: Proximate and Ultimate Causes of Animal Behavior
Segment 3: Female Lion Pregnancy and Birth Rate

Professor: Carolee Caffrey
Course: Biology 2: Principles of Modern Biology

Here, Professor Caffrey gives both the proximate and ultimate explanations of another behavior observed in female lions—their low rate of pregnancy and birth.

TASK 12: Watch the lecture and fill in the missing information from the following outline. Include only the most important information.

I. Interesting observation: Despite their high rate of sexual activity when in estrus, female lions have a very low rate of pregnancy and birth.

    A. Description of sexual activity in lions: _____

    _____

    B. Problems with pregnancy and birth rate

       1. Pregnancy rate is really low.

       2. When lions do get pregnant, _____

       3. Very few cubs _____

II. Question: What are the explanations for this phenomenon?

    A. Proximate explanations

       1. The proximate explanation is not that _____

       2. It's a "female thing." There are two possible explanations.

          a. The female lion may be sexually receptive but _____

          b. A zygote may be produced but _____

    B. _____ explanation: Why are females designed so apparently inefficiently?

       1. Facts

          a. Because the female has a low chance of getting pregnant, every copulation is devalued.

          b. _____

       2. Implications

          a. Therefore, for the male, _____

          b. The devaluation of copulation helps _____

          c. Because every male is potentially the father of every cub, _____

          _____

The following passage is a research report outlining two biologists' observations of and experiments on a behavior unique to male ground squirrels: emigration from the place where they were born. The report further explains the proximate and ultimate causes of this behavior.

TASK 13: This report, like many scientific reports, consists of fairly fixed categories of information, including *background on the problem, research questions, experimental procedures,* and *findings.* These categories are identified in the first section (paragraphs 1-6) of the reading. As you read the second section, "Physiological Mechanisms," put brackets [ ] around each of these categories and label them appropriately in the margin.

WHY MALE GROUND SQUIRRELS DISPERSE

Kay E. Holekamp and Paul W. Sherman

[1]   [When they are about two months old, male Belding's ground squirrels *(Spermophilus beldingi)* leave the burrow where they were born, never to return. Their sisters behave quite differently, remaining near home throughout their lives.] [Why do juvenile males, and only males, disperse?] [This deceptively simple question, which has intrigued us for more than a decade, has led us to investigate evolutionary and ontogenetic explanations. Only recently have answers begun to emerge.

[2]   Dispersal, defined as a complete and permanent emigration from an individual's home range, occurs sometime in the life cycle of nearly all organisms. There are two major types: breeding dispersal, the movement of adults between reproductive episodes, and natal dispersal, the emigration of young from their birthplace. Natal dispersal occurs in virtually all birds and mammals prior to first reproduction. In most mammals, young males emigrate while their sisters remain near home (the females are said to be philopatric).

[3]   From 1974 to 1985 we studied three populations of *S. beldingi* near Yosemite National Park in the Sierra Nevada mountains of California. In each population, the animals were above ground for only four or five months during the spring and summer; during the rest of the year they hibernated. Females bore a single litter of five to seven young per season, and reared them without assistance from males. Most females began to breed as one-year-olds, but males did not mate until they were at least two. Females lived about twice as long as males.]

[4]   [During each field season ground squirrels were trapped alive, weighed, and examined every two to three weeks. About 5,300 different ground squirrels were handled. The animals were marked individually and observed unobtrusively through binoculars for nearly 6,000 hours. Natal dispersal behavior was measured by a combination of direct observations, livetrapping, radio telemetry, and identification of animals killed on nearby roads. The day on which each emigrant was last seen within its mother's home range was defined as its date of dispersal.]

[5]   [Observations of marked pups revealed that natal dispersal was a gradual process. Young first emerged from their natal burrow and ceased nursing when they were about four weeks old. Two or three weeks later some youngsters began making daily excursions away from, and evening returns to, the natal burrow. Eventually these young stopped returning, restricting their activities entirely to the new home range; by definition, dispersal had occurred.

[6]   Natal dispersal is clearly a behavior exhibited by males. In our studies, every one of over 300 surviving males dispersed by the end of its second summer; a large majority (92%) dispersed before their first hibernation, by the age of about 16 weeks. In contrast, only 5% of over 250 females had dispersed from their mother's home range. The universality of natal dispersal by males suggested no flexibility in its occurrence; however, there was variation among individuals in the age at which dispersal occurred.]

Physiological Mechanisms

[7]   We began our analysis of natal dispersal in *S. beldingi* by considering physiological mechanisms. We were most interested in the effects of hormones on dispersal. We wondered whether androgens (male steroids which affect certain tissues in utero or immediately after birth) would influence the development of dispersal behavior. According to our hypothesis, exposing female squirrels to androgens just prior to or just after birth should masculinize subsequent behavior, including natal dispersal. We tested this idea by capturing pregnant females and housing them at a field camp until they gave birth. Soon after birth, female pups were injected with a small amount of testosterone

propionate dissolved in oil; a control group was given oil only. After treatment, the pups and their mothers were taken back to the field, where the mothers found suitable empty burrows and successfully reared their young.

[8]   Twelve of the female pups treated with androgens were located when they were at least 60 days old, and 75% of them had dispersed. The distances they had traveled and their dispersal paths closely resembled those of juvenile males. By comparison, only 8% of untreated juvenile females in the same study area had dispersed by day 60, whereas 60% of juvenile males from the transplanted litters and 74% of the males from unmanipulated litters born in the same area had dispersed by day 60.

Ontogenetic Processes

[9]   We suspected that natal dispersal was triggered by internal factors. In particular, we hypothesized that males might stay home until they attained sufficient size or energy reserves to permit survival during the rigors of emigration. This hypothesis predicts that juvenile males will disperse when they attain a threshold body mass and that dispersers should be heavier, or exhibit different patterns of weight gain, than predispersal males of equivalent ages.

[10]   Our data were consistent with this hypothesis. Emigration dates were correlated with the time at which males reached a minimum body weight of about 125 grams. Emigrant juveniles were significantly heavier than male pups that had not dispersed. Most males attained the threshold weight during their natal summer, and dispersed then. Only the smallest males, who did not put on sufficient weight in the first summer, overwintered in their natal area. All these males dispersed the following season once they had become heavy enough.

Effects on Fitness and Survival

[11]   Do juvenile males disperse to avoid future nuclear family incest? The nonrandom movements of males away from the natal area clearly resulted in complete avoidance of kin as mates. Furthermore, during post-breeding dispersal, the males who had bred with the most females moved farthest. Under this hypothesis, the males who had sired the most female pups in an area would have the most to gain by emigrating. The observed patterns seem to be most consistent with avoiding inbreeding.

[12]   Belding's ground squirrels are not unusual in the rarity of close inbreeding. Inbreeding is minimized in most mammals and birds, often via the mechanism of sex-specific natal dispersal. But why are males the dispersive sex in mammals generally and ground squirrels particularly? The answer probably relates to the fact that females have a greater need for high-quality, well-located burrows for procreation. The depth and dryness of nest burrows, their proximity to food and their degree of protection from predators are vital to pup survival. The significance of the burrow, in turn, favors females who seek out and defend high-quality nest sites and who remain in them from year to year. The quality of a burrow is of negligible significance to the males, who do not take primary responsibility for parenting. To avoid predators and inclement weather, and to forage, males can move frequently without jeopardizing the survival of their young. Thus the sexual bias in natal dispersal might occur because inbreeding is harmful to both sexes and males incur lower costs by leaving home.

Source: (1993). In Paul W. Sherman and John Alcock (Eds.), *Exploring animal behavior* (pp. 41–48). Sunderland, MA: Sinauer Associates.

TASK 14: Read the text again, scanning for specific details about the ground squirrels and the scientists' experiment. Write this information in the space provided. The first one has been done for you.

1. approximate age when males permanently emigrate from their natal burrows   _2 months old_

2. period of time squirrels spend above ground   _____

3. average size of a ground squirrel litter   _____

4. total number of squirrels trapped by the researchers   _____

5. scientific methods used to measure patterns of dispersal   _____

6. percentage of males who have dispersed by the age of approximately sixteen weeks   _____

7. percentage of females who have dispersed from their mother's home range by the age of approximately sixteen weeks   _____

8. the male hormone that physically contributes to male squirrel dispersal   _____

9. experiment designed to measure the effect of male hormones on dispersal   _____

10. average weight of male pups when they disperse   _____

TASK 15: In your own words, summarize the research hypotheses and findings from this study of *S. beldingi* ground squirrels. Label each hypothesis and finding appropriately in terms of whether it leads to proximate or ultimate explanations about male ground squirrel dispersal behavior. Some examples have been done for you.

HYPOTHESIS	RESEARCH FINDINGS	PROXIMATE OR ULTIMATE?
Hypothesis 1: Male hormones influence patterns of dispersal. If females are exposed to male hormones, they should exhibit the same dispersal behavior as males.	**Findings:**	
Hypothesis 2:	**Findings:** Males left their natal burrows permanently when they had reached a body weight of 125 grams. This usually occurred by the end of the first summer of their lives. Only very small males remained in their natal burrow during the following winter.	
Hypothesis 3:	**Findings:**	proximate

Targeting Grammar: Passives in Explanations

WHERE PASSIVES ARE FOUND

Verbs occur in the passive voice instead of the active voice in academic text passages that do one of the following:

- describe the procedures followed in an experiment

    During each field season ground squirrels **were trapped** alive, weighed, and examined every two to three weeks.

    About 5,300 different ground squirrels **were handled.**

- present explanations, generalizations, and hypotheses

    Inbreeding **is minimized** in most mammals and birds, often via the mechanism of sex-specific natal dispersal.

    The ubiquity of natal dispersal seems consistent with the hypothesis that it **has been favored** directly by natural selection in various lineages.

Note that passive verbs contain some form of the auxiliary verb *be* (*is, are, was, were, has/have been, had been*, etc.) + the past participle of the main verb. A modal may also precede the *be* verb (*could be, might have been*, etc.). In the passive voice, the "doer," or "agent," of the verb can be stated or not. If it is explicitly stated, it appears in a *by*-phrase.

Inbreeding **is minimized** in most mammals and birds. [no agent]
  (subj.)   (*be*) (past part.)

Ground squirrels **were trapped** alive. [understood agent: "by researchers"]
  (subj.)   (*be*) (past part.)

Natal dispersal **seems to have been favored** by natural selection.
  (subj.)   (*be*)   (past part.)   (agent)

CHOOSING ACTIVE OR PASSIVE VOICE

When composing explanations, writers choose between active and passive voice as a tool to focus their readers' attention. Note the difference in focus between the active voice and passive voice versions of the *S. beldingi* experimental procedures:

1. The active voice focuses attention on the "doer" of the action, in this case, either the researchers themselves or the ground squirrels.

ACTIVE VOICE: FOCUS ON THE DOER

From 1974 to 1985 we **studied** three populations of *S. beldingi* near Yosemite National Park in the Sierra Nevada mountains of California. In each population, the animals **were** above ground for only four or five months during the spring and summer; during the rest of the year they **hibernated**. Females **bore** a single litter of five to seven young per season, and **reared** them without assistance from males. Most females **began** to breed as one-year-olds, but males **did not mate** until they were at least two. Females **lived** about twice as long as males.

2. The passive voice focuses attention on the research procedure itself. Here, the agent is understood to be the researchers.

PASSIVE VOICE: FOCUS ON THE PROCEDURE

During each field season ground squirrels **were trapped** alive, weighed, and examined every two to three weeks. About 5,300 different ground squirrels **were handled**. The animals **were marked** individually and **observed** unobtrusively through binoculars for nearly 6,000 hours. Natal dispersal behavior **was measured** by a combination of direct observations, livetrapping, radio telemetry, and identification of animals killed on nearby roads. The day on which each emigrant **was last seen** within its mother's home range **was defined** as its date of dispersal.

TASK 16: Rewrite the following sentences, changing the verbs from active to passive. If the agent is unnecessary or easily understood in the passive sentence, omit it. The first one has been done for you.

1. Researchers define *dispersal* as a complete and permanent emigration from the home range.

   <u>Dispersal is defined as a complete and permanent emigration from the home range.</u>

2. Male *S. beldingi* squirrels exhibit natal dispersal behavior.

   _____

3. Soon after the birth of the female pups, researchers injected them with testosterone.

   _____

4. After the testosterone treatment, they took the pups and their mothers back to the field.

   _____

5. The researchers located twelve of the androgen-treated female pups at the age of sixty days.

   _____

6. In the scientists' view, internal factors triggered natal dispersal.

   _____

7. The scientists correlated emigration dates with the minimum body weight of the male pups.

   _____

Task 17: Review the lecture notes you completed in Task 12. Then, taking the perspective of an animal behavior researcher, write five sentences in the passive voice explaining the low pregnancy and birth rate among female lions. The first one has been done for you.

1. From an evolutionary perspective, female lions are designed inefficiently because they produce so few young.

2. _____

_____

3. _____

_____

4. _____

_____

5. _____

_____

6. _____

_____

 ## Targeting Vocabulary: Abstract Nouns with Prepositions

WHAT ARE ABSTRACT NOUNS?

Because academic texts focus on concepts and behaviors, they often feature *abstract nouns*—nouns that express the concept or process associated with an action. These nouns are derived from other parts of speech, usually verbs. For example, when people move to a new country, we say they *emigrate*. The process associated with this action is called *emigration*. When a verb is transformed into a noun, certain suffixes are added to create the abstract noun *(-ence/ance, -al, -ment, -ation/tion/sion, -ure, -ison):*

VERB	ABSTRACT NOUN	VERB	ABSTRACT NOUN
avoid	avoid**ance**	survive	surviv**al**
move	move**ment**	vary	vari**ation**
expose	expos**ure**	compare	compar**ison**

Note: adding a suffix often involves some change to the spelling of the verb, such as dropping the final silent *e*.

PREPOSITIONS THAT ACCOMPANY ABSTRACT NOUNS

Abstract nouns are often followed by a prepositional phrase—most frequently beginning with the preposition *of*. However, other prepositions, including *between, about*, and *on*, may also follow abstract nouns.

Knowing which preposition to use with an abstract noun is a matter of usage and must be learned. The best way to do this is to learn it when you learn the noun. If you are unsure of the proper preposition, consult a dictionary for ESL learners, which gives this information and tells whether the noun is countable or uncountable. Frequently an example phrase is also included.

Dictionary Entries

prevention *n.* [U, *of*] the act or action of PREVENTing; *the prevention of crime*

comparison *n.* [U/C, *between*] similarity or the statement of points of similarity and difference; *There is little comparison between New York and Los Angeles.*

TASK 18: Below is a list of verbs from this chapter. Write the abstract noun form of the verb and the preposition that accompanies it in the column provided. Some nouns may be followed by more than one preposition. Consult a dictionary if necessary. The first one has been done for you.

VERB	⇒	NOUN	VERB	⇒	NOUN
1. appear	⇒	appearance of	12. investigate	⇒	
2. assist	⇒		13. observe	⇒	
3. combine	⇒		14. occur	⇒	
4. correlate	⇒		15. predict	⇒	
5. defend	⇒		16. procreate	⇒	
6. define	⇒		17. reproduce	⇒	
7. emphasize	⇒		18. resemble	⇒	
8. evaluate	⇒		19. restrict	⇒	
9. explore	⇒		20. secrete	⇒	
10. hibernate	⇒		21. select	⇒	
11. identify	⇒		22. suggest	⇒	

Integrating Perspectives

ANALYZING THROUGH DISCUSSION

REST

MEW

CHOKING

OBLIQUE
WITH LONG CALL

FORWARD

FACING AWAY

UPRIGHT

HUNCHED

Principal Display Postures of Herring Gulls

Task 19: In groups, discuss the gull behaviors pictured on page 34 and make guesses about the meaning of each posture. Below are some possible purposes for such postures. Use any knowledge you might have about the behavior of birds in general and of gulls in particular.

- to signal sexual receptivity (done by females)
- to threaten an enemy or intruder
- to sound an alarm to alert other gulls to danger
- to request food
- to appease another gull who is angry or ready to attack
- to encourage young gulls to feed
- to attract females and warn other males away (done by males)
- to demonstrate power to an enemy
- to advertise a nest site to females (done by males)

EVALUATING THROUGH WRITING

Task 20: In both the lion species and *S. beldingi* ground squirrels, males leave their natal groups, with females remaining at home to rear young. Choose one of these species and write a paragraph in which you hypothesize about the proximate and ultimate explanations for this difference in behavior between males and females. You may want to look back at the questions about proximate and ultimate causes of animal behavior in Task 4 on page 20.

EXPANSION:
THE COSTS AND BENEFITS
OF ADAPTIVE BEHAVIOR

This chapter extends the understanding of animal adaptive behavior by looking at its costs and benefits. Different categories of behavior are examined, including those that are cooperative, altruistic, selfish, and aggressive.

Exploring the Concepts

EXPLORING THROUGH VISUAL IMAGES

TASK 1: This chart examines the costs and benefits of social acts. It categorizes these acts as cooperative, selfish, altruistic, or spiteful and examines the costs and benefits of each act. Examine the table with a partner. Find an example from your experience with humans or animals that illustrates each type of social act.

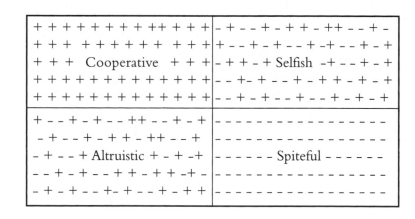

EXPLORING BACKGROUND KNOWLEDGE

One way of viewing a course of action or behavior that is applied in many academic disciplines is the *cost/benefit analysis*. This strategy looks at its advantages and disadvantages as well as its short- and long-term benefits and consequences.

TASK 2: With a partner or in a small group, select two of the actions listed below and on page 37. Perform a cost/benefit analysis of each action by filling in the chart provided.

- **War:** throwing yourself on a grenade to save the life of a friend
- **Business:** lying about your qualifications on a job application
- **Society:** not giving money to a homeless person who requests help

- **Marriage:** giving up a job you like because your spouse is offered a job in another location
- **Education:** stealing someone's idea and passing it off as your own
- **Sports:** playing your position in a team sport so that others do not need to compensate and can attend to the responsibilities of their own positions
- **Law:** defending a client that you know is guilty
- **Medicine:** refusing to treat a gravely ill patient because that patient has a communicable, life-threatening disease

ACTION	ADVANTAGES	DISADVANTAGES	BENEFITS		CONSEQUENCES	
			long-term	short-term	long-term	short-term
1.						
2.						

EXPLORING THROUGH WRITING

Consider the first sentence in Description 1 on page 38, which communicates its meaning through rich word choice.

One way to improve your writing is to find words with precise meanings. A useful tool for this purpose is a thesaurus, which gives synonyms, antonyms, and derivatives of the word you are looking up. You may also find secondary entries, cross-references, and more, depending on how the thesaurus is set up. If you want to find a different word with a similar meaning—or an antonym—look up the word you know, and the thesaurus will give you this information.

ACADEMIC STRATEGY:

USING A THESAURUS

Consider the first sentence in Description 1 on page 38, which communicates its meaning through rich word choice.

> The **popular stereotype** of jackals as **skulking scavengers** with **base** and **reprehensible behavior** is **belied,** as is so often the case, by long-term observations.

A less precise way to write this sentence would be:

> The idea that jackals are evil, sneaky hunters is proven wrong by long-term observation.

Let's say the writer had first written *sneaky* and wanted a word with a slightly different meaning and a more formal tone. The writer would then look up *sneaky* (or *sneak*) in a thesaurus and see *skulk,* among other choices, as a synonym.

Note: A danger in using a thesaurus is that the synonyms associated with a given word are often simply listed with no distinction of meaning provided. This is especially true in pocket thesauruses or the thesaurus tool built into many word processing programs. When choosing a more precise word, therefore, it's best to look it up in a dictionary before using it.

TASK 3: These two descriptions illustrate two different types of animal behavior. Select one and use the cost/benefit framework in Task 1 to categorize the animal's behavior. On a separate piece of paper, write a paragraph summarizing these costs and benefits. Vary some of the words you choose by using a thesaurus.

Description 1

The popular stereotype of jackals as skulking scavengers with base and reprehensible behavior is belied, as is so often the case, by long-term observations. Jackals are one of the few species of mammals in which males and females form long-term pair-bonds, often lasting a lifetime. They hunt together, share food, groom each other, jointly defend their territory, and provision and defend their pups together. Some of the pups stay with their parents and at the age of one year help raise the next litter, their full brothers and sisters.

Source: Patricia D. Moehlman (1993). Social organization in jackals. In Paul W. Sherman and John Alcock (Eds.), *Exploring animal behavior* (pp. 209–218). Sunderland, MA: Sinauer Associates.

Description 2

Occasionally, the pen of natural selection writes a murder mystery onto the pages of evolution. But unlike a typical Agatha Christie novel, this story reveals the identity of the murderer in the first scene. The mystery lies not in the "whodunit," but in why.

The case at hand involves the murder of nestling birds by their older siblings. Observers in the field have frequently noted brutal assaults by elder nestmates on their siblings, and the subsequent deaths of the younger birds. The method of execution varies among different species, ranging from a simple push out of the nest to a daily barrage of pecks to the head of the younger, smaller chick. Such killings present a challenge to the student of evolutionary biology: Does siblicide promote the fitness of the individuals that practice it, or is such behavior pathological? In other words, are there certain environmental conditions under which killing a close relative is an adaptive behavior? Moreover, are there other behaviors or biological features common to siblicidal birds that distinguish them from nonsiblicidal species?

Source: Douglas W. Mock, Hugh Drummond, and Christopher H. Stinson (1993). Avian siblicide. In Paul W. Sherman and John Alcock (Eds.), *Exploring animal behavior* (p. 197). Sunderland, MA: Sinauer Associates.

Working with Sources

UNDERSTANDING THROUGH READING

"Behavioral Ecology" provides a cost/benefit framework used by behavioral ecologists to explain why animals display certain behaviors while avoiding others.

TASK 4: Before you read the excerpt, look at the three headings below taken from the reading. Make predictions about the information that each heading will introduce. Then, next to each excerpt in the chart, write the number of the heading where you think the excerpt will be found.

1—Costs and Benefits of Behavior
2—Benefits of Social Life
3—Costs of Group Living

HEADING	EXCERPTS
_____	1. A male elephant seal that displays aggressive behavior is more likely to be injured than a male that avoids fights.
_____	2. By hunting in groups, the ancestors of modern man were able to kill large mammals they could not have subdued alone.
_____	3. When attacked by wolves, musk oxen form a circle with the young animals inside.
_____	4. Association with sick persons increases humans' chances of contracting a communicable disease.
_____	5. A male elephant seal that defends his parcel of the beach exhausts his fat reserves faster than a male that does not defend his territory.
_____	6. A given behavior pattern may be advantageous for animals of one species but disadvantageous for animals of another species.

The following reading uses the economic framework of cost/benefit analysis to examine animal behavior. It further presents four categories of social acts that animals engage in: altruistic, selfish, cooperative, and spiteful.

TASK 5: Before reading "Behavioral Ecology," think of an example of human behavior for each of the four categories of social acts. Decide which behaviors benefit the individual and which benefit the social group and/or humanity in general. Then read the following passage to discover how these concepts apply to animal behavior.

BEHAVIORAL ECOLOGY

William K. Purves, Gordon H. Orians, and H. Craig Heller

Costs and Benefits of Behavior

[1]   Fitness is a central concept in the study of evolution. The fitness of a genotype or phenotype is its reproductive contribution to subsequent generations *relative* to the contribution of other genotypes or phenotypes. How an individual behaves exerts a major influence on its survival and reproductive success; for example, a male elephant seal that cannot defeat his rivals will never mate. Which behavior patterns evolve depends on how they help an animal compared with other types of behavior in the same circumstances.

[2]   Ecologists interested in the evolution of behavior analyze their observations in terms of costs and benefits. Such analyses are based on the principle that an animal has only a limited amount of time and resources to devote to different kinds of acts. A certain behavior may be costly to the animal that performs it, but it may also benefit the animal. The **energetic cost** of a behavior is the difference between the energy the animal would have expended had it rested and the energy expended in performing the behavior. A male elephant seal that rises on his forelimbs, roars, and fights with rivals expends more energy than a resting male. He therefore exhausts his fat reserves faster than if he had not attempted to defend a parcel of beach.

[3]   The **risk cost** of a behavior is the increased chance of being injured or killed as a result of performing it, compared with resting. A displaying male

elephant seal is more likely to be injured by a rival than a male that avoids fights. The **opportunity cost** of a behavior is the sum of the benefits the animal forfeits by not being able to perform other behavior during the same time interval. A male elephant seal cannot search for food while he defends a section of beach, and the longer he stays the more time he needs to regain his energy reserves once he returns to the sea.

[4] An animal generally does not perform a behavior for which the total costs are greater than the sum of the **benefits:** the improvements in survival and reproductive success that the animal achieves by performing the behavior. Measuring these costs and benefits directly is difficult, but ecologists can find out which costs and benefits are most important for different species by observing how their behavior changes when environmental conditions change. Ecologists believe not that animals consciously calculate costs and benefits, but that through many generations, natural selection molds behavior in accordance with costs and benefits.

Dealing with Individuals of the Same Species

[5] Individuals of sexually reproducing species must mate in order to produce offspring. Associations for reproduction may consist of little more than a coming together of eggs and sperm, but individuals of many species associate for longer times to provide care for offspring. Associating with individuals of one's own species may also improve survival for reasons unrelated to reproduction.

[6] Social behavior evolves when the cooperation of individuals of the same species results in a higher rate of survival and more offspring than are possible for solitary individuals. Determining the effects of group living on survival and reproductive success is not easy, however. A given behavior pattern may be advantageous for individuals of one species but disadvantageous for those of another species, or even for the same individuals at a different time or place.

Benefits of Social Life

[7] Social life may improve hunting success or expand the range of prey that can be captured. For example, by hunting together, animals of some species, such as African hunting dogs, are able to capture prey too large for any one of them to subdue alone. White pelicans cooperate to maneuver prey into places where they are easier to catch. Cooperative hunting was a key component of the evolution of human sociality. By hunting in groups, our ancestors were able to kill large mammals they could not have subdued as individual hunters. These social humans could also defend their prey and themselves from other carnivores.

[8] Individuals of many species are better protected from predators if they live in groups. Predators may be able to find a group of animals more easily than they can a solitary animal, but a group may defend itself better when it is found. When attacked by wolves, musk oxen form a circle, with the young animals inside. The wolves have a great difficulty penetrating the formidable barrier of the large heads and massive horns of the adult animals. Musk ox group size is larger in areas where wolves are abundant than where wolves are scarce. The cost of grouping is that feeding efficiency is poorer in larger groups; the benefit of grouping is that predator defense is better.

Costs of Group Living

[9] An almost universal cost associated with group living is higher exposure to disease and parasites. Long before the causes of diseases were known, people sensed that association with sick persons increased the chances of contracting the illness. Quarantine has been employed as a means of combating the spread of illness for as long as we have had written records. The diseases of wild animals are not well known, but most of those that have been studied are also spread by close contact.

[10] Like the benefits, the costs of group living depend on circumstances. Individuals in groups may compete for food, interfere with one another's foraging, injure one another's offspring, or inhibit one another's reproduction. The effects of group living on survival and reproductive success of an individual also depend on its age, sex, size, and physical condition. Individuals may be larger or smaller than the average for their age and sex. Variation in skills, competitive abilities, and attractiveness to potential mates is often associated with these size differences.

Types of Social Acts

[11] Individuals living in social groups perform many different types of acts. These acts can be grouped into four categories according to their effects on individuals. An **altruistic act** benefits another individual at a cost to the performer. A **selfish act** benefits the performer and inflicts a cost on another individual. A **cooperative act** benefits both the performer and the recipient. A **spiteful act** inflicts costs on both. These terms are purely descriptive; they do not imply conscious motivation or awareness on the part of the animal.

[12] Many current studies of the social behavior of animals attempt to measure the relative costs and benefits of social acts, how the effects of the acts are distributed among the individuals of the group, and how individuals are related genetically. If a genetic basis for a cooperative or selfish act exists, and if performing it increases the fitness of the performer, then the genes governing the act will increase in frequency in the

lineage. In other words, cooperative or selfish behavior will evolve.

[13]   Altruism has long been the subject of a lively debate among biologists interested in animal behavior and understanding how altruistic behavior patterns could have evolved is not easy. Charles Darwin was puzzled by reproductive altruism in social insects. How can an act that *lowers* the performer's chances for survival or for passing on its own genes evolve into a behavior pattern? An individual may influence its fitness in two different ways. First, it may produce its own offspring, contributing to its **individual fitness.** Second, it may help the survival of relatives that bear the same alleles because they are descended from a common ancestor. This process is called **kin selection.** Together, individual fitness and kin selection determine the **inclusive fitness** of the individual. Altruistic acts eventually may evolve into altruistic behavior patterns. When the benefits of increasing the reproductive success of related individuals exceed the costs of decreasing the altruist's own reproductive success, then the altruist's inclusive fitness is enhanced.

Source: (1995). *Life: The science of biology* (4th ed.) (pp. 1058; 1063–1064). Sunderland, MA: Sinauer Associates.

TASK 6: To create a study guide for the reading, write a definition of the key terms below and create your own example to illustrate each. The definitions should be in your own words. An example has been done for you.

risk cost   individual fitness

opportunity cost   kin selection

benefit   ~~energetic cost~~

energetic cost

Definition - The energetic cost of a behavior is the difference between the energy the animal uses when it performs an act and the energy the animal would have used if it had remained at rest.

Example - A dog that trees a squirrel and stands barking under the tree, with little or no chance of catching or killing it, expends more energy than a dog who lies napping under the same tree.

TASK 7: Read the following description of the behavior of wild African dogs. Explain the *energetic, risk,* and *opportunity costs* associated with the behavior of the sentinel dog. Make predictions about the consequences of this dog's behavior in terms of *individual fitness* and *kin selection.*

Wild dogs in Africa hunt in packs of approximately eight dogs. One of the dogs has the task of sentinel; i.e., it is his job to warn the other dogs about approaching dangers. This sentinel dog goes ahead of or falls behind his packmates and is therefore separated from the pack in order to perform his duty.

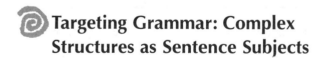 ## Targeting Grammar: Complex Structures as Sentence Subjects

English sentence subjects can be simple nouns, noun phrases, or more complex structures. Here are examples of two more complex structures.

EMBEDDED *Wh-*QUESTIONS

A noun clause used as a subject can contain an embedded *wh*-question. For example, the question "What are the risk costs of this behavior?" can be transformed into an embedded question to create a subject noun clause.

What the risk costs of this behavior are is an important scientific question.

(embedded *wh*-question)

GERUND CLAUSE

Another type of complex subject structure is a gerund clause. A gerund is a verbal—the present participle form ending in *-ing*—that is used as a noun (*eating, surviving*). A subject clause containing a gerund can include an object and a modifying adverb phrase.

> **Explaining** altruistic behavior in evolutionary terms is not easy.
>   (gerund)   (object)   (adverbial)

Note: These complex structures are considered one unit in the sentence and act as singular subjects. Notice that the verb in the main clause is, therefore, in the third person singular form.

> **How an animal behaves** influences its survival and reproductive success.
>   (embedded *wh*-question)   (verb) ↑

TASK 8: Each item contains two sentences. Using the cues provided, combine the two sentences into one sentence by using either a noun clause or a gerund structure as the subject of the new sentence. You may need to make additional changes to the original sentences. The first two have been done for you.

1. An animal performs only certain altruistic acts. This is triggered by the action's evolutionary benefits.

   Which altruistic acts an animal performs is triggered by the action's evolutionary

   benefits.

2. Behavioral ecologists measure the costs and benefits of animal behavior. This is difficult.

   Measuring the costs and benefits of animal behavior is difficult for behavioral

   ecologists.

3. Natural selection molds behavior. This involves a conscious calculation of the behavior's costs and benefits.

   How _____

   _____

4. Many animal species live in groups. This involves both costs and benefits.

   Living _____

   _____

5. The effects of social acts are distributed among individuals. This is the subject of current study.

   How _____

   _____

6. A male elephant seal defends his territory. This depletes his energy reserves.

   Defending _____

   _____

UNDERSTANDING THROUGH LISTENING

VIDEO

Lecture: Proximate and Ultimate Causes of Animal Behavior
Segment 4: Lion Infanticide—Costly or Beneficial?

Professor: Carolee Caffrey
Course: Biology 2: Principles of Modern Biology

In this final segment of her lecture, Professor Caffrey analyzes the costs and benefits of an apparently negative behavior, the slaughter of lion cubs by a male coalition that takes control of the lion pride.

TASK 9: In the previous lecture segment, Professor Caffrey noted that there are two basic ways to increase survivorship: "have lots of kids or kill the kids of others." With a partner or in a small group, explain what this means, giving examples of any animals you know that exhibit this behavior. Discuss why animals would choose to "kill the kids of others" rather than have their own.

TASK 10: Watch the lecture and take notes on the most important information. Using your notes, fill in the missing information in the following diagram about the infanticide cycle in lion prides. Some of the information may be from earlier lecture segments.

Infanticide in Lion Prides

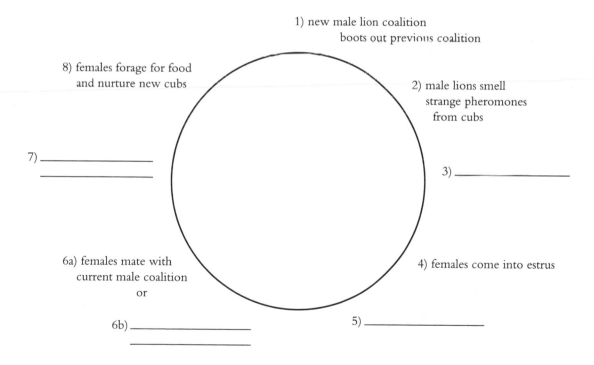

1) new male lion coalition boots out previous coalition

8) females forage for food and nurture new cubs

2) male lions smell strange pheromones from cubs

7) _____
_____

3) _____

6a) females mate with current male coalition
or

4) females come into estrus

6b) _____
_____

5) _____

TASK 11: Review the chart in Task 1 that presents a classification system for animal behavior and write a journal entry that does the following:

• classifies lion infanticide according to the chart
• explains the costs and benefits of infanticide to male and female lions

Hint: Pay particular attention to phases 3 and 6 of the infanticide cycle.

In his essays, Lewis Thomas, the famous sociobiologist, often makes the connection between concepts in biology and the human experience. This passage compares altruistic behavior in animals and humans.

TASK 12: Many reading passages address the universal questions *Who? What? When? Where? How?* and *Why?* As you read the Thomas passage, take notes on the information that helps you to answer each of these questions about the subject of altruism. The first question has been answered for you.

Who? Although altruism is often associated with human behavior, bees and other social insects also exhibit such behavior. Other species such as birds, moose, baboons, and dogs also sacrifice themselves for others of their same species.

ALTRUISM

Lewis Thomas

[1] Altruism has always been one of biology's deep mysteries. Why should any animal, off on its own, specified and labeled by all sorts of signals as its individual self, choose to give up its life in aid of someone else? Nature, long viewed as a wild, chaotic battlefield swarmed across by more than ten million different species, comprising unnumbered billions of competing selves locked in endless combat, offers only one sure measure of success: survival. Survival, in the cool economics of biology, means simply the persistence of one's own genes in the generations to follow.

[2] At first glance, it seems an unnatural act, a violation of nature, to give away one's life, or even one's possessions, to another. And yet, in the face of improbability, examples of altruism abound. When a worker bee, patrolling the frontiers of the hive, senses the nearness of a human intruder, the bee's attack is pure, unqualified suicide; the sting is barbed, and in the act of pulling away the insect is fatally injured. Other varieties of social insects, most spectacularly the ants and higher termites, contain castes of soldiers for whom self-sacrifice is an everyday chore.

[3] It is easy to dismiss the problem by saying that "altruism" is the wrong technical term for behavior of this kind. The word is a human word, pieced together to describe an unusual aspect of human behavior, and we should not be using it for the behavior of mindless automata. A honeybee has no connection to creatures like us, no brain for figuring out the future, no way of predicting the inevitable outcome of that sting.

[4] But the meditation of the 50,000 or so connected minds of a whole hive is not so easy to dismiss. A multitude of bees can tell the time of day, calculate the geometry of the sun's position, argue about the best location for the next swarm. Bees do a lot of close observing of other bees; maybe they know what follows stinging and do it anyway.

[5] Altruism is not restricted to the social insects, in any case. Birds risk their lives, sometimes lose them, in efforts to distract the attention of predators from the nest. Among baboons, zebras, moose, wildebeests, and wild dogs there are always stubbornly fated guardians, prepared to be done in first in order to buy time for the herd to escape.

[6] It is genetically determined behavior, no doubt about it. Animals have genes for altruism, and those genes have been selected in the evolution of many creatures because of the advantage they confer for the continuing survival of the species. It is, looked at in this way, not the emotion-laden problem that we feel when we try to put ourselves in the animal's place; it is just another plain fact of life, perhaps not as hard a fact as some others, something rather nice, in fact, to think about.

[7] J. B. S. Haldane, the eminent British geneticist, summarized the chilly arithmetic of the problem by announcing, "I would give up my life for two brothers or eight cousins." This calculates the requirement for ultimate self-interest: the preservation and survival of an individual's complement of genes. Trivers, Hamilton, and others have constructed mathematical models to account nicely for the altruistic behavior of social insects, quantifying the self-serving profit for the genes of the defending bee in the act of tearing its abdomen apart. The hive is filled with siblings, ready to carry the *persona* of the dying bee through all the hive's succeeding generations. Altruism is based on kinship; by preserving kin, one preserves one's self. In a sense.

[8] Haldane's prediction has the sound of a beginning sequence: two brothers, eight (presumably) first cousins, and then another series of much larger numbers of more distant relatives. Where does the influence tail off? At what point does the sharing of the putative altruist's genes become so diluted as to be

meaningless? Would the line on a graph charting altruism plummet to zero soon after those eight cousins, or is it a long, gradual slope? When the combat marine throws himself belly-down on the live grenade in order to preserve the rest of his platoon, is this the same sort of altruism, or is this an act without any technically biological meaning? Surely the marine's genes, most of them, will be blown away forever; the statistical likelihood of having two brothers or eight cousins in that platoon is extremely small. And yet there he is, belly-down as if by instinct, and the same kind of event has been recorded often enough in wartime to make it seem a natural human act, normal enough, even though rare, to warrant the stocking of medals by the armed services.

[9]   At what point do our genetic ties to each other become so remote that we feel no instinctual urge to help? I can imagine an argument about this, with two sides, but it would be a highly speculative discussion, not by any means pointless but still impossible to settle one way or the other. One side might assert, with total justification, that altruistic behavior among human beings has nothing at all to do with genetics, that there is no such thing as a gene for self-sacrifice, not even a gene for helpfulness, or concern, or even affection. These are attributes that must be learned from society, acquired by cultures, taught by example. The other side could maintain, with equal justification, since the facts are not known, precisely the opposite position: we get along together in human society because we are genetically designed to be social animals, and we are obliged, by instructions from our genes, to be useful to each other. This side would argue further that when we behave badly, killing or maiming or snatching, we are acting on misleading information learned from the wrong kinds of society we put together; if our cultures were not deformed, we would be better company, paying attention to what our genes are telling us.

[10]   For the purposes of the moment I shall take the side of the sociobiologists because I wish to carry their side of the argument a certain distance afield, beyond the human realm. I have no difficulty in imagining a close enough resemblance among the genomes of all human beings, of all races and geographic origins, to warrant a biological mandate for all of us to do whatever we can to keep the rest of us, the species, alive. I maintain, despite the moment's evidence against the claim, that we are born and grow up with a fondness for each other, and we have genes for that. We can be talked out of it, for the genetic message is like a distant music and some of us are hard-of-hearing. Societies are noisy affairs, drowning out the sound of ourselves and our connection. Hard-of-hearing, we go to war. Stone-deaf, we make thermonuclear missiles. Nonetheless, the music is there, waiting for more listeners.

[11]   But the matter does not end with our species. If we are to take seriously the notion that the sharing of similar genes imposes a responsibility on the sharers to sustain each other, and if I am right in guessing that even very distant cousins carry at least traces of this responsibility and will act on it whenever they can, then the whole world becomes something to be concerned about on solidly scientific, reductionist, genetic grounds. For we have cousins more than we can count, and they are all over the place, run by genes so similar to ours that the differences are minor technicalities. All of us, men, women, children, fish, sea grass, sandworms, dolphins, hamsters, and soil bacteria, everything alive on the planet, roll ourselves along through all our generations by replicating DNA and RNA, and although the alignments of nucleotides within these molecules are different in different species, the molecules themselves are fundamentally the same substance. We make our proteins in the same old way, and many of the enzymes most needed for cellular life are everywhere identical.

[12]   This is, in fact, the way it should be. If cousins are defined by common descent, the human family is only one small and very recent addition to a much larger family in a tree extending back at least 3.5 billion years. Our common ancestor was a single cell from which all subsequent cells derived, most likely a cell resembling one of today's bacteria in today's soil. For almost three-fourths of the earth's life, cells of that first kind were the whole biosphere. It was less than a billion years ago that cells like ours appeared in the first marine invertebrates, and these were somehow pieced together by the joining up and fusion of the earlier primitive cells, retaining the same blood lines. Some of the joiners, bacteria that had learned how to use oxygen, are with us still, part of our flesh, lodged inside the cells of all animals, all plants, moving us from place to place and doing our breathing for us. Now there's a set of cousins!

[13]   Even if I try to discount the other genetic similarities linking human beings to all other creatures by common descent, the existence of these beings in my cells is enough, in itself, to relate me to the chestnut tree in my backyard and to the squirrel in that tree.

[14]   There ought to be a mathematics for connections like this before claiming any kinship function, but the numbers are too big. At the same time, even if we wanted to, we cannot think the sense of obligation away. It is there, maybe in our genes for the recognition of cousins, or, if not, it ought to be there in our intellects for having learned about the matter. Altruism, in its biological sense, is required of us. We have an enormous family to look after, or perhaps that assumes too much, making us sound like official gardeners and zookeepers for the planet, responsibilities for which we are probably not yet grown-up enough. We may need new technical terms for

concern, respect, affection, substitutes for altruism. But at least we should acknowledge the family ties and, with them, the obligations. If we do it wrong, scattering pollutants, clouding the atmosphere with too much carbon dioxide, extinguishing the thin carapace of ozone, burning up the forests, dropping the bombs, rampaging at large through nature as though we owned the place, there will be a lot of paying back to do and, at the end, nothing to pay back with.

Source: (1983). *Late night thoughts on listening to Mahler's ninth symphony* (pp. 101–107). New York: Viking.

TASK 13: Thomas cites the British geneticist Haldane, who says, "I would give up my life for two brothers or eight cousins." Think of a human example and an animal example that might exemplify Haldane's statement. Discuss with a partner what your examples suggest about the limits of altruistic behavior in humans and in animals. Are they the same or different?

Targeting Vocabulary: Shades of Meaning

A good way to learn vocabulary is to learn words in their *semantic fields*, or groups of words with closely related meanings. A semantic field comprises some words with a general meaning and other words with related (stronger or weaker) connotations.

Examine the following sentence from "Altruism":

> This side would argue further that when we behave badly, killing or **maiming** or snatching, we are acting on misleading information learned from the wrong kinds of society we put together; if our cultures were not deformed, we would be better company, paying attention to what our genes are telling us.

In this sentence, the very specific verb *maim* belongs to the semantic field *to injure* and carries the connotation *to wound a part of the body such that it becomes useless.* Compare this meaning with the meanings of other words in the same semantic field.

SEMANTIC FIELD FOR *TO INJURE*

wound - to damage the body

maim - to wound a part of the body such that it becomes useless

maul - to wound by tearing the flesh (usually associated with animals)

injure - to damage something so that it doesn't function properly

disfigure - to spoil the appearance of a person (especially the face)

cripple - to damage the legs or nerves so that walking or moving is difficult or impossible

disable - to cause someone to be unable to use his or her arms or legs

In the above semantic field, *injure* has the most general meaning while all other words are more specific and, therefore, have a more restricted use.

TASK 14: Below are words from the unit that have specific connotations. Fill in the chart as shown in the example, creating semantic fields. In the middle column, write a + if the word has a positive connotation and a – if it has a negative connotation. Consult a thesaurus if necessary.

SPECIFIC WORD	PART OF SPEECH/MEANING	+/–	GENERAL WORD	OTHER SPECIFIC WORDS
1. base	adjective; a bad thing done for selfish and dishonest reasons	–	bad	cowardly; contemptible
2. brutal				
3. chaotic				
4. inflict				
5. violate				
6. altruistic				
7. reprehensible				
8. spiteful				
9. deprive				
10. formidable				
11. enhance				

ⓔ Targeting Grammar: *-ing* Participial Phrases with *by*

One type of participial phrase begins with the *-ing* form of the verb. This participial phrase modifies the subject of the main clause and functions as an adverb.

> **Patrolling the frontiers of the hive,** a ***worker bee*** can sense human intruders.
> (*-ing* participial phrase)   (subject)

Participial phrases with *-ing* verb forms express several different meanings. A common meaning is "how" or "by means of." These phrases occur after the preposition *by*.

> **By scattering pollutants,** ***people*** destroy their relationship with other forms of life.
> (*-ing* participial phrase)   (subject)

The preposition *by* is often deleted from introductory participial phrases. However, *by* cannot be deleted when the participial phrase follows the main clause.

> (**By**) patrolling the frontiers of the hive, a worker bee can sense human intruders.

> A worker bee can sense human intruders **by** patrolling the frontiers of the hive.

TASK 15: Complete the following sentences with a participial phrase. Use the cues in parentheses and add any other words that are needed or that fit the context. Use the preposition *by* when necessary. The first one has been done for you.

1. (ground squirrels, trap, observe) <u>Trapping and observing young ground squirrels,</u> researchers could determine how they dispersed from their natal burrows.

2. (animals, deprive, opportunity to learn) Scientists attempt to prove that a certain behavior is genetically determined _____.

3. (white substance, rectal pouch, deposit, grass) Hyenas mark their paths as they move through the jungle _____.

   (*Note:* add a comma before a final participial phrase if you do not use *by*.)

4. (circle, form, young inside) Musk oxen defend themselves against wolves in groups _____.

5. (family ties, acknowledge, other living beings) Humans may become more responsible in preserving nature _____.

Integrating Perspectives

APPLYING THE CONCEPTS

Following is a description of an unusual behavior in the animal world—sexual abstinence. In this behavior, either male or female wolves choose not to breed.

TASK 16: According to Lewis Thomas, "Animals have genes for altruism, and those genes have been selected in the evolution of many creatures because of the advantage they confer for the continuing survival of the species." Read the passage on page 49. With a partner or in a small group, discuss the advantages of sexual abstinence for wolves.

Female wolves do not breed until they are two years old, and males not until they are three. Until they are of breeding age, most of the adolescents remain with their parents; but even when they are of age to start a family they are often prevented from doing so by a shortage of homesteads. There is simply not enough hunting territory available to provide the wherewithal for every female to raise a litter. Since an overpopulation of wolves above the carrying capacity of the country to maintain would mean a rapid decline in the numbers of prey animals—with consequent starvation for the wolves themselves—they are forced to practice what amounts to birth control through continence. Some adult wolves may have to remain celibate for years before a territory becomes available. However, because the period of urgent amorous appetite is short—only about three weeks out of the year—these bachelors and spinsters probably do not suffer any great feeling of sexual deprivation. Moreover, their desire for domesticity and the companionship of other adults, as well as pups, is apparently met by the communal nature of the family group. Indeed, some wolves seem to prefer the "uncle" or "aunt" status, since it gives them the pleasure of being involved in rearing a family without incurring the full responsibilities of parenthood.

Source: Farley Mowat (1979). *Never cry wolf* (pp. 122–123). New York: Bantam.

ANALYZING THROUGH DISCUSSION

TASK 17: Choose one of the following animal behaviors that you have read about. Label the behavior using the chart in Task 1. In small groups, analyze the costs and benefits of the behavior, both to the individual performing the behavior and to future generations.

- Jackals mate for life, and some jackal offspring even stay with their families to help raise young born in the generation after their own.
- Praying mantis females eat the head of the male during the reproductive act.
- Male ground squirrels leave their natal burrows when they are strong enough to survive on their own.
- Young male lion cubs leave their natal pride when they are strong enough and join a coalition of other males.
- A coalition of male lions who have newly taken over a lion pride will kill all the dependent infants of the former coalition.
- Older nestling birds will often kill their newly hatched younger siblings.

EVALUATING THROUGH LITERATURE

Mark and Delia Owens have written a best-selling book, *Cry of the Kalahari*, which presents their research on animals in Botswana's famous Kalahari Desert.

TASK 18: In the passage on page 50, the Owens provide a rich sketch of the behavior of a lioness who has strayed from her natal pride (the Springbok Pan Pride) into the Blue Pride. Study the cast of characters; then read the description of Happy's behavior as she attempts to attract two Blue Pride males, Muffin and Moffet.

CAST OF CHARACTERS

Happy – a Springbok Pan Pride female in estrus who has strayed into Blue Pride territory

Muffin – a receptive Blue Pride male

Moffett – a receptive Blue Pride male, companion of Muffin

Diablo – head male of the Springbok Pan Pride

Dixie – another Springbok Pan Pride male

Liesa
Gypsy
Spicy
Spooky
} Blue Pride females

LIONS WITH NO PRIDE

Mark Owens and Delia Owens

[1]   Midnight takeoff: Cast in soft moonlight, the pewter desert fell away below us. Except for our gas lantern, set out on the airstrip to guide us home, not another light on earth could be seen as we sailed over the quiet, forgotten world of the Kalahari. Our faces glowing eerie red from the cockpit instrument lights, we followed the night movements of the lions and hyenas below.

[2]   Straining to recognize the subtle landmarks beneath us, we found Happy of the Springbok Pan Pride one night, on the boundary of the Blue Pride's territory. Within two weeks after Muffin and Moffet had killed Satan, another male, Diablo, had taken over the Springbok Pan Pride. The females had adjusted to their new male, and in recent weeks we had even seen Happy and some of the others mating with him. But now, as we circled overhead in the moonlight, we could see that Happy was within a few yards of Muffin and Moffet, who were patrolling the border of their territory. We were curious to know whether the two males would chase this foreign female back into her own territory or mate with her—if she was in estrus. In the Serengeti, male lions will court females from other prides, but we had never had the opportunity to observe this in the Kalahari. We flew back to camp, and then drove south to look for the lions.

[3]   When we found Muffin and Moffet, they were walking fast through brambles near Cheetah Pan, their noses to the ground. They stopped abruptly and looked up; Happy's eyes met theirs at less than thirty yards. The two lions stared intently at her for a few seconds, their tails twitching. Happy stood above the males on a low, scrub-covered sand ridge.

[4]   The lioness walked slowly forward, her head tall above the grass, her ears perked. Chests rumbling and tails lashing, Muffin and Moffet sprang to their feet and chased her for over 100 yards. But Happy was too fast for them, and when they broke off the charge she stopped just out of reach. They stared aggressively at her, raking their hind paws through the grass and roaring.

[5]   Again Happy walked cautiously toward them, and again they chased her, roaring and swatting the air just behind the tuft of her long tail. After each chase she ventured closer to them, but they seemed less and less inclined to pursue her. When she managed to get within twenty yards of them, Muffin and Moffet lay down side by side and watched what amounted to a feline burlesque.

[6]   Her hindquarters swaying sinuously, eyes half closed and jaws parted, Happy slunk toward the mesmerized males. Muffin quickly stood and strutted toward her, but she galloped away. When he stopped, she turned and wound her way toward them again, this time passing within a few yards of their noses. Muffin stood as tall as he could and, with all the savoir-faire he could muster, swaggered toward Happy. She lowered her hindquarters suggestively, inviting him to mount her. But when he stepped to her rear she suddenly spat and cuffed him hard across the nose. Muff roared and drew back, his ears flat and his long canines exposed, as Happy minced away, her tail flicking flirtatiously. After a few more attempts by both males to gain her favor, Muffin and Moffet seemed to tire of the game, and they walked back north into their own territory. Happy followed about thirty yards behind, apparently unconcerned that she was on foreign soil.

[7]   We knew that Liesa, Gypsy, Spicy, and Spooky of the Blue Pride were finishing a warthog kill on the crest of West Dune. Muffin and Moffet, with Happy trailing by fifteen yards, were moving directly toward them.

[8]   Since it was not unusual for male lions in the Serengeti to associate occasionally with females of another pride, it had not been totally surprising to see Muffin and Moffet interact with Happy. However, we knew that Serengeti pride females form closed social groups that do not accept new female members or tolerate foreign females in their territory. There the pride is sacrosanct: a stable social unit of closely related lionesses and their young, who associate with the male or males who help defend the territory. A lioness may be kicked out and become nomadic, but these nomads do not join other prides. In the Serengeti, a single pride lasts for generations, with the same kin line, and at any one time, it has in its membership great-grandmothers, grandmothers, mothers, daughters, aunts, and female cousins.

[9]   Now Muffin, Moffet, and Happy padded steadily toward the crest of West Dune. We followed in the truck, preparing our flashes, cameras, and the tape recorder for the coming fight between Happy and the Blue Pride females.

[10]   By the time we could see the four Blue Pride females in the spotlight ahead, they had finished the warthog and were casually licking one another's faces. The two males greeted the lionesses, smelled the skeleton, and then lay down a few yards away. Happy sauntered past Spicy and Spooky and lay down next to Muffin and Moffet. Incredibly, there was not the slightest sign of aggression on the part of any of the lionesses. We switched off the tape recorder and pulled the cameras back inside the truck. It was astonishing: A foreign female had ambled into the heart of the Blue Pride camp, and its members had hardly noticed!

[11]   For the next four days, Happy was courted, first by Muffin and then by Moffet, just as though she were a Blue Pride female. During the heat of the day Muffin lay as near to her as he could, watching her every move. If she sought out better shade, he strutted so close beside her that their bodies rubbed together. Sometimes he would initiate copulation by standing at her rear. More often, however, she would walk back and forth in front of him, her tail flicking and hindquarters swaying, or she would brush her body along his before crouching in front of him. When he stood over her to copulate, he nibbled at her neck and she growled and flattened her

ears. As soon as Muffin had finished, he would step back quickly to avoid getting clouted by Happy's paw, for invariably she would whirl around, snarling fiercely, and swat at him. Then, lying on her back, her legs extended, she would roll over and over in the grass, her eyes closed in apparent ecstasy. They mated in this stereotypic fashion every twenty to thirty minutes for part of two days and all of two nights. Small wonder that Muffin did not object when Moffet took over the courtship at sunset on the third day.

[12]   During the day Happy rested—Muffin or Moffet always at her side—under the same bush as Spicy, looking very much as if she belonged. Then, on the fifth night, she walked south alone and returned to Diablo, Dixie, and the others of the Springbok Pan Pride.

[13]   This mixing of females between prides had never been reported in lions. Was this wandering lioness an aberration, a passing "stranger in the night"? Was her behavior unique? We could hardly think so. Since Happy had been so readily accepted by the Blue Pride females, it appeared that such exchanges of lionesses between prides might occur quite regularly.

Source: (1984). *Cry of the Kalahari* (pp. 238-241). Boston: Houghton Mifflin.

TASK 19: Do you believe that Happy was just a "passing stranger in the night" and that her behavior was unique? Alternatively, do you believe that the exchange of lionesses occurs more regularly? To answer this second question, consider the costs and benefits of this behavior for Happy, her offspring, and the Blue Pride lions. Compare your answers with a partner's.

EVALUATING THROUGH WRITING

This unit has provided illustrations of a range of animal behaviors, such as older nestlings killing younger siblings, worker bees giving up their lives to protect the queen bee, and adult wolves helping to raise the siblings of others. The unit has also provided both a cost/benefit framework within which to analyze these behaviors and a larger lens through which to view a behavior's evolutionary consequences.

TASK 20: Choose one of the following topics and write an analytical essay. Use examples from the unit to support your analysis. Consult the Academic Strategy box on page 52 to help you develop your ideas.

1. In this unit, we have seen several examples of *selfish* behavior. Choose one of these and write an essay in which you analyze the behavior's costs and benefits. Comment on why such behavior is expected behavior in animals.

2. In this unit, we have seen several examples of *altruistic* behavior. Choose one of these (not wolves) and write an essay in which you analyze the behavior's costs and benefits. Comment on why such behavior seems unusual in animals.

3. In this unit, we have seen several examples of *cooperative* behavior. Choose one of these and write an essay in which you analyze the behavior's costs and benefits. Comment on why such behavior is more typical in certain animal species.

ACADEMIC STRATEGY:

DEVELOPING IDEAS FOR AN ANALYTICAL ESSAY

When writing an analytical paper, the writer's task is to divide the topic in a way that explains it more clearly. One common way of analyzing a topic is to examine costs and benefits associated with it.

You can develop ideas for a cost/benefit analysis paper in the following way:

- Identify the topic and consider what a reader needs to understand about it. This could include a definition and/or an explanation about why this topic involves costs and benefits.

  The topic is altruistic behavior. Readers need to know that it is any "selfless" action or behavior that has costs to the performer and benefits to the recipient.

- Find an example that illustrates your topic.

  Wolves who do not mate because of food shortages and who instead become "aunts" or "uncles" to other wolf pups are a good example of altruistic behavior.

- Make a list of the short- and long-term costs.

  Short-term costs: The wolf does not have his/her own young. This wolf may be perceived as different by other wolves because wolves place a high value on the group and on family.

  Long-term costs: Because these wolves do not breed, their own genes are not passed on to future generations.

- Make a list of the short- and long-term benefits.

  Short-term benefits: With "aunt" or "uncle" status, the wolf does get to participate in child-rearing. Because the wolf does not produce offspring, there is more food to go around, thus saving both the wolf and his or her close relatives. This is an immediate benefit to survivorship. It may also help the pack to have an "extra pair of hands" for protection and hunting.

  Long-term benefits: The gene pool of the pack will survive. In addition, this wolf ensures that, at the least, his or her relatives' genes will survive.

- Look beyond the costs and benefits you have listed. Think of the larger picture. What is the larger meaning that you want your analysis to convey to readers?

  Though the costs to the individual wolf are great, they are outweighed by the short- and long-term benefits to the pack. Thus, this seemingly puzzling behavior makes sense within the picture of wolf survivorship.

INSIGHTS FROM SOCIOLOGY

INTRODUCTION:
THE RULES
OF CIVIL INATTENTION

Sociologist Erving Goffman studied how and why we act the way we do in our everyday lives. When he examined the smallest aspects of social behavior, he found that our social life is well organized and runs smoothly because we follow certain unwritten rules, or rules dictated by custom and culture.

Exploring the Concepts

EXPLORING THROUGH VISUAL IMAGES

TASK 1: Look at this picture of people in an elevator. What unwritten rules of behavior are these people following? Discuss with a partner or small group.

EXPLORING THROUGH DISCUSSION

Targeting Vocabulary: Describing Contacts with People

The verb phrases below can be used to describe the ways in which we make or avoid contact with people. Many of these verbs are followed by prepositions: They are *two-word verbs.*

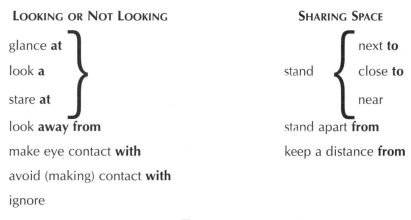

LOOKING OR NOT LOOKING

glance **at**

look **a**

stare **at**

look **away from**

make eye contact **with**

avoid (making) contact **with**

ignore

SHARING SPACE

stand { next **to** / close **to** / near

stand apart **from**

keep a distance **from**

TALKING

talk **to** someone **about** something

converse/chat **with** someone **about** something

discuss something **with** someone

ask someone something

tell someone something

comment **on** something **to** someone

remark **on** something **to** someone

Note: about is not used after *discuss.*

TASK 2: Take turns asking a partner the following questions about hypothetical situations. In your answers, try to use a variety of the phrases above.

1. You get on an elevator with a stranger of the opposite sex. How would you position yourself in the elevator in relation to that person?

2. The worst has happened! You are stuck in an elevator with three strangers. You have been informed by an intercom in the elevator that it will take thirty minutes to get the elevator operating again. What are some ways you might spend your time?

3. A very attractive person about your age smiles at you in the grocery checkout line. What would you probably do?

4. While you are waiting for the bus, you notice that a stranger keeps staring at you. It's making you uncomfortable. What would you do?

5. As you take a seat on the first day of a new class, you listen to a person next to you talking to another classmate. You decide that you want to say something to that person next to you. What would you say?

EXPLORING BACKGROUND KNOWLEDGE

Strangers meet face-to-face in many public places, such as city sidewalks or streets; buses, taxis, or subways; food markets, shopping centers, or clothing stores; at the zoo, the beach, or the park.

TASK 3: To answer the following questions, discuss with your classmates some of the "unwritten" rules that influence behavior with strangers in a public place in your culture.

1. How close can a stranger stand to you before you begin to feel uncomfortable?

2. Is it appropriate to make eye contact with a stranger? How long can you look at a stranger before you begin to feel uncomfortable? Can both men and women make eye contact with strangers?

3. What situations allow strangers to talk to one another (i.e., to ask the time of day, to give a stranger something he or she has accidentally dropped, etc.)?

4. How long do conversations with strangers usually last?

5. How do you signal that you do or do not want to talk to a stranger?

Working with Sources

UNDERSTANDING THROUGH READING

In the following passage, Erving Goffman describes how people act toward strangers in public places. He outlines three possible ways that people may react to someone they don't know. According to Goffman, the third alternative, which he terms *civil inattention,* is the most appropriate "unwritten" rule controlling how strangers in American culture act toward one another in a face-to-face public encounter.

TASK 4: Skim the reading to locate the three ways that people react to strangers. Then read the text and determine how civil inattention differs from the other two reactions. Be prepared to explain this difference to your classmates.

CIVIL INATTENTION

Erving Goffman

[1] When persons are mutually present and not involved together in conversation or other focused interaction, it is possible for one person to stare openly and fixedly at others, gleaning what he can about them while frankly expressing on his face his response to what he sees. It is also possible for one person to treat others as if they were not there at all, as objects not worthy of a glance, let alone close scrutiny. Here we have "nonperson" treatment; it may be seen in our society in the way we sometimes treat children and mental patients.

[2] Currently, in our society, this kind of treatment is to be contrasted with the kind generally felt to be more proper in most situations, which will here be called "civil inattention." What seems to be involved is that one gives to another enough visual notice to demonstrate that one appreciates that the other is present (and that one admits openly to having seen him), while at the next moment withdrawing one's attention from him so as to express that he does not constitute a target of special curiosity or design.

[3] In performing this courtesy the eyes of the looker may pass over the eyes of the other, but no "recognition" is typically allowed. Where the courtesy is performed between two persons passing on the street, civil inattention may take the special form of eyeing the other up to approximately eight feet.

[4]   By according civil inattention, the individual implies that he has no reason to suspect the intentions of the others present and no reason to fear the others, be hostile to them, or wish to avoid them.

[5]   Civil inattention is so delicate an adjustment that we may expect constant evasion of the rules regarding it. Dark glasses, for example, allow the wearer to stare at another person without that other being sure that he is being stared at. One person can look at another out of the corner of his eyes. The fan and para-sol once served as similar aids in stealing glances. It should be added, too, that the closer the onlookers are to the individual who interests them, the more exposed his position (and theirs), and the more obligation they will feel to ensure him civil inattention. The further they are from him, the more license they will feel to stare at him a little.

Source: (1963). *Behavior in public places* (pp. 83–85). New York: Free Press of Glencoe.

TASK 5: Which of the statements follow the definition of civil inattention? Circle *Yes* or *No* according to whether the statement is part of the definition or not.

Yes   No   1. A person acknowledges the presence of another momentarily.

Yes   No   2. A person stares fixedly at another.

Yes   No   3. A person withdraws his attention from another after a brief initial acknowledgment.

Yes   No   4. Dark glasses are used to view another person without being noticed for an extended period of time.

Yes   No   5. There is no acknowledgment at all of the other's presence.

Yes   No   6. When people are in close proximity to each other they cannot regard each other openly.

Yes   No   7. At distances of eight feet or more two strangers can regard each other openly.

Yes   No   8. A stranger is treated as a nonperson.

⊚ Targeting Grammar: Introducing Explanations with *It* Constructions

Explanations are frequently introduced in English using certain phrases that begin with *it*. This type of construction allows the writer (1) to emphasize the explanation by putting it at the end of the sentence and (2) to avoid taking responsibility for the information. Notice the following patterns.

IT + BE + ADJECTIVE
- **It is possible** for one person to stare openly and fixedly at others.
- **It is conceivable** that people feel physically threatened if someone stares fixedly at them.

IT + (MODAL) PASSIVE CONSTRUCTION
- **It is known** that mental patients are usually treated as nonpersons.
- **It should be added** that the closer the onlookers are to the individual who interests them, the more obligation they feel to accord civil inattention.

TASK 6: Write a journal entry in which you discuss whether Goffman's concept of civil inattention operates in your culture or in the place where you live. Give an example of a place where you most frequently experience civil inattention (i.e., on a subway train or a bus, in a market, etc.) and provide explanations for how people behave there. Try to use a variety of *It* constructions in your writing.

UNDERSTANDING THROUGH LISTENING

VIDEO

Lecture: Stranger Intervention
Segment 1: The Relational Wedge

Professor: Kerry Ferris
Course: Sociology 3: The Sociology of Everyday Life
Texts: *Behavior in Public Places* by Erving Goffman and
Social Problems by Phillip W. Davis

In this segment of her lecture on stranger intervention, Professor Ferris, a sociologist, defines the notion of a relational wedge in public situations. She provides several examples to explain how this phenomenon allows an individual to initiate an interaction with a stranger.

 Targeting Vocabulary: Key Terms

TASK 7: The words in this task are from the lecture and readings in this chapter.

- Put a √ by the words you know fairly well.
- Put an X by words you've seen before but whose meaning you aren't sure of.
- Put a ? next to unfamiliar words.

Compare your list with several classmates' lists. Give definitions of some of the words you know but other students do not. Have your classmates do the same.

VERB	NOUN	ADJECTIVE
___ deny (a request)	___ civil inattention	___ explicit
___ differentiate (oneself)	___ interaction	___ tolerable
___ initiate (conversation)	___ norm	___ unwritten
___ merit	___ petitioner	___ vulnerable
___ accord	___ public aid	___ risky
___ bid	___ relational wedge	___ ratified
___ fulfill (a request)	___ social intercourse	___ implicit
___ interact		___ palatable
___ intervene		___ mute
___ petition		___ legitimate
___ ignore		___ unspoken

TASK 8: Watch the lecture and take notes. As you listen, focus on how relational wedges break the pattern of civil inattention.

The format of most content courses at the university includes not only the lecture itself but also an opportunity for students to raise questions about the information in the lecture and the related course readings. Often, large lecture courses will have discussion sections that allow students to work with content in a more interactive way. Both types of classrooms provide a context for students to ask *clarification questions,* i.e., questions that help students better understand ideas or concepts that are difficult for them.

ACADEMIC STRATEGY:

ASKING CLARIFICATION QUESTIONS IN A LECTURE OR DISCUSSION SECTION

Here are several common ways to ask for clarification:

- Introducing clarification questions:

  I might have missed this, but . . .
  You might have already said this, but . . .
  I'm not sure whether . . .

- Asking for clarification:

  I'm confused about the difference between X and Y.
  Could you explain the idea of X again?
  I'm not sure I completely understood X. Could you repeat it?
  I didn't quite get what you meant by X.

- Paraphrasing ideas for additional clarification:

  Are you saying that [any time a person looks at a stranger, that is a relational wedge?]
  I still don't understand why [civil inattention is seen as normal behavior].
  The way I understand it, [we cannot legitimately talk to strangers in public without a relational wedge]. *Is that correct?*

TASK 9: Based on the reading "Civil Inattention" and the lecture by Professor Ferris, formulate four clarification questions that you would ask Professor Ferris. Take turns asking your questions to other class members to see if they can answer them.

TASK 10: On a separate paper, write a definition of the term *relational wedge,* giving examples of the different types of relational wedges that oblige strangers to interact with other strangers.

TASK 11: At the end of this lecture segment, Professor Ferris recounts an experience at the San Francisco airport in which a stranger in need was helped. With a partner, explain the type of relational wedge present in this experience. Why couldn't the person who helped ignore the stranger?

Integrating Perspectives

ANALYZING THROUGH VISUAL IMAGES

TASK 12: This cartoon illustrates an extreme case of civil inattention—people ignoring a potential suicide. With a partner, discuss how the concept of civil inattention applies to this situation. Why do you think Wiley has labeled the cartoon "Urban Compassion"?

NON SEQUITUR By Wiley

APPLYING THE CONCEPTS

TASK 13: Read the following two cases. For the second case, describe briefly how the concept of civil inattention applies and what relational wedges are present. The first case has been done for you.

Case 1

Four people were contacted to participate in a survey about a new product. These subjects who came to fill out the survey were met by a woman. As the subjects were led into the room where the survey would be conducted, they passed an office. Through its open door was a desk and bookcases piled high with papers and filing cabinets. The subjects entered the adjacent room and were given a questionnaire to fill out. The woman told the subjects that she would be working next door for about 10 minutes while they completed the questionnaires. She left after opening the collapsible curtain which divided the two offices. About four minutes later, the subjects heard the woman climb up on a chair to reach for a stack of papers on the bookcase. They then heard a loud crash and a scream as the chair collapsed and she fell to the floor. "Oh, my God, my foot . . . I . . . can't move . . . it. Oh . . . my ankle," the woman moaned. "I . . . can't get this . . . thing . . . off me."

Source: Bibb Latané and John M. Darley (1973). Bystander "apathy." In John Helmer and Neil A. Eddington (Eds.), *Urbanman: The psychology of urban survival* (pp. 73–74). New York: The Free Press.

Case 2

A mother and her thirteen-year-old daughter stopped at a supermarket in a Denver suburb. As they approached the store, they heard piercing screams coming from a dilapidated old-model car. A child's voice was pleading, "No! No! Please . . . don't. Don't please!" The cries were punctuated by the sound of sickening thuds; they saw a large, bearded man in the front seat of the parked car, presumably the child's father, punching the child with terrific force with his clenched fist. Although they could not see enough of the child to determine his age or even his sex because he was lying on the front seat, they guessed that he was about five or six years old. After several punches the child was silent, but the man continued to beat him.

Source: Joanna Simms (1989, May). Witness to child abuse. *Parents Magazine*, 90–94.

Case 1: The woman and the people filling out the questionnaire are strangers; therefore, the rules of civil inattention would normally apply. In other words, the four people and the woman would briefly acknowledge each other's presence and then ignore each other. But civil inattention is broken because a relational wedge occurs when the woman cries out in pain within the hearing of the strangers.

Case 2: _____

_____

_____

_____

_____

_____

Evaluating through Writing

Task 14: Write a journal entry about a time when you were confronted by a stranger needing assistance. What did you do? Go beyond the story to analyze the situation, using the concepts of *civil inattention* and *relational wedge*. Answer the following questions:

- Why did the people in this situation no longer merit civil inattention?
- In order to intervene, what factors did you need to consider?
- What were the possible consequences of intervening? of **not** intervening?

EXPLORATION:
BYSTANDER APATHY

How readily would you step in to help a stranger in need in a public place? In this chapter, you will examine the factors that complicate people's decisions to intervene.

Exploring the Concepts

EXPLORING THROUGH VISUAL IMAGES

TASK 1: The cartoon below reveals something about the way people often behave when confronted by a stranger in need of help. In small groups, discuss what the cartoonist is saying about people's responses. Do you believe that this is typical?

EXPLORING THROUGH DISCUSSION

In the following vignettes from the short story "Witness," the first-person narrator expresses views that are similar to those of the cartoonist in Task 1.

TASK 2: After reading all the vignettes, choose the adjective below that you think best describes the narrator's reaction when confronted with strangers in trouble. Be prepared to defend your choice.

concerned   cynical

realistic   cautious

I adopt a "wait and see" attitude.

Most of the time, these things just go away by themselves. Why jump to unnecessary conclusions?

I sit up in bed. I buff my nails. I try to guess where those ear-piercing screams are coming from. The garden below my window? The park? The TV next door? It's fun to play detective.

A woman getting bludgeoned to death and a cat in heat sound remarkably similar.

It's easy to be fooled. Rooftop slaying or children playing?

Most people don't realize dialing 911 costs 50 cents. Let the neighbors call.

* * * *

In the park I hold the *Times* in front of my face. What is that couple doing over there? Are they struggling or *dancing*? Vicious assault or April Fool's Day gag?

It's not polite to stare.

I never take a stand until I've heard both sides of a story.

She runs away, he catches up, pins her to the ground, a knife to her throat. I glance at my watch, I've got to be going.

Nobody likes a busybody.

* * * *

I say to the guy reading the newspaper next to me, Do you see what I see? He says, Do you see what *I* see? We shudder. Teamwork.

We agree. Serves her right for taking a walk so late at night in a changing neighborhood.

He should have given him his wallet the first time he asked.

Sometimes you get what's coming to you.

* * * *

From a safe distance, I size up the assailant. Isn't it the thought that counts?

I could go to a lot of trouble for nothing. What if my photograph doesn't get in the paper? The mayor doesn't praise my heroism?

Rule: I never intervene if I'm on the way to the office. I'd mess up my suit.

* * * *

In the morning a cardboard figure lay in the grass where the girl had been murdered. The neighbors and I looked at each other with surprise, "I thought you called."

Don't blame us. Blame the system.

We're good people. We're a community. We donate money to the Wildlife Preservation Fund each year. We care.

Nothing like this has ever happened in our neck of the woods before.

What a shame. She was such a lovely girl.

Oh well, that's life in the big city.

That's par for the course.

If you can't stand the heat get out of the kitchen.

A cop at my door. He asks me questions. I cut him short. Officer, I say, I'm one of those lucky people who can sleep through anything.

Source: Lisa Blaushild (1992). Witness. In David Cavitch (Ed.), *Life studies* (4th ed.) (pp. 285–287). Boston: Bedford.

TASK 3: Look at the four pictures. In groups or with a partner, discuss which person you think is most likely to hold the same views as the narrator of "Witness." Be prepared to defend your choice.

⟳ Targeting Vocabulary: Colloquial Language

The author of "Witness" uses colloquial language to express the "do-nothing, see-nothing" attitude of the narrator.

TASK 4: Read the phrases from the story in the left-hand column and write your "translation" in the right-hand column. The first one has been done for you.

WHAT THE AUTHOR SAYS	WHAT SHE MEANS
1. I adopt a "wait and see" attitude.	I don't act immediately. I want to see if a situation resolves itself without my help.
2. Why jump to unnecessary conclusions?	
3. I never take a stand until I've heard both sides of a story.	
4. [It] serves her right. . . .	
5. Sometimes you get what's coming to you.	
6. Isn't it the thought that counts?	
7. That's par for the course.	
8. If you can't stand the heat get out of the kitchen.	

TASK 5: Do you agree or disagree with the author's attitude? For each statement, put a √ in the column that best represents your attitude. Then compare your answers with a partner's.

STATEMENT	STRONGLY AGREE	AGREE	NEUTRAL	DISAGREE	STRONGLY DISAGREE
1. Most of the time problems just go away by themselves.	____	____	____	____	____
2. It's not polite to stare.	____	____	____	____	____
3. Nobody likes a busybody.	____	____	____	____	____
4. It's the thought that counts.	____	____	____	____	____

EXPLORING THROUGH WRITING

TASK 6: What if everyone in a society held the same views as the narrator of "Witness"? On a separate piece of paper, write a journal entry about the possible social or moral consequences of a "do-nothing, see-nothing" attitude. You may want to consider consequences in one or more of the following areas of public life:

* safety in public places (no response to attacks or purse stealings)
* common courtesy (unwillingness to give directions or the time to strangers or assist disabled or elderly people in need)
* neighborliness (ignoring neighbors' requests for help)
* emergency situations (no response to victims of natural disasters like earthquakes or floods)

Working with Sources

UNDERSTANDING THROUGH LISTENING

VIDEO

> **LECTURE:** Stranger Intervention
> **SEGMENT 2:** Trouble in Public Aid Situations
>
> **PROFESSOR:** Kerry Ferris
> **COURSE:** Sociology 3: The Sociology of Everyday Life
> **TEXTS:** *Behavior in Public Places* by Erving Goffman and
> *Social Problems* by Phillip W. Davis

In this segment of the lecture, Professor Ferris gives some examples of people's reluctance to ask for or give public aid.

TASK 7: Watch the lecture. In each of the following situations, specify the reasons that people are reluctant to engage in interactions with strangers. The first one has been done for you.

Example 1: Asking for the time

The petitioner is reluctant to ask a stranger for the time because the stranger might

either ignore the request completely or answer rudely.

Example 2: Asking for directions

_____

_____

Example 3: Asking for money

_____

_____

TASK 8: In which of the situations in Task 7 would you be most or least likely to ask a stranger for aid? to give aid? Check the boxes that apply. Add any circumstances that might influence your decision. Then discuss your decisions and reasons with a partner.

SITUATIONS	VERY LIKELY	SOMEWHAT LIKELY	NOT VERY LIKELY	HIGHLY UNLIKELY	CIRCUMSTANCES THAT WOULD INFLUENCE YOUR DECISION
Asking for the time					
Giving the time					
Asking for directions					
Giving directions					
Asking for money					
Giving money					

TASK 9: All the situations in Task 7 share the common denominator that people are reluctant to engage in social interaction with strangers. Which one of the following reasons do you think best accounts for this reluctance? Do your classmates agree with you? If not, why not? Be prepared to defend your choice in a discussion with your classmates.

_____ People's lives are busy. They are often too rushed.

_____ People are basically self-absorbed and uninterested in the lives of others.

_____ People fear being taken advantage of by others.

_____ People don't feel competent or qualified to help.

_____ People fear that they will be asked to give additional help after the initial request.

UNDERSTANDING THROUGH READING

In the following reading, Latané and Darley provide a sociological perspective on why people do not intervene to give aid in public situations.

TASK 10: Read the text. On a separate piece of paper, take notes on the five characteristics of emergencies.

BYSTANDER "APATHY"

Bibb Latané and John M. Darley

[1]   On a March night in 1964, Kitty Genovese was set upon by a maniac as she came home from work at 3 A.M. Thirty-eight of her Kew Gardens neighbors came to their windows when she cried out in terror—none came to her assistance. Even though her assailant took over half an hour to murder her, no one even so much as called the police.

[2]   This story became the journalistic sensation of the decade. "Apathy," cried the newspapers. "Indifference," said the columnists and commentators. "Moral callousness," "dehumanization," "loss of concern for our fellow men," added preachers, professors, and other sermonizers. Movies, television specials, plays, and books explored this incident and many more like it. Americans became concerned about their lack of concern.

[3]   But can these epithets be correct? We think not. Although it is unquestionably true that witnesses in such emergencies have often done nothing to save the victims, "apathy," "indifference," and "unconcern" are not entirely accurate descriptions of their reactions. The thirty-eight witnesses to Kitty Genovese's murder did not merely look at the scene once and then ignore it. Instead they continued to stare out their windows at what was going on. Caught, fascinated, distressed, unwilling to act but unable to turn away, their behavior was neither helpful nor heroic; but it was not indifferent or apathetic either.

[4]   There are certainly strong forces leading us to act. Empathy or sympathy, innate or learned, may cause us to share, at least in part, a victim's distress. If intervention were easy, most of us would be willing to relieve our own discomfort by alleviating another's suffering.

[5]   Even if empathy or sympathy were not strong enough to lead us to help in emergencies, there are a variety of social norms which suggest that each of us has a responsibility to each other, and that help is the proper thing to do. "Do unto others as you would have them do unto you," we hear from our earliest years. Although norms such as these may not have much influence on our behavior in specific situations, they may imbue us with a general predisposition to try to help others.

[6]   Indeed, in many nonemergency situations, people seem surprisingly willing to share their time and money with others. According to the Internal Revenue Service, Americans contribute staggering sums to a great variety of charitable organizations each year. Even when tax deductions don't fan the urge to help, people still help others. When Columbia students asked 2,500 people on the streets of New York for 10 cents or 20 cents, over half of these people gave it.

[7]   If people are so willing to help in nonemergency situations, they should be even more willing to help in emergencies when the need is so much greater. Or should they? Emergencies differ in many ways from other types of situations in which people need help, and these differences may be important. The very nature of an emergency implies certain psychological consequences.

Characteristics of Emergencies

[8]   Perhaps the most distinctive characteristic of an emergency is that it involves threat or harm. Life, well-being, or property is in danger. Even if an emergency is successfully dealt with, nobody is better off afterwards than before. Except in rare circumstances, the best that can be hoped for if an emergency occurs is a return to the status quo. Consequently, there are few positive rewards for successful action in an emergency. At worst, an emergency can claim the lives not only of those people who are initially involved in it, but also of anybody who intervenes in the situation. This fact puts pressures on individuals to ignore a potential emergency, to distort their perceptions of it, or to underestimate their responsibility for coping with it.

[9]   The second important feature of an emergency is that it is an unusual and rare event. Fortunately, although he may read about them in newspapers, or watch fictionalized accounts on television, the average person probably will encounter fewer than half a dozen serious emergencies in his lifetime. Unfortunately when he does encounter one, he will have had little direct personal experience in handling such a situation. Unlike the stereotyped patterns of his everyday behavior, an individual facing an emergency is untrained and unrehearsed.

[10]   In addition to being rare, emergencies differ widely, one from another. There are few common requirements for action between a drowning, a fire, or an automobile accident. Each emergency presents a

different problem, and each requires a different type of action. Consequently, unlike other rare events, our culture provides us with little secondhand wisdom about how to deal with emergencies.

[11]   The fourth basic characteristic of emergencies is that they are unforeseen. They "emerge," suddenly and without warning. Being unexpected, emergencies must be handled without the benefit of forethought and planning and an individual does not have the opportunity to think through in advance what course of action he should take when faced with an emergency. He must do this thinking in the immediacy of the situation, and has no opportunity to consult others as to the best course of action or to alert others who are especially equipped to deal with emergencies. The individual confronted with an emergency is thrown on his own resources. We have already seen that he does not have much in the way of practiced responses or cultural stereotypes to fall back upon.

[12]   A final characteristic of an emergency is that it requires instant action. It represents a pressing necessity. If the emergency is not dealt with immediately, the situation will deteriorate. The threat will transform itself into damage; the harm will continue or spread. There are urgent pressures to deal with the situation at once. The requirement for immediate action prevents the individual confronted with an emergency from leisurely considering the possible courses of action open to him. It forces him to come to a decision before he has had time to consider his alternatives. It places him in a condition of stress.

[13]   The picture we have drawn is a rather grim one. Faced with a situation in which there is no benefit to be gained for himself, unable to rely on past experience, on the experience of others, or on forethought and planning, denied the opportunity to consider carefully his course of action, the bystander to an emergency is in an unenviable position. It is perhaps surprising that anyone should intervene at all.

Social Determinants of Bystander Intervention

[14]   Most emergencies are, or at least begin as, ambiguous events. A quarrel in the street may erupt into violence, but it may be simply a family argument. A man staggering about may be suffering a coronary or an onset of diabetes; he may simply be drunk. Smoke pouring from a building may signal a fire; on the other hand, it may be simply steam or air conditioner vapor. Before a bystander is likely to take action in such ambiguous situations, he must first define the event as an emergency and decide that intervention is the proper course of action.

[15]   In the course of making these decisions, it is likely that an individual bystander will be considerably influenced by the decisions he perceives other bystanders to be taking. If everyone else in a group of onlookers seems to regard an event as nonserious and the proper course of action as nonintervention, this consensus may strongly affect the perceptions of any single individual and inhibit his potential intervention.

[16]   The definitions that other people hold may be discovered by discussing the situation with them, but they may also be inferred from their facial expressions or their behavior. A whistling man with his hands in his pockets obviously does not believe he is in the midst of a crisis. A bystander who does not respond to smoke obviously does not attribute it to fire. An individual, seeing the inaction of others, will judge the situation as less serious than he would if alone.

[17]   But why should the others be inactive? Unless there were some force inhibiting responses on the part of others, the kind of social influence process described would, by itself, only lead to a convergence of attitudes within a group. If each individual expressed his true feelings, then, even if each member of the group were entirely guided by the reactions of the others, the group should still respond with a likelihood equal to the average of the individuals.

[18]   An additional factor is involved, however. Each member of a group may watch the others, but he is also aware that others are watching him. They are an audience to his reactions. Among American males, it is considered desirable to appear poised and collected in times of stress. Being exposed to the public view may constrain the actions and expressions of emotion of any individual as he tries to avoid possible ridicule and embarrassment. Even though he may be truly concerned and upset about the plight of a victim, until he decides what to do, he may maintain a calm demeanor.

[19]   The constraints involved with being in public might in themselves tend to inhibit action by individuals in a group, but in conjunction with the social influence process described above, they may be expected to have even more powerful effects. If each member of a group is, at the same time, trying to appear calm and also looking around at the other members to gauge their reactions, all members may be led (or misled) by each other to define the situation as less critical than they would if alone. Until someone acts, each person sees only other nonresponding bystanders, and is likely to be influenced not to act himself. A state of "pluralistic ignorance" may develop.

[20]   It has often been recognized that a crowd can cause contagion of panic, leading each person in the crowd to overreact to an emergency to the detriment of everyone's welfare. What we suggest here is that a crowd can also force inaction on its members. It can suggest, implicitly but strongly, by its passive behavior, that an event is not to be reacted to as an emergency, and it can make any individual uncomfortably aware of what a fool he will look for behaving as if it is.

[21]   This line of thought suggests that individuals may be less likely to intervene in an emergency if they witness it in the presence of other people than if they see it alone. It suggests that the presence of other people may lead each person to interpret the situation as less serious, and less demanding of action than he would if alone. The presence of other people may alter each bystander's perceptions and interpretations of the situation.

[22]   Once an individual has noticed an emergency and interpreted it as being serious, he still has to decide what, if anything, he will do about it. He must decide that he has a responsibility to help, and that there is some form of assistance that he is in a position to give. He is faced with the choice of whether he himself will intervene. His decision will presumably be made in terms of the rewards and costs of the various alternative courses of action open to him.

[23]   In addition to affecting the interpretations that he places on a situation, the presence of other people can also alter the rewards and costs facing a bystander. Perhaps most importantly, the presence of other people can alter the cost of not acting. If only one bystander is present at an emergency, he carries all of the responsibility for dealing with it; he will feel all of the guilt for not acting; he will bear all of any blame others may level for nonintervention. If others are present, the onus of responsibility is diffused, and the individual may be more likely to resolve his conflict between intervening and not intervening in favor of the latter alternative.

[24]   When only one bystander is present at an emergency, if help is to come it must be from him. Although he may choose to ignore them (out of concern for his personal safety, or desire "not to get involved"), any pressures to intervene focus uniquely on him. When there are several observers present, however, the pressures to intervene do not focus on any one of the observers; instead the responsibility for intervention is shared among all the onlookers and is not unique to any one. As a result, each may be less likely to help.

[25]   "There's safety in numbers," according to an old adage, and modern city dwellers seem to believe it. A feeling so widely shared should have some basis in reality. Is there safety in numbers? If so, why? Two reasons are often suggested: Individuals are less likely to find themselves in trouble if there are others about, and even if they do find themselves in trouble, others are likely to help them deal with it. While it is certainly true that a victim is unlikely to receive help if nobody knows of his plight, our research casts doubt on the suggestion that he will be more likely to receive help if more people are present. In fact, the opposite seems to be true. A victim may be more likely to get help, or an emergency be reported, the fewer people who are available to take action.

[26]   Although the results of our research may shake our faith in "safety in numbers," they also may help us begin to understand a number of frightening incidents where crowds have listened to, but not answered, a call for help. Newspapers have tagged these incidents with the label "apathy." We have become indifferent, they say, callous to the fate of suffering others. Our society has become "dehumanized" as it has become urbanized. These glib phrases may contain some truth, since startling cases such as the Genovese murder often seem to occur in our large cities, but such terms may also be misleading. Our research suggests a different conclusion. It suggests that situational factors, specifically factors involving the immediate social environment, may be of greater importance in determining an individual's reaction to an emergency than such vague cultural or personality concepts as "apathy" or "alienation due to urbanization." We have found that the failure to intervene may be better understood by knowing the relationship among bystanders rather than that between a bystander and the victim.

[27]   Our research may explain why the failure to intervene seems to be more characteristic of large cities than rural areas. Bystanders to urban emergencies are more likely to be, or at least to think they are, in the presence of other bystanders than witnesses of non-urban emergencies. Bystanders to urban emergencies are less likely to know each other or to know the victim than are witnesses of nonurban emergencies. When an emergency occurs in a large city, a crowd is likely to gather; the crowd members are likely to be strangers; and it is likely that no one will be acquainted with the victim. These are exactly the conditions that make the helping response least likely.

Source: John Helmer and Neil A. Eddington (Eds.) (1973). *Urbanman: The psychology of urban survival* (pp. 62–91). New York: The Free Press.

When using information from a source text, academic writers are expected to *paraphrase,* or use their own words, as much as possible. The following three strategies are useful ones for transforming an original text into your own words:

- Use different word forms.
- Use synonyms.
- Change the sentence structure.

Let's consider the following sentence:

Original text: The presence of other people may lead each person to interpret the situation as less serious than he would if alone.

It contains two key words that can be changed to different word forms.

presence (n.)	⇒	present (adj.)
interpret (v.)	⇒	interpretation (n.)

It also contains several key words that can be replaced by synonyms:

person	⇒	individual
people	⇒	others
alone	⇒	by himself, by herself

Finally, the sentence structure of the original sentence can be changed from one independent clause to a dependent clause plus an independent clause. To do this, it is necessary to think about the logical relationship expressed in the sentence. The original sentence contains the verb phrase "may lead to," indicating a condition/result relationship. When paraphrasing this sentence, therefore, we can use a dependent clause beginning with *if* or *when.*

Using these three strategies, we arrive at the following paraphrase for the original sentence:

Paraphrased text: **When** others are present, an individual's interpretation of an emergency situation may be less serious than if he were by himself.

Since the tendency in academic writing today is to avoid sexist language, we might want to paraphrase this sentence further to avoid the personal pronouns *he* and *himself.* This is commonly achieved by rewriting the sentence using the plural subject *they* and making any other necessary changes:

Paraphrased text: When others are present, individual**s'** interpretation**s** of emergency situation**s** may be less serious than if **they** were by **themselves**.

TASK 11: On a separate piece of paper, paraphrase each of the following sentences from "Bystander 'Apathy'" using the paraphrasing strategies on page 71. Note that there is more than one possible paraphrase for each sentence.

1. This consensus may strongly affect the perceptions of any single individual and inhibit his potential intervention.

2. Situational factors are of great importance in determining an individual's reaction to an emergency.

3. There are [*sic*] a variety of social norms which suggest that each of us has a responsibility to each other and that help is the proper thing to do.

TASK 12: Latané and Darley mention numerous interrelated factors that determine whether people intervene in an emergency situation. In groups or with a partner, decide what you think are the three most important factors. Share these with a classmate.

Targeting Vocabulary: Describing Emotions and Reactions

The following vocabulary from "Bystander 'Apathy'" expresses how people respond in emergency situations. These noun, adjective, and adverb forms are typically used with certain verb phrase patterns.

NOUN	ADJECTIVE	ADVERB
apathy	apathetic	apathetically
callousness	callous	callously
compassion	compassionate	compassionately
concern	concerned	(in a concerned manner)
empathy	empathetic	empathetically
indifference	indifferent	indifferently; (with indifference)
sympathy	sympathetic	sympathetically
unconcern/lack of concern	unconcerned	(in an unconcerned manner)

TASK 13: Use the nouns, adjectives, or adverbs in the lists to fill in the blanks in the sentences. There may be more than one correct word following the verb. The first one has been done for you.

1. verb pattern: *respond* + adverb

    The witnesses in the Kitty Genovese stabbing <u>responded with indifference.</u>

2. verb pattern: *react* + adverb

    Strangers often react _____ when small children are involved in an emergency situation.

3. verb pattern: *act* + adverb

    Urban dwellers seem to act _____ even when confronted with violent crimes.

4. verb pattern: *behave* + adverb

    The New Yorkers who witnessed Kitty Genovese's murder behaved _____.

5. verb pattern: *display* + noun

   Sociologists study why people display _____ in emergency situations.

6. verb pattern: *demonstrate* + noun

   When confronted with an emergency, people often do not demonstrate _____ for the victims.

7. verb pattern: *show* + noun

   Why don't people show more _____ for the plight of others?

8. verb pattern: *exhibit* + noun

   A stranger who exhibits _____ for another stranger is often deemed a hero.

9. verb pattern: *express* + noun

   Most neighbors will express _____ for the safety and well-being of those who live around them.

TASK 14: Describe an emergency situation in which you or someone you know intervened. Then list the criteria (as set forth by Latané and Darley) that qualify this as an emergency. An example has been done for you:

Emergency Situation: Once I was cross-country skiing with my family. It was snowing and the visibility wasn't very good. As we approached some trees, we noticed two sleeping bags covered with snow. It turned out that there were two boys asleep in the bags. We shook them to wake them up and took them back to our cabin. They told us they had been hiking and got tired so they decided to rest. We decided that we should take them to the emergency room at the nearest hospital. We then phoned their parents to tell them about the situation. Later we found out that they both had frostbite on their toes and fingers.

Criteria of an Emergency Situation: This situation involved a threat or harm to the two boys. It was unusual to come across two sleeping bags in the snow; this situation was further unforeseen because it interrupted our fun. We knew that we needed to intervene because the boys would have frozen to death. It required instant action. The situation presented several complex problems to be solved. We needed to decide whether to approach the sleeping bags or just ignore them. We also needed to decide who should take responsibility for the emergency situation and what to do with the boys. Finally, we needed to determine how serious their medical condition was and how to contact their families.

Emergency Situation: _____

_____

_____

_____

Criteria of an Emergency Situation: _____

_____

_____

_____

⊚ Targeting Grammar: Using Modal Verbs to Describe Possibility in the Past

We often use modal verbs such as *could* or *might* to describe possibility.

Talking with strangers **could** be dangerous.

Standing too close to a stranger **might** be offensive.

When we speculate about the possible causes of past actions, we generally use the modals *could, may,* or *might* followed by *have* + past participle.

	MODAL	+	*HAVE*	+	PAST PARTICIPLE	
The boy	**could**		have		**wanted**	attention.
The stranger	**may**		have		**needed**	help.
The woman	**might**		have		**been**	drunk.

To discuss possible consequences of a past action, consequences that did not actually happen, we use *could* or *might*.

	MODAL	+	*HAVE*	+	PAST PARTICIPLE	
He	**could**		have		**threatened**	me.
She	**might**		have		**been**	upset.

Here is the progressive (*-ing*) form with *might* and *could*.

	MODAL	+	*HAVE*	+	*BEEN*	+	VERB *-ING*	
The man	**might**		have		**been**		**lying**	when he said his car was out of gas.
The stranger	**could**		have		**been**		**trying**	to make friends.

Task 15: Each of the following pairs of sentences describes an intervention situation that happened in the past and a consequence that could have occurred as a result. Each sentence stating a consequence has a verb error. Using the information in the examples on page 74, correct each error in the italicized verb so that it expresses a consequence that could have happened in the past but did not necessarily occur.

SITUATION	POSSIBLE CONSEQUENCE
1. I helped an old woman cross the street because she looked a little confused.	She *might have call* me a male chauvinist. Correction: _____
2. I asked a man who was on the bus to turn down his radio.	He *could being* very angry. Correction: _____
3. I told a man who was hitting a woman in a parking lot to stop.	He *may have told* me to mind my own business. Correction: _____
4. I asked a girl if she could lend me a dollar.	She *might say* I was asking for too much. Correction: _____
5. I stared at a woman who was shoplifting groceries in a store.	She *could have became* hostile toward me. Correction: _____

Task 16: Go back to the situation you described in Task 14. Use the factors you have listed in Task 12 to help describe what might have caused you (or the person involved) *not* to intervene. Write a paragraph on a separate piece of paper. An example has been done for you.

> In the case of the frozen boys in the snow, we wouldn't have intervened if we hadn't viewed it as an emergency situation (e.g., if it hadn't been cold and snowing). We probably also wouldn't have intervened if there had been other people present at the scene because we might have thought that they would take action. We also might have looked to those other people for clues as to what to do. For example, if they had skied past the bags, we might have done the same thing.

Integrating Perspectives

EVALUATING THROUGH DISCUSSION

TASK 17: Here is a letter sent to an advice columnist by someone who needed help from strangers. From the list below, select the reason that best explains why no one intervened. Put a √ on the line. Be prepared to defend your choice in a discussion with your classmates.

Whatever Happened to Neighbors Who Care?

Dear Abby:

While my husband interns at a local hospital, I manage a small convenience store. One night recently I had to work from midnight to 6 A.M. because a clerk called in sick. Just after 1 A.M., I was robbed.

A couple confronted me, tied and gagged me and robbed the store. Before leaving, they hung up the "Closed" sign and turned out the lights, leaving me helpless on the floor, bound from my ankles to my shoulders. I was unable to struggle free, so I just lay there until daybreak. I was finally able to work myself to a standing position and hopped to the front door.

Somehow, I got it open and hopped out onto the parking lot. I continued hopping up and down, hoping to attract the attention of drivers going by. (I fell several times.) You would think that someone would stop and come to my aid— no one could miss that I was tied up—but no one wanted to get involved.

Finally, someone did stop and untie me.

I'm sorry to be spilling my anger out on you, but after being robbed at gunpoint, bound and gagged for four hours and then facing indifference from the people in my neighborhood, I'm furious. Thanks for letting me get that off my chest.

ELIZABETH IN A RAGE

Source: (1995, Friday, August 4). Dear Abby. *The Los Angeles Times.*

_____ Bystanders or passersby thought she needed medical attention, but they didn't feel qualified to give it to her.

_____ They didn't think her problem was any of their business.

_____ They didn't see anyone else who stopped to help her.

_____ They were afraid that she was going to trick them, take their money, or even kill them.

_____ Perhaps they drove past but then called the police.

_____ Because it was so early (only daybreak), they were afraid to stop. If this had happened in the middle of the day, they would have helped her.

_____ Many of the bystanders were alone and, therefore, didn't want to stop.

TASK 18: Latané and Darley's research suggests that bystanders influence other bystanders in two ways: (1) whether an individual bystander interprets the situation as an emergency, and (2) how a bystander weighs the costs and benefits of helping a stranger. Look again at the Dear Abby column about the woman who was robbed. Speculate with a partner or in a small group about the following:

- how the bystanders who see this woman in trouble on the side of the road could influence each other *not* to interpret this as an emergency
- why it was more costly to themselves to intervene than *not* to intervene

EVALUATING THROUGH WRITING

TASK 19: Without looking at Abigail Van Buren's response that follows, write your own response to Elizabeth in a Rage. Read your response aloud in a small group. Then compare your group's responses to the following one that was published in *The Los Angeles Times*. Which response do you like best? Why?

My response:

Dear Elizabeth,

_____

_____

_____

_____

_____

_____

_____

_____

Abby's response:

Dear Elizabeth: Don't apologize. That's what I'm here for. And your anger is justified. I'm relieved that you were not physically injured in what had to have been an emotionally devastating incident. Those who wouldn't come to your aid should be ashamed of themselves. Consider channeling your righteous anger into organizing a neighborhood watch program composed of those residents who are willing to get involved.

EXPANSION:

TO INTERVENE OR NOT TO INTERVENE?

The readings and the lecture segment in this chapter present situations that, whether an emergency or not, require some kind of response. Bystanders must decide whether to intervene in what are sometimes unclear circumstances.

Exploring the Concepts

EXPLORING VISUAL IMAGES

TASK 1: Look at the following photo. Would you step in? Discuss your response and your reasons for it with three classmates.

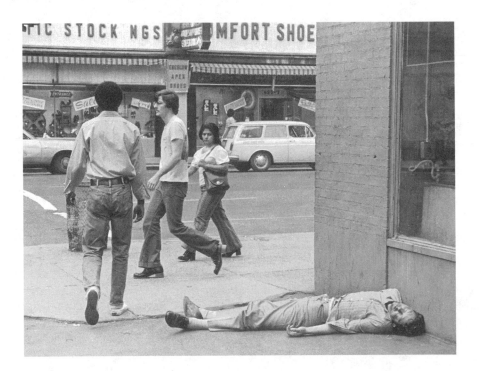

EXPLORING THROUGH DISCUSSION

The decision to intervene in public situations is not a straightforward matter. In part, deciding to intervene depends on how you feel about the action you see, on how other bystanders are behaving, and on whether or not you define the situation you see as an emergency.

TASK 2: Next to each public situation in the left column, circle *Yes, No,* or *Maybe* to indicate whether you would intervene. Then write the circumstances that would influence your decision. Discuss your answers with your classmates, and be prepared to defend your answers. The first one has been done for you.

	SITUATION	WOULD YOU INTERVENE?			WHAT CIRCUMSTANCES WOULD INFLUENCE YOUR DECISION?
IN NEED OF HELP	You see a woman or a man sitting on a park bench looking lonely.	Yes	(No)	Maybe	I wouldn't intervene because I think some people like to be left alone or need time to themselves. Also, no one else is paying attention to this person. There appears to be no emergency.
	You see a woman or a man sitting on a park bench crying.	Yes	No	Maybe	
	You see a woman or a man lying on the street.	Yes	No	Maybe	
CHILD PUNISHMENT	You see a parent scolding his or her child.	Yes	No	Maybe	
	You see a parent slapping his or her child across the face.	Yes	No	Maybe	
	You see a parent spanking his or her child.	Yes	No	Maybe	
ALTERCATIONS	You see a man and a woman having a heated argument.	Yes	No	Maybe	
	You see a man or a woman slapping his or her partner across the face.	Yes	No	Maybe	
	You see two men fighting in a bar.	Yes	No	Maybe	

Working with Sources

Because of their special training, doctors have the ability and professional responsibility to help strangers with medical emergencies. Yet in today's society, doctors face potential legal consequences if they intervene.

TASK 3: As you read the article, consider the rewards and costs of intervening that confront the doctor in this emergency situation.

A DOCTOR'S DILEMMA

James N. Dillard

[1] It was a bright, clear February afternoon in Gettysburg, Pennsylvania. A strong sun and layers of down did little to ease the biting cold. Our climb to the crest of Little Roundtop wound past somber monuments, barren trees and polished cannon. From the top, we peered down on the wheat field where men had fallen so close together that one could not see the ground. Rifle balls had whined as thick as bee swarms through the trees, and cannon shots had torn limbs from the young men fighting there. A frozen wind whipped tears from our eyes. Despite the cold, it was hard for my friend, Amy, and me to leave this place.

[2] Driving east out of Gettysburg on a country blacktop, the gray Bronco ahead of us passed through a rural crossroad just as a small pickup truck tried to take a left turn. The Bronco swerved, but slammed into the pickup on the passenger side. We immediately slowed to a crawl as we passed the scene. The Bronco's driver looked fine, but we couldn't see the driver of the pickup. I pulled over on the shoulder and got out to investigate.

[3] The right side of the truck was smashed in, and the side window was shattered. The driver was partly out of the truck. His head hung forward over the edge of the passenger-side window, the front of his neck crushed on the shattered windowsill. He was unconscious and starting to turn blue. His chest slowly heaved against a blocked windpipe.

[4] A young man ran out of the house at the crossroad. "Get an ambulance out here," I shouted against the wind. "Tell them a man is dying."

[5] I looked down again at the driver hanging from the windowsill. There were six empty beer bottles on the floor of the truck. I could smell the beer through the window. I knew I had to move him, to open his airway.

I had no idea what neck injuries he had sustained. He could easily end up a quadriplegic (unable to walk or to move). But I thought: he'll be dead by the time the ambulance gets here if I don't move him and try to do something to help him.

[6] An image flashed before my mind. I could see the courtroom and the driver of the truck sitting in a wheelchair. I could see his attorney pointing at me and thundering at the jury: "This young doctor, with still a year left in his residency training, took it upon himself to play God. He took it upon himself to move this gravely injured man, condemning him forever to this wheelchair. . . ." I imagined the millions of dollars in award money. And all the years of hard work lost. I'd be paying him for the rest of my life. Amy touched my shoulder. "What are you going to do?"

[7] The automatic response from long hours in the emergency room kicked in. I pulled off my overcoat and rolled up my sleeves. The trick would be to keep enough traction straight up on his head while I moved his torso, so that his probably broken neck and spinal-cord injury wouldn't be made worse. Amy came around the driver's side, climbed half in and grabbed his belt and shirt collar. Together we lifted him off the windowsill.

[8] He was still out cold, limp as a rag doll. His throat was crushed and blood from the jugular vein was running down my arms. He still couldn't breathe. He was deep blue-magenta now, his pulse was rapid and thready. The stench of alcohol turned my stomach, but I positioned his jaw and tried to blow air down into his lungs. It wouldn't go.

[9] Amy had brought some supplies from my car. I opened an oversize intravenous needle and groped on the man's neck. My hands were numb, covered with freezing blood and bits of broken glass. Hyoid bone—God, I can't even feel the thyroid cartilage, it's gone . . . OK, the thyroid gland is about there, cricoid rings are here . . . we'll go in right here. . . .

[10] It was a lucky first shot. Pink air sprayed through the IV needle. I placed a second needle next to the first.

The air began whistling through it. Almost immediately, the driver's face turned bright red. After a minute, his pulse slowed down and his eyes moved slightly. I stood up, took a step back and looked down. He was going to make it. He was going to live. A siren wailed in the distance. I turned and saw Amy holding my overcoat. I was shivering and my arms were turning white with cold.

[11]   The ambulance captain looked around and bellowed, "What the hell . . . who did this?", as his team scurried over to the man lying in the truck.

[12]   "I did," I replied. He took down my name and address for his reports. I had just destroyed my career. I would never be able to finish my residency with a massive lawsuit pending. My life was over.

[13]   The truckdriver was strapped onto a backboard, his neck in a stiff collar. The ambulance crew had controlled the bleeding and started intravenous fluid. He was slowly waking up. As they loaded him into the ambulance, I saw him move his feet. Maybe my future wasn't lost.

[14]   A police sergeant called me from Pennsylvania three weeks later. Six days after successful throat-reconstruction surgery, the driver had signed out, against medical advice, from the hospital because he couldn't get a drink on the ward. He was being arraigned on drunk-driving charges.

[15]   A few days later, I went into the office of one of my senior professors, to tell the story. He peered over his half glasses and his eyes narrowed. "Well, you did the right thing medically of course. But, James, do you know what you put at risk by doing that?" he said sternly. "What was I supposed to do?" I asked.

[16]   "Drive on," he replied. "There is an army of lawyers out there who would stand in line to get a case like that. If that driver had turned out to be a quadriplegic, you might never have practiced medicine again. You were a very lucky young man."

[17]   The day I graduated from medical school, I took an oath to serve the sick and the injured. I remember truly believing I would be able to do just that. But I have found out it isn't so simple. I understand now what a foolish thing I did that day. Despite my oath, I know what I would do on that cold roadside near Gettysburg today. I would drive on.

Source: (1995, June 12). My turn: A doctor's dilemma. *Newsweek*, 12.

TASK 4: With a partner, discuss the rewards and costs that the doctor faced. Share your ideas with the rest of the class.

TASK 5: "A Doctor's Dilemma" is a true story about a public aid situation. With a group, discuss the ways in which the following concepts from the first two chapters of this unit apply to the situation.

• civil inattention

• relational wedge

• characteristics of an emergency

• the effects of other bystanders

Here is an example for *civil inattention*.

> The doctor was unable to maintain civil inattention because the man in the truck was unconscious and bleeding, thereby indicating a need for help. Any time an explicit or implied call for help is displayed, a stranger is invited to intervene.

TASK 6: In this doctor's place, would you have intervened? Why or why not? Discuss your answer with a partner.

Targeting Grammar: Adverbials Expressing Concession

Writers often qualify statements they make by citing conflicting information or points of view. For example, Dr. Dillard states, "Despite the cold, it was hard for my friend, Amy, and me to leave this place." In other words, we would normally expect people to leave a cold place, but this didn't happen. The two pieces of information are conflicting. Such conflicting information is often introduced or joined by words or phrases that express *concession*. Here are some common concessive adverbials in two sentence patterns.

PATTERN 1

CONCESSIVE ADVERBIAL	DEPENDENT CLAUSE	INDEPENDENT CLAUSE
Although/Even though	intervening in an emergency situation is not the norm,	there are circumstances that compel people to intervene.
Despite/In spite of	the norm of civil inattention,	there are many circumstances that cause us to interact with strangers.

PATTERN 2

INDEPENDENT CLAUSE	CONCESSIVE ADVERBIAL	DEPENDENT CLAUSE
People seldom ignore children in trouble	although/even though	they will generally ignore adults.
We cannot say that all people are apathetic or uncaring	despite/in spite of	the human tendency not to intervene.

TASK 7: Reread "A Doctor's Dilemma." Find three situations in which the author presents conflicting information or points of view. Use both patterns 1 and 2 for concessive adverbials to express this information. The first one has been done for you.

Although

Pattern 1: Although the doctor knew that he faced a possible lawsuit, he still administered medical care to the accident victim.

Pattern 2: The doctor administered medical care to the accident victim although he knew that he faced a possible lawsuit.

Even though

Pattern 1: _____

_____

Pattern 2: _____

_____

Despite

Pattern 1: _____

_____

Pattern 2: _____

_____

In spite of

Pattern 1: _____

_____

Pattern 2: _____

_____

UNDERSTANDING THROUGH LISTENING

VIDEO

> **LECTURE:** Stranger Intervention
> **SEGMENT 3:** Intervention in Child Punishment
>
> **PROFESSOR:** Kerry Ferris
> **COURSE:** Sociology 3: The Sociology of Everyday Life
> **TEXTS:** *Behavior in Public Places* by Erving Goffman and
> *Social Problems* by Phillip W. Davis

In this segment of her lecture, Professor Ferris discusses the problems that are created when a stranger intervenes in public child punishment. She further presents the negotiation that often ensues between the parent or caretaker and the stranger who wants to stop the punishment.

TASK 8: Before you watch the lecture, make a list of some problems or trouble that might arise if a stranger intervenes when a parent or caretaker is punishing a child in public.

Task 9: Watch the lecture by Professor Ferris. Take notes and then give a brief explanation of each interactional process and an example of what might be said by either the parent or the intervener. The first one has been done for you.

1. Establishing wrongful child treatment

Explanation: <u>The stranger must decide that the punishment he or she is witnessing</u>

<u>is inappropriate or excessive.</u>

Claim: <u>The stranger may say to the parent, "You shouldn't be doing that."</u>

2. Undue intervener interest

Explanation: _____

_____

_____

Claim: _____

_____

_____

3. Protection of parental differences

Explanation: _____

_____

_____

Claim: _____

_____

_____

4. Determining if the child abuse label fits

Explanation: _____

_____

_____

Claim: _____

_____

_____

The next reading passage, "Stranger Intervention into Child Punishment in Public Places," is an example of a type of academic text called the *scientific research report*. You may eventually be asked to write this type of text if you do research. The contents and organization of the scientific research report are predictable and include statements or information about the following:

ACADEMIC STRATEGY:

READING A RESEARCH REPORT

- the problem to be studied and why this problem is of interest

- the purpose of or rationale for the present study

- a summary of other research that has been done

- the design of the experiment, including the subjects and how and what type of information was obtained

- the variables/factors tested in the experiment

- the highlights of important information found in the experiment

- what the findings tell us about the problem

- areas for further research

TASK 10: Read "Stranger Intervention into Child Punishment in Public Places." Then mark the numbers of the paragraphs where the following information is found. The first one has been done for you.

¶ 1, 2, 3   1. the problem to be studied and the general interest of this problem

_____ 2. the purpose of or rationale for the present study

_____ 3. a summary of other research that has been done

_____ 4. the design of the experiment

_____ 5. the variables/factors tested in the experiment

STRANGER INTERVENTION INTO CHILD PUNISHMENT IN PUBLIC PLACES

Phillip W. Davis

[1]   When they think the punishment of a child in public has gone too far, some people employ "hate stares" (Goffman 1963:83–83), a few others search for help from someone in charge, but only a minority initiate a face-to-face encounter (Gelles and Straus 1988:127). According to the National Committee for Prevention of Child Abuse (NCPCA 1990), for example, only 17 percent of its sample said they had "stopped someone they did not know from hitting a child," and this figure may be inflated by the vague wording of the question and a desire to report socially desirable actions. Given what we know about the prescription of noninvolvement among strangers in public (Edgerton 1979; Emerson 1970; Goffman 1963; Lofland 1989) and the low probability of involvement in all sorts of emergency and helping situations

(Dovidio 1984; Latané and Darley 1970), it is not surprising that most people do not step in to voice their complaints and control other peoples' [sic] caretaking.

Child Punishment and Public Intervention

[2]   Within the family system, where the traditional parent role includes the right to exercise control over children (Goode 1971; Shehan and Less 1990), parental force is legally protected so long as it is noninjurious and "reasonable" (NCCAN 1980). Physical punishment is practiced by the vast majority of parents (see example, Wauchope and Straus 1990), with the prevailing attitude being that slapping and spanking children is natural, normal, and necessary (Straus, Gelles, and Steinmetz 1980).

[3]   While no one is in favor of "too much punishment" (Hardin and Ireland 1989), there is no clear cutting point between acceptable and excessive levels. It is widely recognized that cultural standards of abuse are varied, legal criteria are ambiguous, professional definitions are problematic, and labeling is selective (Gelles 1975; Gil 1970; Giovanonni and Becerra 1979; Johnson 1986; Korbin 1980). These uncertainties pose a vast array of emotional, relational, medical, and legal issues for parents, children, agencies, communities, institutions, and strangers—issues made more complex as more phenomena are regarded as maltreatment.

Methods and Data

[4]   The data for this study of child punishment come from semi-structured interviews with 37 people who directly intervened in child punishment situations on at least one occasion. Another seven were with people who witnessed the intervention of others, six of whom also participated in some way. The interviews resulted in detailed, retrospective descriptions of 50 face-to-face interventions. Interveners ranged in age from 19 to 45 and tended to have some college education. Of the interveners, 29 (78%) were women.

[5]   Interviewees were asked when the event occurred, as best they could recall. The interval between the interview and the time of the event ranged from the same day to 12 years. Seven interventions occurred between four and twelve years prior to the interview; 11 between two and three years. It should be stressed that more than half the interventions occurred within a year of the interview, and several within weeks.

Location and Activities

[6]   According to the given wisdom, this kind of thing—public punishment of a child—happens in grocery stores. Markets are, in fact, the most common location cited by interviewees, but department stores and shopping malls were also common. Less often,

people intervened in parks, in parking lots, on city sidewalks, in waiting rooms, in restaurants, at a zoo, by a highway roadside, at a beach, on a rapid transit platform, on a bus, on a train, and in a church cry room. In a little over half of the instances, interveners were already standing or walking very close to the family when the adult hit, dragged, shook, or kicked the child. Several interventions, quite literally, occurred "in passing." One couple jogging toward a crowded bus-stop watched a mother pull a boy from a bus, yell at him, and spank him hard as she dragged him up the sidewalk. The joggers stopped for a moment to argue and then resumed jogging. Other interveners were shopping near the adult and child in the same market aisle. Many said they "went over" to the pair, but usually just a short distance.

[7]   According to interviewees, the encounter does not usually involve anyone but the intervener and punitive parent. Both were without adult companions in three out of five instances. Several interveners had their own children with them at the time. Interveners *never* asked another shopper or bystander for help at any point, even though others were usually in view.

Scenes and Reactions

[8]   Two observational studies (Brown 1979; Davis 1990) indicate public punishment situations are short lived, with most hitting episodes involving a single hit in the absence of crying or complaining by the child, or yelling or explaining by the adult (Davis 1990). Even with multiple hits and the use of objects, the application of force lasts only a couple of seconds. As Goffman (1971) puts it, justice in public is summary. From an audience standpoint, the low visibility of the scene could easily make intervention seem "unnecessary."

[9]   When interveners chance across punishment situations, what do they see that leads them to step in and speak up? Most interveners say they witnessed something more than a mild spanking. I mention this because the negative intervener stereotype is of busybodies that "butt-in" at the slightest tap. In fact, only two interviewees described scenes in which the only force was a simple spank on the bottom. A few children were slapped on the hands, but repeatedly. In rough behavioral terms, half the interviewees say they saw adults hitting children hard or repeatedly with their hands. In one out of five interventions the parent used a belt or switch. In over a fourth of the instances, interviewees said the child was hit on the face or head.

[10]   Most interveners say they did not think much about whether to intervene, but instead, they found themselves "stepping over" and "stepping in," the words "just coming out" of their mouths. Several described the actions as having been "instinctive" or "a matter of reflexes."

[11]   Several watched as the adult continued to hit the child repeatedly, sometimes rapid-fire and sometimes spread out over a period of time. For these people, their comments suggest the building of *intervention momentum* (see Adler 1981) in which they tolerated the initial hitting, hoping it would stop. After seconds or minutes or heightening tension, they reach a point where, as they put it, they just had to say something.

[12]   Most interveners were bothered more by the manner, style, and context of what the adult did than by the fact [that] the child was being physically punished, even though nearly half the interveners believed that no physical punishment is acceptable. They cited the facts that the adult used an object, hit the child in the face, did not stop after the first hit, or scowled and yelled angrily while hitting. Others felt the punishment did not fit the infraction or were dismayed that the parent would hit the child for failing to stop crying after a preceding hit. Interveners chance across the punishment scene, step from the public audience role, and then typically enter into unsubtle debates, disputes, and arguments over the deviant import of the situation.

Source: (1991). *Social problems, 38*(2), 227–246.

TASK 11: Complete these statements so that they accurately correspond to the information presented in the reading. The first one has been done for you.

1. When people see someone hitting a child in a public place, <u>only an average of 17</u>

   <u>percent intervene to stop the punishment.</u>

2. American parents think that children should be punished by _____

   _____

   _____

3. The boundary between acceptable and unacceptable levels and types of punishment is

   _____

   _____

4. The data in this study consisted of _____

   _____

   _____

5. People decided to intervene because _____

   _____

   _____

6. The decision to intervene when a child is being punished in public is difficult
   because _____

   _____

   _____

7. The places where strangers witnessed children being punished included _____

   _____

   _____

Targeting Vocabulary: Expressing Tendencies

Throughout this unit, discussions of stranger intervention describe tendencies for people to behave in certain ways under certain types of circumstances.

> People **tend** to politely ignore strangers in public places.

> **There is a tendency for** most people to keep some distance between themselves and strangers.

Here are some phrases that express tendencies:

PHRASE	EXAMPLE
to tend to (do something)	Most people **tend** to avoid extended eye contact with strangers.
to have a tendency to (do something)	**We have a tendency** to look at strangers only for a short period of time.
there + to be a tendency for (someone) to do/not to do (something)	**There is a tendency for** strangers not to speak to each other in the subway.
to be likely to (do something)	People **are likely** to keep a certain distance between themselves and strangers in public places.
to be prone to (do something)	**Are** Americans more **prone to** looking directly at strangers than people from Japan are?

TASK 12: The following statements about the study reported in "Stranger Intervention into Child Punishment in Public Places" are inaccurate. Find the information needed to correct each statement and write the paragraph number where you found it. Then rewrite each sentence so that it accurately states information from the article. Use one of the phrases from the chart to express tendencies. The first one has been done for you.

1. Most of the interveners in the study had no college education.

    Paragraph: _4_

    Correction: _The interveners tended to have some college education._

2. Public punishment of children happens most often in parking lots.

    Paragraph: ___

    Correction: _____

    _____

3. Most stranger interventions into child punishment involve several other people besides the intervener and the punitive parent.

    Paragraph: ___

    Correction: _____

    _____

4. Public punishment situations often last a long time.

Paragraph: ___

Correction: _____

_____

5. Most interveners in the study carefully reflected about what to do before they took action.

Paragraph: ___

Correction: _____

_____

6. Interveners are often bothered more by the fact that a child is being punished than they are by the manner of the adult's behavior.

Paragraph: ___

Correction: _____

_____

Integrating Perspectives

APPLYING THE CONCEPTS

TASK 13: Using the explanations about intervention in child punishment situations in "Stranger Intervention into Child Punishment in Public Places" on pages 85–87 and in lecture segment 3 on page 83, explain why the woman in the cartoon is unable to remain silent. Share your explanations with a partner or a small group.

TASK 14: Create a typical child punishment situation that a stranger might witness and then write a brief dialogue that might ensue between a parent or caretaker and the stranger. An example has been done for you.

Situation observed: <u>You're in the supermarket and you observe a child seated in a shopping cart crying uncontrollably. The child's mother is visibly angry at the child and slaps him in the face.</u>

Stranger: <u>Is there anything wrong? Can I help you?</u>

Parent: <u>No, nothing's wrong.</u>

Stranger: <u>If there's nothing wrong, why did you just slap your little boy?</u>

Parent: <u>It's really none of your business. He's my kid and I'll discipline him however I want to.</u>

Situation observed: _____

_____

_____

Stranger: _____

_____

Parent: _____

_____

Stranger: _____

_____

Parent: _____

_____

ANALYZING THROUGH DISCUSSION

TASK 15: Read the following list of advice from child abuse experts about how to intervene in child punishment situations. With a partner, discuss which pieces of advice you would be most likely to follow. Which ones would make you feel uncomfortable? Share your answers with the rest of the class.

- Speak in a calm tone. Shouting and making loud accusations will probably only incite the abuser to react with more violence.

- Some abusers are not aware of the extent to which their words or actions are hurtful to children; give an abuser the opportunity to save face. For example, you could say, "You probably don't realize how your words are affecting your child."

- Express a sincere interest in the child. For example, you could start by saying, "I couldn't help noticing your daughter's lovely red hair," rather than focusing first on the abuser's unacceptable behavior.

- Approach the parent with empathy: "I respect that you have a tough job, and I would like to help you."

- Do not confront the abuser physically or verbally and do not threaten any kind of action.

- Give strong, disapproving looks to parents who are hurting their children.

- Say something positive to the child or give the child a sympathetic, this-is-not-your-fault look.

Sources: Joanna Simms (1989, May). Witness to child abuse, *Parents Magazine*, 90–94.
Lynn Smith (1995, August 2). When you see a parent lose it, what do you do? *Los Angeles Times*, 34–38.

TASK 16: What advice do you think Phillip Davis, author of "Stranger Intervention into Child Punishment in Public Places," would offer? On separate paper, create an advice list consistent with Davis's research findings. Share your list with the class.

EVALUATING THROUGH LITERATURE

In this short story, the author recounts a less dramatic, but more usual, case of bystander apathy.

TASK 17: Read the story to identify the dilemma the protagonist faced. What would you have done in the protagonist's place? Discuss your answers with a partner or small group.

WILSHIRE BUS

Hisaye Yamamoto

[1]   Wilshire Boulevard begins somewhere near the heart of downtown Los Angeles and, except for a few digressions scarcely worth mentioning, goes straight out to the edge of the Pacific Ocean. It is a wide boulevard and traffic on it is fairly fast. For the most part, it is bordered on either side with examples of the recent stark architecture which favors a great deal of glass. As the boulevard approaches the sea, however, the landscape becomes a bit more pastoral, so that the university and the soldiers' home there give the appearance of being huge country estates.

[2]   Esther Kuroiwa got to know this stretch of territory quite well while her husband Buro was in one of the hospitals at the soldiers' home. They had been married less than a year when his back, injured in the war, began troubling him again, and he was forced to take three months of treatments at Sawtelle before he was able to go back to work. During this time, Esther was permitted to visit him twice a week and she usually took the yellow bus out on Wednesdays because she did not know the first thing about driving and because her friends were not able to take her except on Sundays. She always enjoyed the long bus ride very much because her seat companions usually turned out to be amiable and if they did not, she took vicarious pleasure in gazing out at the almost unmitigated elegance along the fabulous street.

[3]   It was on one of these Wednesday trips that Esther committed a grave sin of omission which caused her later to burst into tears and which caused her acute discomfort for a long time afterwards whenever something reminded her of it.

[4]   The man came on the bus quite early and Esther noticed him briefly as he entered because he said gaily to the driver, "You robber. All you guys do is take money from me every day, just for giving me a short lift!"

[5]   Handsome in a red-faced way, greying, medium of height, and dressed in a dark grey sport suit with a yellow-and-black flowered shirt, he said this in a nice, resonant, carrying voice which got the response of a scattering of titters from the bus. Esther, somewhat amused and classifying him as a somatotonic, promptly forgot about him. And since she was sitting alone in the first regular seat, facing the back of the driver and the two front benches facing each other, she returned to looking out the window.

[6]   At the next stop, a considerable mass of people piled on and the last two climbing up were an elderly Oriental man and his wife. Both were neatly and somberly clothed and the woman, who wore her hair in a bun and carried a bunch of yellow and dark red chrysanthemums, came to sit with Esther. Esther turned her head to smile a greeting (*well, here we are, Orientals together on a bus*), but the woman was watching, with some concern, her husband who was asking directions of the driver.

[7]   His faint English was inflected in such a way as to make Esther decide he was probably Chinese, and she noted that he had to repeat his question several times before the driver could answer it. Then he came to sit in the seat across the aisle from his wife. It was about then that a man's voice, which Esther recognized soon as belonging to the somatotonic, began a loud monologue in the seat just behind her. It was not really a monologue, since he seemed to be addressing his seat companion, but this person was not heard to give a single answer. The man's subject was a figure in the local sporting world who had a nice fortune invested in several of the shining buildings the bus was just passing.

[8]   "He's as tight-fisted as they make them, as tight-fisted as they come," the man said. "Why, he wouldn't give you the sweat of his. . . ." He paused here to rephrase his metaphor, ". . . wouldn't give you the sweat off his palm!"

[9]   And he continued in this vein, discussing the private life of the famous man so frankly that Esther knew he must be quite drunk. But she listened with

interest, wondering how much of this diatribe was true, because the public legend about the famous man was emphatic about his charity. Suddenly, the woman with the chrysanthemums jerked around to get a look at the speaker and Esther felt her giving him a quick but thorough examination before she turned back around.

[10]   "So you don't like it?" the man inquired, and it was a moment before Esther realized that he was now directing his attention to her seat neighbor.

[11]   "Well, if you don't like it," he continued, "why don't you get off this bus, why don't you go back where you came from? Why don't you go back to China?"

[12]   Then, his voice growing jovial, as though he were certain of the support of the bus in this at least, he embroidered on this theme with a new eloquence, "Why don't you go back to China, where you can be coolies working in bare feet out in the rice fields? You can let your pigtails grow and grow in China. Alla samee, mama, no tickee no shirtee. Ha, pretty good, no tickee no shirtee!"

[13]   He chortled with delight and seemed to be looking around the bus for approval. Then some memory caused him to launch on a new idea: "Or why don't you go back to Trinidad? They got chinks running the whole she-bang in Trinidad. Every place you go in Trinidad. . . ."

[14]   As he talked on, Esther, pretending to look out the window, felt the tenseness in the body of the woman beside her. The only movement from her was the trembling of the chrysanthemums with the motion of the bus. Without turning her head, Esther was also aware that a man, a mild-looking man with thinning hair and glasses, on one of the front benches was smiling at the woman and shaking his head mournfully in sympathy, but she doubted whether the woman saw.

[15]   Esther herself, while believing herself properly annoyed with the speaker and sorry for the old couple, felt quite detached. She found herself wondering whether the man meant her in his exclusion order or whether she was identifiably Japanese. Of course, he was not sober enough to be interested in such fine distinctions, but it did matter, she decided, because she was Japanese, not Chinese, and therefore in the present case, immune. Then she was startled to realize that what she was actually doing was gloating over the fact that the drunken man had specified the Chinese as the unwanted.

[16]   Briefly, there bobbled on her memory the face of an elderly Oriental man whom she had once seen from a streetcar on her way home from work. (This was not long after she had returned to Los Angeles from the concentration camp in Arkansas and been lucky enough to get a clerical job with the Community Chest.) The old man was on a concrete island at Seventh and Broadway, waiting for his streetcar. She had looked down on him

benignly as a fellow Oriental, from her seat by the window, then been suddenly thrown for a loop by the legend on a large lapel button on his jacket. I AM KOREAN, said the button.

[17]   Heat suddenly rising to her throat, she had felt angry, then desolate and betrayed. True, reason had returned to ask whether she might not, under the circumstances, have worn such a button herself. She had heard rumors of I AM CHINESE buttons. So it was true then; why not I AM KOREAN buttons, too? Wryly, she wished for an I AM JAPANESE button, just to be able to call the man's attention to it, "Look at me!" But perhaps the man didn't even read English, perhaps he had been actually threatened, perhaps it was not his doing—his solicitous children perhaps had urged him to wear the badge.

[18]   Trying now to make up for her moral shabbiness, she turned towards the little woman and smiled at her across the chrysanthemums, shaking her head a little to get across her message (*don't pay any attention to that stupid old drunk, he doesn't know what he's saying, let's take things like this in our stride*). But the woman, in turn looking at her, presented a face so impassive yet cold, and eyes so expressionless yet hostile, that Esther's overture fell quite flat.

[19]   Okay, okay, if that's the way you feel about it, she thought to herself. Then the bus made another stop and she heard the man proclaim ringingly, "So clear out, all of you and remember to take every last one of your slant-eyed pickaninnies with you!" This was his final advice as he stepped down from the middle door. The bus remained at the stop long enough for Esther to watch the man cross the street with a slightly exploring step. Then, as it started up again, the bespectacled man in front stood up to go and made a clumsy speech to the Chinese couple and possibly to Esther. "I want you to know," he said, "that we aren't all like that man. We don't all feel the way he does. We believe in an America that is a melting pot of all sorts of people. I'm originally Scotch and French myself." With that, he came over and shook the hand of the Chinese man.

[20]   "And you, young lady," he said to the girl behind Esther, "you deserve a Purple Heart or something for having to put up with *that* sitting beside you."

[21]   Then he, too, got off.

[22]   The rest of the ride was uneventful and Esther stared out the window with eyes that did not see. Getting off at last at the soldiers' home, she was aware of the Chinese couple getting off after her, but she avoided looking at them. Then, while she was walking towards Buro's hospital very quickly, there arose in her mind some words she had once read and let stick in her craw: People say, do not regard what he says, now he is in liquor. Perhaps it is the only time he ought to be regarded.

[23]   These words repeated themselves until her saving detachment was gone every bit and she was filled once again in her life with the infuriatingly helpless, insidiously sickening sensation of there being in the world nothing solid she could put her finger on, nothing solid she could come to grips with, nothing solid she could sink her teeth into, nothing solid.

[24]   When she reached Buro's room and caught sight of his welcoming face, she ran to his bed and broke into sobs that she could not control. Buro was amazed because it was hardly her first visit and she had never shown such weakness before, but solving the mystery handily, he patted her head, looked around smugly to his roommates, and asked tenderly, "What's the matter? You've been missing me a whole lot, huh?" And she, finally drying her eyes, sniffed and nodded and bravely smiled and answered him with the question, yes weren't women silly?

(1950)

Source: (1988). *Seventeen syllables and other stories* (pp. 34–38). Latham, NY: Kitchen Table: Women of Color Press.

TASK 18: The story "Wilshire Bus" puts the issue of bystander apathy into a context that we can all relate to—a situation in which we might find ourselves every day. Hold a class debate about whether the events portrayed in this story qualify as a "public aid" situation. Consider the following questions:

- Do you find a relational wedge?
- Is there a clear reason to suspend civil inattention?
- Does this qualify as an emergency?
- Do you find the kind of intervention momentum described in Davis's article?
- Is there pressure from bystanders?

Divide the class into two large groups. One group will take the position that it *does qualify* as a public aid situation. The other group will take the opposite position. Defend your position by using information from the readings and lectures in the unit.

EVALUATING THROUGH WRITING

TASK 19: Choose one of the following topics and write an essay. First, do the activities in Tasks 20 and 21 as prewriting. Refer to the Academic Strategy box on page 94 for tips on how to gain readers' understanding.

1. The story "Wilshire Bus" illustrates that bystander apathy is present even in our everyday interactions, situations that do not necessarily qualify as "emergencies." Using the research about public aid situations and stranger intervention, explain why none of the bus passengers came to the aid of the Chinese woman.

2. In her letter to "Dear Abby," Elizabeth in a Rage states that the reason no one helped her was because "no one wanted to get involved." She seems to feel that passersby were simply apathetic and indifferent to her situation. Write an essay that explains why "apathy" and "indifference" are not sufficient explanations for why no one would help this woman.

3. Look again at some of the child punishment scenarios presented in the Davis reading and in this unit. Write an essay in which you examine why strangers break the general rules of nonintervention and intervene when they witness parents punishing their children in an excessive way.

4. James Dillard, the physician in "A Doctor's Dilemma," helps an accident victim despite serious reservations. Write an essay in which you apply both the definition of emergency situations given by Latané and Darley and the social determinants of bystander intervention to explain why Dr. Dillard intervened.

Sociologists are trained to go deeper than the surface to find universal causes of the human behavior that they observe in individuals. When they write about these universal causes, successful writers take into account the views and preconceptions of their readers. Most readers have opinions, based on experience and common knowledge, about what causes certain human behavior.

To gain readers' understanding, writers begin with these opinions, then present the deeper causes that they have found to underlie actions. Researchers use certain phrases and sentences to effect transitions from commonsense explanations to scientific reasons.

- These glib phrases may contain some truth, since startling cases such as the Genovese murder often seem to occur in our large cities, **but such terms may also be misleading.**

- While it is certainly true that a victim is unlikely to receive help if nobody knows of his plight, our research casts doubt on the suggestion that he will be more likely to receive help if more people are present. **In fact, the opposite seems to be true.**

TASK 20: Decide what you believe to be your readers' commonsense beliefs about the causes or consequences of the behavior in the situation you have chosen from Task 19. List these beliefs below.

_____

_____

_____

TASK 21: On a separate piece of paper, list all of the sociological factors that could contribute to the causes of the behavior in the topic you have chosen in Task 19. Once you have listed the obvious causes, examine each for underlying or hidden causes or factors. Refer to the readings by Goffman, Davis, or Latané and Darley to help you develop causes. Essay topic 1 from Task 19 has been done for you as an example.

CAUSES	ANALYSES
1. Perhaps the bus passengers did not define this as an "emergency."	1. As discussed in Latané and Darley, emergencies or crises "begin as ambiguous events." The bystanders must first decide that the situation qualifies as an emergency. No one was in danger of being harmed or of dying (as was the case in the child abuse cases we have read and in the traffic accident witnessed by the doctor and his friend). Latané and Darley also maintain that "it is likely that an individual bystander will be influenced by the decisions he considers others to be taking." The passengers on this bus all sat silently. No one became angry with the man who was harassing the elderly Chinese couple. Since no intervention momentum built among these passengers, everyone seemed to tolerate the verbal insults to the couple—even the couple themselves.

Insights from Political Science

Introduction:

Power and Influence in World Politics

The goal of any country's foreign policy is to gain and retain power and influence over other states. What makes a foreign policy successful? The sources in this chapter explore this question as well as the changes that will influence international power in the post–cold war era.

Exploring the Concepts

EXPLORING THROUGH VISUAL IMAGES

TASK 1: The 1985 hit song "We Are the World" conveys the message that cooperation is the key to world peace. What message does this cartoon convey about the way that countries attempt to achieve world peace? What other means of power do countries have to influence other states? With a partner, make a list of some possible means of power.

"WE ARE THE WORLD, WE ARE THE WORLD!"

Exploring Background Knowledge

TASK 2: The author of the excerpt that follows makes a distinction between *power* and *influence*. With a partner or in a small group, choose four of the historical world figures from the list below. Put a P next to the people you think had power; put an I next to the people you think had influence. You may decide that some figures had both. Be prepared to defend your choices.

Power and influence generally go hand in hand. Anyone who has the clout to make decisions with the stroke of a pen has influence over the way we live and think. . . . To hold power is to have at your disposal blunt instruments. But without influence, power dies out at the end of its own channels of command. To have influence is to gain assent, not just obedience; to attract a following, not just an entourage; to have imitators, not just subordinates. Power gets its way (when it gets it). Influence makes its way.

Source: Richard Lacayo (1996, June 17). Power: Now for the folks who have clout. *Time, 147,* 81–82.

_____ Winston Churchill	_____ Napoleon Bonaparte
_____ Confucius	_____ Alexander the Great
_____ Mahatma Gandhi	_____ Martin Luther King, Jr.
_____ Evita Peron	_____ Golda Meir
_____ Nelson Mandela	_____ Jimmy Carter
_____ Catherine the Great of Russia	_____ Adolph Hitler

Targeting Vocabulary: Key Terms

The readings and lectures in this unit deal with abstract topics, including *power, evil, morality, cooperation, conflict,* and *competition.* Here is a list of words associated with these topics.

affiliation	decency	harmony	righteousness
alliance	depravity	hegemony	rivalry
antagonism	discord	honor	strength
argument	disunity	hostility	struggle
collaboration	domination	joint effort	uprightness
command	ethics	might	vice
contention	force	morals	virtue
corruption	friction	opposition	worth

TASK 3: Put each abstract word from the previous Targeting Vocabulary under the heading with which it is most closely associated. Some examples have been done for you. You may want to consult a dictionary or thesaurus.

EVIL	POWER	MORALITY	COOPERATION	COMPETITION/CONFLICT
depravity	strength	uprightness	alliance	antagonism

EXPLORING THROUGH DISCUSSION

Aphorisms are short quotations or wise sayings, usually by famous people. They express a point of view in very few words. Below are aphorisms about the subject of power.

a. Power is not only what you have but what the enemy thinks you have.
   Saul Alinsky (1909–1972), U.S. radical activist. Rules for Radicals, "Tactics" (1971).

b. But the relationship of morality and power is a very subtle one. Because ultimately power without morality is no longer power.
   James Baldwin (1924–1987), U.S. author. A dialogue (1973; with Nikki Giovanni), from a conversation in London, November 4, 1971.

c. Political power grows out of the barrel of a gun.
   Mao Zedong (1893–1976), founder of the People's Republic of China. "Problems of War and Strategy," speech November 6, 1938 (published in *Selected Works,* vol. 2, 1961).

d. I hope our wisdom will grow with our power, and teach us, that the less we use our power the greater it will be.
   Thomas Jefferson (1743–1826), U.S. president. Letter, June 12, 1815.

e. You cannot have power for good without having power for evil too. Even mother's milk nourishes murderers as well as heroes.
   George Bernard Shaw (1856–1950), Anglo-Irish playwright, critic. Cusins, in *Major Barbara,* Act 3.

Source: (1993). *The Columbia dictionary of quotations.* New York: Columbia University Press.

TASK 4: Which aphorisms on page 97 correspond to the following statements? Put the letter of the aphorism(s) in the blank provided. An example has been done for you.

_____ You don't need to actually have power to be powerful.

_____ Power is often gained by force.

_____ The power to do good co-exists with the power to do evil.

_____ Controlling the use of one's power is the wisest course of action.

___*b*___ People who exercise force for negative ends do not truly have power.

TASK 5: With a partner or in a small group, read the aphorisms about power on page 97. Select one that interests you the most. What is the writer's viewpoint about power? Do you agree or disagree? Be prepared to present your interpretation and reaction to the class.

EXPLORING THROUGH WRITING

TASK 6: In your journal, write your own aphorism about power. Then share it with your classmates.

Working with Sources

UNDERSTANDING THROUGH LITERATURE

The U.S. Civil War, the war between the North and the South, took place from 1861 to 1865 and was one of the bloodiest wars ever waged. General William Tecumseh Sherman of the Union (Northern) army ordered his men to march from the captured city of Atlanta to Savannah. Cutting a path through the state of Georgia to the Atlantic Ocean, the army marauded and plundered the Southern civilian population.

TASK 7: General Sherman is considered one of the greatest generals of the United States. Consider the qualities that might make a great general. For each of the following adjectives, put an X along the continuum to indicate the degree to which you think a great general possesses these qualities. Compare your answers with a classmate's.

logical	LOW		1	2	3	4	5	6	7	HIGH
patriotic	LOW		1	2	3	4	5	6	7	HIGH
single-minded	LOW		1	2	3	4	5	6	7	HIGH
proud	LOW		1	2	3	4	5	6	7	HIGH
charismatic	LOW		1	2	3	4	5	6	7	HIGH
ambitious	LOW		1	2	3	4	5	6	7	HIGH
decisive	LOW		1	2	3	4	5	6	7	HIGH
level-headed	LOW		1	2	3	4	5	6	7	HIGH
compassionate	LOW		1	2	3	4	5	6	7	HIGH

TASK 8: The following excerpt is the preface to the novel *Sherman's March* by Cynthia Bass. She writes from the first person viewpoint of General Sherman as he recalls his military administratorship of Memphis, Tennessee. As you read about his occupation of Memphis, underline any passages that show Sherman's power and influence over the South.

PREFACE TO *SHERMAN'S MARCH*

Cynthia Bass

Sherman's March—1: Sherman's March to the Sea, Atlanta–Savannah, autumn of 1864. Considered the first widespread use of civilian warfare. **2:** Total war.

[1]   When Memphis fell in the summer of '62, I was appointed military administrator. It was an honor I neither coveted nor sought; I am a soldier, nothing more. But since I am a soldier I know how to follow commands, and I undertook readily the task of restoring order to a conquered city. I issued proclamations guaranteeing the safety of the people of Memphis, and promised any citizen with a complaint against our Northern troops an immediate public hearing, with myself in attendance. I signed such proclamations personally, in my own name, William Tecumseh Sherman.

[2]   Under my administration Memphis blossomed. Schools reopened; theaters resumed performances; shopkeepers emerged from their cellars to reclaim their countertops—shocked, I'm sure, to find their wares still neatly stacked on their shelves, and their money still safe in its hiding place. I persuaded the city fathers to return to their posts, and urged the religious leaders to open the doors of their churches. In all aspects, in all decisions, civil as well as military, I favored the side of moderation, of reason.

[3]   But soon enough I was to learn the foolishness of such policy. At the very moment I was treating the people of Memphis with so great a benignity I was condemned on the floor of the U.S. Senate for insufficient ardor in the face of the enemy, the citizens of that city were setting

their hearts against my army. Patrols were attacked and captured on moonless nights, found dying (but not quite dead) in empty fields, bleeding from unspeakable wounds. Rifles disappeared; depots exploded; cannons were examined and found to be jimmied or jammed. Slowly at first, not wanting to know, I began to suspect that those same good citizens who came to me at noon with such politesse were roaming the countryside at midnight, slashing my soldiers' throats with my own stolen sabers, shooting my men in the stomach with my own stolen guns.

[4]   In late September I received *incontrovertible evidence* that guerrillas from the nearby village of Randolph had fired upon two of my steamboats. Thanks to my trust and respect for the citizens of Memphis, these boats were unarmed; they could not return a single shot in their own defense. They simply bobbled, helpless and clear in the sights of their unseen enemy.

[5]   But I was not helpless. I immediately ordered the village of Randolph burnt to the ground—all save one house, which remained to mark the spot. Then I announced to the people of Memphis that for every boat fired on, I would expel from the city ten families, chosen by lot. I vowed that henceforth any guerrillas caught by my soldiers would be found, themselves put on boats, and used by my men for target practice.

[6]   It has now been two years since I ordered the burning of Randolph. Today Atlanta smolders, an evacuated husk. Every flame, every paneless window, every shell, for one purpose only.

[7]   This war must stop. Every day we gnaw one another like two baffled dragons; night falls, and we scoop up stomachs and bury eyes. Meanwhile the real enemies—the civilians—understand nothing. Worse than nothing. They send off their children for us to torture, then call them martyrs, and us barbarians. Cocooned from real suffering by distance and custom, they urge on the slaughter from the untouched shade of their peaceful verandas.

[8]   But war has no place for peace. Thus did the teachers of Memphis instruct me. Treated kindly, a soldier responds with kindness; treated kindly, a civilian responds with treason. Thus kindliness in the midst of warfare—bypassing the land between battlefields, sparing the illusion of everyday life—is an error. All it does is hurt your own people, enrich the undertakers, and prolong the killing on either side. War cannot be waged civilly, and still be war.

[9]   All that will end this war quickly is more war. Harder war, stricter war, crueler, deeper. Into the occupied zones. Into the cities, into the countryside. War until the people themselves sample its sting—not in their minds, not in their mourning or songs, but in reality. In their own bodies for once, and not their soldiers'. We must take the pain from the battlefield, and bring the war home.

[10]   I can do it. I can begin ending the war right now. I have the troops. I have the rifles. I have the cannons, I have the will. I have Atlanta. Give me the rest.

[11]   The heart of the Southern Confederacy lies beating before me. Let me wade in that heart. Let me bathe in its blood.

[12]   I can make Georgia howl!

Source: (1994). *Sherman's march* (pp. 3–6). New York: Villard.

TASK 9: This passage describes Sherman's change in attitude from a trust in the civilian population to disillusionment and distrust of all citizens of the Confederacy. With a partner, discuss how and why this change in attitude came about.

TASK 10: Skim the passage to find the following quotes. Indicate whether each quote reflects Sherman's trust in the civilian population or not by circling *Trust* or *Distrust* in the middle column. Then in the right-hand column, write a paraphrase of Sherman's quote. The first one has been done for you.

QUOTE	TRUST OR DISTRUST?	PARAPHRASE
1. "I issued proclamations guaranteeing the safety of the people of Memphis. . . ."	(Trust) Distrust	I gave orders to ensure that none of the citizens of Memphis would be harmed.
2. "I can make Georgia howl!"	Trust Distrust	
3. "In all aspects, in all decisions, civil as well as military, I favored the side of moderation, of reason."	Trust Distrust	
4. ". . . kindliness in the midst of warfare— bypassing the land between battlefields, sparing the illusion of everyday life—is an error."	Trust Distrust	
5. ". . . I undertook readily the task of restoring order to a conquered city."	Trust Distrust	
6. "War cannot be waged civilly, and still be war."	Trust Distrust	

TASK 11: How did Sherman's thinking change as a result of the events in Memphis? On a separate piece of paper, write a paragraph in which you explain whether or not Sherman was justified in undertaking his "march to the sea." Consider the quotes in Task 10.

TASK 12: In the novel, Bass paints an ambiguous portrait of Sherman, never exactly revealing whether the motives for his actions were selfish or honorable. Examine the possible motives below. Which one do you think represents Sherman's *true* motive for his devastation of Georgia? Find evidence in the text to support your opinion. Compare your choice to a partner's.

- Sherman wanted revenge on the people of Memphis who had attacked his patrols and fired upon his steamboats.
- Sherman believed that war needed to be waged in a ruthless fashion in order to be won.
- Sherman believed that he needed to move quickly and decisively in order to bring the war to a quick end.

Targeting Grammar: Repetition of Structures

To emphasize or highlight an idea, writers often repeat a grammatical structure, substituting different words. Almost any element of sentence grammar can be repeated. Below are some examples from "Preface to *Sherman's March*" with the repeated grammatical element(s) labeled:

¶ 2 **In all aspects, in all decisions,** civil as well as military, I favored the side **of moderation, of reason.**
Repeated element: prepositional phrase

¶ 9 War until the people themselves sample its sting—**not in their minds, not in their mourning or songs,** but in reality.
Repeated element: *not* + prepositional phrase

¶ 9 **Harder war, stricter war, crueler, deeper.**
Repeated elements: (comparative) adjective + noun; (comparative) adjective

¶ 8 **Treated kindly,** a soldier responds with kindness; **treated kindly,** a civilian responds with treason.
Repeated element: participial phrase

¶ 8 Treated kindly, **a soldier responds with kindness;** treated kindly, **a civilian responds with treason.**
Repeated element: subject + verb + prepositional phrase

¶ 10 **I can do it. I can begin ending the war right now.**
Repeated element: subject + modal + verb + object

¶ 11 **Let me** wade in that heart. **Let me** bathe in its blood.
Repeated element: imperative

TASK 13: Complete the repeated grammatical structures from "Preface to *Sherman's March*" and write the paragraph number where you found them. Underline the repeated elements in each. The first one has been done for you.

1. (¶ _3_) <u>Rifles disappeared</u>; <u>depots exploded</u>; <u>cannons were examined</u> and found to be jimmied or jammed.

2. (¶ __) Every flame, _____

_____

3. (¶ __) Under my administration, Memphis blossomed. _____

_____

4. (¶ __) I have the troops. _____

_____

5. (¶ __) Into the occupied zones. _____

_____

TASK 14: On a separate piece of paper, create three sentences with repeated structures by imitating sentences in Task 13. Substitute your own ideas or content for the author's. An example has been done for you.

> Rifles disappeared; depots exploded; cannons were examined and found to be jimmied or jammed.

> Imitation: Students appeared; assignments proliferated; their papers were graded and found to be interesting or insightful.

Targeting Vocabulary: Collocations

The following are *collocations,* or words that often occur together in a kind of set phrase.

undertake the task of (-*ing* verb)	burn (*something*) to the ground
restore order to	spare the illusion of
issue a proclamation/an order	wage war against
set one's heart against	prolong the killing/suffering
incontrovertible evidence	

TASK 15: On separate paper, write a summary of the excerpt from "Preface to *Sherman's March*" using these collocations. Underline the collocations that you have used. The summary has been started for you.

> William Tecumseh Sherman was sent to Memphis in 1862 after it was captured by the North. His job was <u>to restore order to</u> the city.

UNDERSTANDING THROUGH LISTENING

VIDEO

> **Lecture:** Power in International Relations*
> **Segment 1:** Power and Influence in International Relations
>
> **Professor:** Steven Spiegel
> **Course:** Political Science 20: World Politics
> **Text:** *World Politics in a New Era* by Steven L. Spiegel

Professor Spiegel presents a basic framework for understanding how one country influences the actions or policies of another. He concludes this discussion with five key questions that countries must consider as they exert influence.

TASK 16: Before you watch the lecture, review the answers you gave in Task 1 to the question "What other means of power do countries have to influence other states?" Compare these answers to the possible means of influencing another country listed below. Place a √ next to each item that you listed in Task 1. For each item that you did not check, give an example from your knowledge of history or world politics.

_____ a country votes for or against a policy in the UN

_____ a country moves troops into or out of a particular location

_____ a country's diplomatic leaders make a statement

_____ a country gives foreign aid money to or withdraws it from another country

_____ a country organizes a conference and selectively invites representatives from other states

_____ a country walks into or out of a conference sponsored by another country

_____ a country boycotts another country's goods

_____ a country eases or imposes tariffs on another country's goods

TASK 17: As you watch Professor Spiegel's lecture, note his main point about power in international politics: A country mobilizes resources to achieve a particular policy goal. He gives several examples of the kinds of power goals countries pursue. List three such examples below. An example has been done for you.

1. The Ayatollah Khomeini led the revolution in Iran to achieve religious ends and save souls.

2. _____

_____

3. _____

_____

4. _____

_____

* Lecture material for this unit is in part taken from K. J. Holsti (1995). *International politics: A framework for analysis* (7th ed.). Englewood Cliffs, NJ: Prentice Hall; and from John T. Rourke (1995). *International politics on the world stage* (5th ed.). Guilford, CT: Dushkin Publishing Group/Brown & Benchmark Publishers.

TASK 18: Watch the lecture again to find the five key questions that countries must answer when attempting to influence another state. Write these questions below. Question 1 has been done for you.

1. <u>What do we want B to do or not to do</u>   ?

2. _____ ?

3. _____ ?

4. _____ ?

5. _____ ?

TASK 19: Take any international incident that intrigues you or that you know about. With a partner or in a small group, ask and answer Professor Spiegel's five key questions from Task 18.

UNDERSTANDING THROUGH READING

As the world has changed since the "end of the cold war," so has the nature of power in world politics. The following reading contrasts traditional types of power with the new types of "soft" power that countries will use to influence one another.

TASK 20: As you read the passage, take notes on the differences between traditional and "soft" power. Divide a piece of paper into two columns, labeling one column *traditional* and the other *soft*.

SOFT POWER

Joseph S. Nye, Jr.

[1]   The dictionary tells us that power means an ability to do things and control others, to get others to do what they otherwise would not. Because the ability to control others is often associated with the possession of certain resources, politicians and diplomats commonly define power as the possession of population, territory, natural resources, economic size, military forces, and political stability. For example, in the agrarian economies of eighteenth-century Europe, population was a critical power resource since it provided a base for taxes and recruitment of infantry.

[2]   Traditionally the test of a great power was its strength in war. Today, however, the definition of power is losing its emphasis on military force and conquest that marked earlier eras. The factors of technology, education, and economic growth are becoming more significant in international power, while geography, population, and raw materials are becoming somewhat less important. . . .

[3]   What can we say about changes in the distribution of power resources in the coming decades? Political leaders often use the term "multipolarity" to imply the return to a balance among a number of states with roughly equal power resources analogous to that of the nineteenth century. But this is not likely to be the situation at the turn of the century.

The Great Power Shift

[4]   The coming century may see continued American preeminence, but the sources of power in world politics are likely to undergo major changes that will create new difficulties for all countries in achieving their goals. Proof of power lies not in resources but in the ability to change the behavior of states. Thus, the critical question for the United States is not whether it will start the next century as the superpower with the largest supply of resources, but to what extent it will be able to control the political environment and get other countries to do what it wants. Some trends in world politics suggest that it will be more difficult in the future for any great power to control the political environment. The problem for the United States will be less the rising challenge of another major power than a general diffusion of power. Whereas nineteenth-century Britain faced new challengers, the twenty-first century United States will face new challenges.

[5]   As world politics becomes more complex, the power of all major states to gain their objectives will be

diminished. To understand what is happening to the United States today, the distinction between power over other countries and power over outcomes must be clear. Although the United States still has leverage over particular countries, it has far less leverage over the system as a whole. It is less well-placed to attain its ends unilaterally, but it is not alone in this situation. All major states will have to confront the changing nature of power in world politics. . . .

[6]   Traditionalist accounts of world politics often speak of an international system that results from the balancing strategies of states. Although *bipolarity* and multipolarity are useful terms, today different spheres of world politics have different distributions of power—that is, different power structures. Military power, particularly nuclear, remains largely bipolar in its distribution. But in trade, where the European Community acts as a unit, power is multipolar. Ocean resources, money, space, shipping, and airlines each have somewhat different distributions of power. The power of states varies as well, as does the significance of nonstate actors in different spheres. For example, the politics of international debt cannot be understood without considering the power of private banks.

[7]   If military power could be transferred freely into the realms of economics and the environment, the different structures would not matter; and the overall hierarchy determined by military strength would accurately predict outcomes in world politics. But military power is more costly and less transferable today than in earlier times. Thus, the hierarchies that characterize different issues are more diverse. The games of world politics encompass different players at different tables with different piles of chips. They can transfer winnings among tables, but often only at a considerable discount. The military game and the overall structure of the balance of power dominate when the survival of states is clearly at stake, but in much of modern world politics, physical survival is not the most pressing issue.

The Changing Face of Power

[8]   These trends suggest a second, more attractive way of exercising power than traditional means. A state may achieve the outcomes it prefers in world politics because other states want to follow it or have agreed to a situation that produces such effects. In this sense, it is just as important to set the agenda and structure the situations in world politics as to get others to change in particular cases.

[9]   This second aspect of power—which occurs when one country gets other countries to *want* what it wants—might be called co-optive or soft power in contrast with the hard or command power of *ordering* others to do what it wants.

[10]   Parents of teenagers have long known that if they have shaped their child's beliefs and preferences, their power will be greater and more enduring than if they rely only on active control. Similarly, political leaders and philosophizers have long understood the power of attractive ideas or the ability to set the political agenda and determine the framework of debate in a way that shapes others' preferences. The ability to affect what other countries want tends to be associated with intangible power resources such as culture, ideology, and institutions.

[11]   Soft co-optive power is just as important as hard command power. If a state can make its power seem legitimate in the eyes of others, it will encounter less resistance to its wishes. If its culture and ideology are attractive, others will more willingly follow. If it can establish international norms consistent with its society, it is less likely to have to change. If it can support institutions that make other states wish to channel or limit their activities in ways the dominant state prefers, it may be spared the costly exercise of coercive or hard power.

[12]   In general, power is becoming less transferable, less coercive, and less tangible. Modern trends and changes in political issues are having significant effects on the nature of power and the resources that produce it. Co-optive power—getting others to want what you want—and soft power resources—cultural attraction, ideology, and international institutions—are not new. In the early postwar period, the Soviet Union profited greatly from such soft resources as communist ideology, the myth of inevitability, and transnational communist institutions. Various trends today are making co-optive behavior and soft power resources relatively more important.

Source: (1994). Soft power. In Glen Hastedt and Kay Knickrehm (Eds.), *Toward the twenty-first century: A reader in world politics* (pp. 136–138). Englewood Cliffs, NJ: Prentice Hall.

---

bipolarity A balance of power between two states. Such a balance of power existed during the cold war between the United States and the former Soviet Union.

Task 21: Below are statements about power in the pre–cold war and post–cold war eras. Cross out the incorrect verb form to create a sentence that correctly represents the author's ideas. Reread the text as necessary to locate the author's point of view. The first one has been done for you.

1. The test of a great power **was/~~is~~** its strength in war.

2. Geography, population, and raw materials **were/are** becoming less important.

3. Factors such as technology, education, and economic growth **were/are** more important sources of power.

4. The world political situation **was/is** one of multipolarity in which there **was/is** a balance between many countries with roughly equal power resources.

5. There **was/will be** a general diffusion of power around the world.

6. The power of all major states to gain their objectives **was/will be** diminished.

7. The United States **had/will have** substantial leverage over the world political system as a whole.

8. In world politics, a country's continued existence **was/is** the most pressing issue.

9. Hard command power **was/will be** more legitimate than power based on ideology and culture.

10. Power in world politics **was/is** less transferable, coercive, and tangible.

Central propositions are sentences that convey the arguments, conclusions, and statements of a text. Every text is composed of such central propositions and sentences that support them. These supporting sentences give evidence or provide elaboration for the author's ideas.

ACADEMIC STRATEGY:

FINDING CENTRAL PROPOSITIONS IN AN ACADEMIC TEXT

FINDING THE CENTRAL PROPOSITION
The key to active reading is finding the writer's central propositions. These propositions are often contained in the sentences that seem the most complex and therefore the most difficult to understand. These sentences tend to be the ones you read more slowly or more than once.

UNDERSTANDING THE CENTRAL PROPOSITION
The next step is understanding what each of these propositions means. After this, readers can combine all these propositions to understand the main idea that the text is conveying. This process is a complex one because it requires the reader to grapple with the ideas and the language in the text. It develops with experience and exposure to a variety of academic text types.

EXAMPLES
It is important to realize that a central proposition is often not contained within one sentence in the text. Instead, it is commonly expressed through a series of statements that are logically connected. For example, in the following excerpt from "Soft Power," the author states:

(1) The dictionary tells us that power means an ability to do things and control others, to get others to do what they otherwise would not. (2) Because the ability to control others is often associated with the possession of certain resources, politicians and diplomats commonly define power as the possession of population, territory, natural resources, economic size, military forces, and political stability. (3) For example, in the agrarian economies of eighteenth-century Europe, population was a critical power resource since it provided a base for taxes and recruitment of infantry.

Note that in this excerpt, the central proposition is expressed in sentences 1 and 2, while sentence 3 can be considered as evidence for the central proposition. This central proposition can be restated as "Power, which means controlling others, often implies the possession of resources; therefore, political power is often defined as the possession of population, economic wealth, military strength, etc." Let's look at another example:

(1) Traditionally the test of a great power was its strength in war. (2) Today, however, the definition of power is losing its emphasis on military force and conquest that marked earlier eras. (3) The factors of technology, education, and economic growth are becoming more significant in international power, while geography, population, and raw materials are becoming somewhat less important.

In this paragraph, all three sentences contribute to the writer's central proposition. The author first states the traditional way in which a country's power was measured. He then contrasts this traditional view with the contemporary perspective on power. In the third sentence, he explains which factors are replacing the previous measure of power. His central proposition can be restated as: "Military force and other traditional measures of power (such as natural resources or population) are no longer the measure of a superpower; instead other factors such as technology, education, and economic growth determine a country's power."

COMMON LOGICAL RELATIONSHIPS

As these examples show, the sentences that make up a central proposition are logically related to one another and reflect a point of view that the author wishes to state. Some of the common logical relationships upon which a central proposition is built are the following: part-whole relationships (e.g., the first example above), cause/effect relationships, comparison/contrast relationships (e.g., the second example above), concessive relationships, and conditional relationships. Good readers can recognize these logical relationships and, as a result, are able to determine the author's central argument.

TASK 22: Review paragraphs 4 and 12 of "Soft Power." On a separate piece of paper, write the central proposition contained in each paragraph. Use paraphrasing strategies to rephrase each central proposition in your own words.

TASK 23: Review the aphorisms about power on page 97. Choose the one that best fits the author's view of "soft power." Be prepared to justify your choice to a partner or small group.

 Targeting Grammar: General versus Specific Article Use

In English, nouns and noun phrases may or may not be preceded by an article. The rules are different for general and specific nouns.

NOUNS WITH GENERAL REFERENCE

Some noun phrases do not refer to specific objects, people, quantities, or ideas. They refer to generalized instances or general concepts and ideas. Such noun reference is common in academic writing because it deals with theories and general truths.

- To test whether the noun is general, put the word *all, any,* or *some* in front of the noun phrase. If this makes sense, then the noun's reference is general.

[All] **Soft co-optive power** is just as important as [all] **hard command power.**

There are different ways to signal that a noun phrase is general.

GENERAL REFERENCE		
NOUN	**ARTICLE**	**EXAMPLE**
uncountable	φ (no article)	φ **Soft co-optive power** is just as important as φ **hard command power.**
singular countable	a, an	Power means *an* **ability to control others**.
plural countable	φ	φ **Modern trends** and φ **changes** are having φ **significant effects** on power.

NOUNS WITH SPECIFIC REFERENCE

Specific nouns and noun phrases refer to objects or people or express quantities or ideas. You cannot put the words *all, any,* or *some* in front of these noun phrases.

- To signal specificity, put the definite article *the* before both uncountable and countable noun phrases.

The **coming century** may see continued American preeminence.
(countable noun)

The **power** of a country often depends on the prestige of its leader.
(uncountable noun)

- When a post-modifier—an *of*-phrase or a relative clause (beginning with *who, which, that*, etc.)—follows the noun, it is often specific.

Traditionally, ***the*** **test** [of ***a*** great power] was its strength in war.

The **ability** [to control others] is often associated with certain resources.

The **hierarchies** [that characterize φ different issues] are very diverse.

The **distinction** [between φ power over other countries and φ power over outcomes] must be clear.

- Some nouns with post-modifiers are not specific in reference. Remember that if the word *any, all,* or *some* makes sense in front of it, the noun is general and requires no article.

Parent*s* [of teenagers] have long known that they can shape their child's beliefs.

It can establish **international norms** [that are consistent with its society].

TASK 24: The following summary of "Soft Power" contains some errors in article usage. Using your knowledge of general versus specific noun reference, correct any inappropriate uses of articles in the underlined noun phrases. When a noun phrase is general reference, pay attention to whether the noun is uncountable or countable. An example has been done for you.

According to the dictionary, (1) ~~the~~ power is (2) the ability to do things and control others. This ability is traditionally associated with (3) the possession of resources such as (4) territory, (5) the natural resources, and (6) the military forces. Today, however, (7) a definition of power is losing its emphasis on (8) military strength and shifting to such factors as (9) technology, (10) education, and (11) economic growth. In this new era, (12) preeminence of superpowers, whose status is based largely on (13) the military capability, will be challenged. Rather than (14) a world divided into (15) superpower camps, there will be (16) general diffusion of power. (17) New test of strength will be (18) a country's ability to control the political environment and get other countries to do what it wants. (19) Ability to control outcomes will be based on (20) the soft power, which will involve (21) the strategic use of money, space, shipping, culture, and ideology.

Integrating Perspectives

ANALYZING THROUGH VISUAL IMAGES

Uncle Sam is the symbol of the U.S. government. He is portrayed as a tall, thin man with a white beard who wears a blue jacket, a top hat, and red-and-white-striped trousers.

TASK 25: What view of world politics and the superpower role does this cartoon portray? Use the concepts from the readings and lecture in this chapter to analyze the cartoonist's point of view. Discuss with a partner.

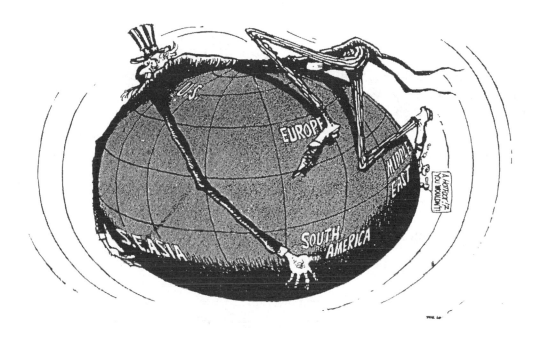

APPLYING THE CONCEPTS

Imagine two hypothetical countries, Altan and Zebron, both with large populations, which have the same foreign policy goal: to influence other countries' actions and policies. Their approaches to achieving this goal are different. Altan views power more traditionally, while Zebron takes a "soft" power approach.

TASK 26: In small groups, brainstorm policies that each country might pursue in each of the following categories. These policies should be consistent with each country's approach toward power. Examples have been done for you.

	ALTAN	ZEBRON
Population	• government promotes population control	• government promotes large families
Economy		
Military		
Territory and Natural Resources		
Political Situation	• has a strong political ideology that has gained worldwide recognition as a by-product of trade • enjoys political stability with a long-standing government that is popularly elected by the citizens	• has a strong political ideology • political stability is reinforced through the police, the military, and laws prohibiting antigovernment activities
Foreign Policy		

TASK 27: Based on the policies you have outlined in Task 26, which country do you think is in a better position to get other countries to do what it wants? In your groups, consider these questions and others you may think of.

- What must a country have to be powerful?
- What type of world power situation exists: multipolarity or bipolarity?
- What role do ideology and culture play?

EVALUATING THROUGH WRITING

TASK 28: Based on your group discussion in Tasks 26 and 27, write a one-page analysis that

- explains which country will have more political influence in the future
- notes the most important factor or factors that will lead to this country's rise to a position of influence

EXPLORATION:

DETERRENCE
IN WORLD POLITICS

One strategy frequently employed by countries in foreign policy is deterrence. Deterrence includes economic, political, or military threats against another country. The readings and lecture segments in this chapter explain why deterrent threats are an important source of power in international politics.

Exploring the Concepts

EXPLORING THROUGH VISUAL IMAGES

TASK 1: As we saw in Segment 1 of the lecture, Professor Spiegel defines the power that countries can use in international relations as follows: "A influences B to do X by __(means)__." With a partner or in a small group, discuss the "means" one country uses to influence another as shown in this cartoon. Do you think that other means can be more effective? Give historical or hypothetical examples to support your opinion.

Exploring through Writing

The author of the following passage believes that the United States is a "warrior nation." She also outlines some underlying motivations for this behavior, which she believes is rooted in human nature.

The Warrior Culture

In what we like to think of as "primitive" warrior cultures, the passage to manhood requires the blooding of a spear, the taking of a scalp or head. Among the Masai of eastern Africa and dozens of other human cultures, a man could not marry until he had demonstrated his capacity to kill in battle. Leadership, too, in a warrior society is typically contingent on military prowess and wrapped in the mystique of death. In the Solomon Islands a chief's importance could be reckoned by the number of skulls posted around his door, and it was the duty of the Aztec kings to nourish the gods with the hearts of human captives.

All warrior peoples have fought for the same high-sounding reasons: honor, glory, or revenge. The nature of their real and perhaps not conscious motivations is a subject of much debate. Some anthropologists postulate a murderous instinct, almost unique among living species, in human males. Others discern a materialistic motive behind every fray: a need for slaves, grazing land, or even human flesh to eat. Still others point to the similarities between war and other male pastimes—the hunt and outdoor sport—and suggest that it is boredom, ultimately, that stirs men to fight.

But, in a warrior culture, it hardly matters which motive is most basic. Aggressive behavior is rewarded whether or not it is innate to the human psyche. Shortages of resources are habitually taken as occasions for armed offensives, rather than for hard thought and innovation. And war, to a warrior people, is of course the highest adventure, the surest antidote to malaise, the endlessly repeated theme of legend, song, religious myth, and personal quest for meaning. It is how men die and what they find to live for.

"You must understand that Americans are a warrior nation," Senator Daniel Patrick Moynihan told a group of visiting Arab leaders in 1990. He said this proudly, and he may, without thinking through the ugly implications, have told the truth.

Source: Barbara Ehrenreich (1995). *The snarling citizen* (pp. 207–208). New York: Harper Perennial.

TASK 2: One of Ehrenreich's key claims is that, in a warrior culture, "Aggressive behavior is rewarded whether or not it is innate to the human psyche." Write a journal entry in which you agree or disagree with Ehrenreich's view. Give examples to support your point of view.

Working with Sources

UNDERSTANDING THROUGH LISTENING 1

VIDEO

> **Lecture:** Power in International Relations
> **Segment 2:** Deterrence in International Relations
>
> **Professor:** Steven Spiegel
> **Course:** Political Science 20: World Politics
> **Text:** *World Politics in a New Era* by Steven L. Spiegel

Professor Spiegel relates the foreign policy concept of *deterrence* to our natural human tendency to try to prevent others from taking certain actions. He also sets out premises that underlie strategic deterrence.

 ## Targeting Vocabulary: Key Vocabulary

The following vocabulary can be used to discuss the concept of deterrence. The words in the groups have similar meanings.

GROUP I	GROUP II	GROUP III	GROUP IV
to threaten	to retaliate against	to deter	to influence someone's actions/behavior
to attempt to frighten	to provoke aggressive behavior	to prevent potential adversaries' actions to prevent from attacking	to have/maintain/ hold a (credible) position
to pose a (credible) threat to	to carry out a reprisal against	to inhibit aggressive behavior	to affect the views and perspectives of
to intimidate		to dissuade	
to bluff		to check	

TASK 3: Here are some examples of hypothetical events involving some form of deterrence between two states. Use the words and expressions from the chart on page 115 to write sentences that explain what the countries are doing. More than one word or expression may be appropriate. An example has been done for you.

1. Country A and Country B share a common border. Although they have not fought a war in fifteen years, they remain enemies because they have different political ideologies. For the past five years, Country A has periodically stationed troops at Country B's border.

   By stationing troops at Country B's border, Country A is attempting to threaten

   Country B.

   _____

   Country A's action is an attempt to inhibit Country B's possible aggressive

   behavior.

   _____

2. Country C invades a small part of Country D to gain access to its oil fields. In return, Country D blockades Country C's harbor, thus preventing all ships from leaving or entering the harbor.

   _____

   _____

   _____

3. Country X aims nuclear missiles at Country Y's capital city, even though it has no intention of firing them.

   _____

   _____

   _____

4. Country F and Country G are longtime enemies because Country G declared independence from Country F and established its own state. Country F, in an attempt to show its sovereignty and power, periodically carries out missile and weapons tests off the coast of Country G (within a 200-mile protected boundary).

   _____

   _____

   _____

5. Countries N and P have been at war for the past five years. Country M is about to tip the balance of power by entering the war on the side of Country P. Before this can happen, terrorists from Country N hijack an airplane belonging to Country M.

   _____

   _____

   _____

METHOD

One effective strategy for taking lecture notes is to make two columns on a page, one for the notes you write as you listen to the lecture, and the other for expanded notes that you make later.

Left column

As you listen to the lecture, write the basic concepts and key terms. Focus on main ideas and don't worry if you miss some details.

Right column

As soon after the lecture as possible, elaborate on your notes with further explanations. Write them opposite the main ideas and concepts that they relate to. These additional notes might include the following:

- examples the lecturer gives
- associations with the main ideas and key terms (from assigned readings or your experience)
- questions you have about the lecture

PURPOSE

The double-entry strategy can help you

- organize the lecture information informally, in a less rigid format than an outline, for example
- be more selective about the information you record during the lecture
- make connections between the course readings and the lecture
- expand your notes to be as comprehensive as possible (This can be done by comparing notes with a classmate.)
- review lecture notes easily and think about them actively

TASK 4: Watch the lecture once and take notes on the key concepts in the left-hand column. Then go back and fill in as much information as you can from memory. Some example notes have been provided for you.

LECTURE CONCEPTS AND TERMS	ELABORATION, EXAMPLES, AND QUESTIONS
deterrence –	
deterrence in our daily lives – We often try to stop others from taking certain actions.	Example 1 – If Spiegel wanted students to drop the course, he could assign lots of papers and exams and then later say papers are optional.
deterrence in the nuclear era –	
Six premises underlying strategic deterrence 1.	
2.	
3.	
4.	
5.	
6.	

TASK 5: With a partner or in a small group, compare your double–entry notes and work together to produce a more complete set of lecture notes.

UNDERSTANDING THROUGH READING 1

TASK 6: In this reading, Professor Spiegel outlines three conditions that must be met for any threat of deterrence to work. Skim the text to locate these three conditions. Then skim it again to locate a general definition of each one.

DETERRENCE

Steven L. Spiegel

[1]   Deterrence attempts to prevent war by discouraging a potential aggressor from attacking. The primary goal for the defender is to convince the challenger that the probable cost of attacking will far exceed any anticipated gain. This is usually accomplished by threatening to militarily retaliate or punish the initiator if it commits the undesired action. More precisely, the defender must signal its **commitment** to punish or retaliate and its **capability** to do so in order to demonstrate the **credibility** of the deterrent threat. If the defender succeeds, the challenger will back down without a shot being fired; if it fails, the challenger will attack.

[2]   The concept of deterrence is commonly associated with nuclear weapons, but its application extends to any situation where one side seeks to prevent another from taking some action that has not already been taken. When a five-year-old boy accosted by bullies attempts to warn them off by threatening, "You better leave me alone or my big brother will beat you up," he is using a strategy of deterrence to deal with a security problem.

[3]   Deterrence can also be used by the strong to prevent the weak from trying to overthrow the established order. Its use dates back thousands of years. In 70 A.D., for example, a Jewish rebellion against Roman rule in Palestine was crushed, but a few managed to escape to the mountain fortress of Masada. Although it could easily have chosen to ignore the remaining rebels, Rome painstakingly and expensively assaulted Masada to demonstrate that it "would pursue rebellion even to mountain tops in remote deserts to destroy its last vestiges, regardless of the cost." Rome's purpose was to deter any other groups in the empire from rebelling. In more recent times, the same argument could be made about the Soviet Union's strong-arm tactics in putting down the 1956 Hungarian revolt; Moscow's harsh action was intended to send a strong and clear message to neighboring Soviet satellites in Eastern Europe.

[4]   Deterrence can be a difficult strategy to successfully implement. It was mentioned previously that three conditions must be met in order for it to work. First, the defending state must define behavior that is unacceptable and communicate its commitment to punish the challenger. Second, the defender must possess the capability to punish an attacker. Finally, the defending state must demonstrate that it is willing to carry out its commitment to retaliate against the attacker; that is, the deterrent threat must have credibility.

[5]   Before we discuss these "three Cs" of successful deterrence, it must be made clear that the concept of deterrence assumes that decision makers are essentially rational. Rational decision making means choosing to act in a way that best enables you to maximize your own position, based on calculations of potential gains and losses, and of probabilities of enemy actions. It does not mean that decisions are made without emotion; obviously, human beings are often influenced by their emotions. But, it does assume that the leader of the challenging nation is capable of weighing the potential benefits of attacking against the costs of the defending nation's probable response, and that the decision to attack or not will be made on the basis of this calculation.

Commitment

[6]   As the first step in successful deterrence, the defending state must make a commitment to punish the challenger if the challenger takes a specified action. In other words, the defender must "draw a line in the sand" and warn the challenger that it will suffer if it crosses it. This commitment must be stated clearly, unambiguously, and before the challenger commits the act of aggression. For example, Israel repeatedly stated that a blockade of the Strait of Tiran, the only waterway passage to its southern port of Eilat, would be regarded as an act of war, and Egyptian attempts to blockade the strait in 1955 and 1967 were contributing factors in both the 1956 and 1967 Arab-Israeli wars.

[7]   It is important that deterrence commitments be definite and specific, as ambiguity may elicit probes by challengers interested in testing a defender's resolve. Prior to the outbreak of World War I, Britain wavered on its commitment to support the Entente (France and Russia) in the event of war against the Triple Alliance (Germany, Austria-Hungary, and Italy). Had Britain clearly voiced its position, Germany might have been dissuaded from attacking France in 1914.

[8]   Deterrence often fails because a defender does not properly signal a commitment to punish or fails to specify the precise retaliatory actions to be undertaken in case of aggression. Prior to Argentina's invasion of the Falkland Islands in 1982, for example, Britain failed to issue any verbal warning or to start any military preparations as a deterrent signal. As a result, the ruling Argentine junta probably doubted Britain's interest in defending a small colony left over from its imperial past, and thus was not deterred from seizing the islands. In this case, deterrence appears to have failed because a defender did not state its commitment to punish, or was ambiguous about its position.

Capability

[9]   The clearest commitment is useless if a state does not have the means to carry it out. Since deterrence revolves around convincing a challenger that the cost of a certain action is not worth the benefit, the challenger must be convinced (or at least strongly suspect) that the defender has the capability to retaliate. Even if a state's deterrent capability is weak, it may try to convince a challenger that its power to punish is greater than it actually is, just as a homeowner might hope to dissuade trespassers by posting a "Beware of Dog" sign even though she doesn't own a dog. This is one reason why some countries refuse to reveal their suspected nuclear capabilities; the very possibility that a defender might respond to an attack with nuclear weapons may be sufficient to deter an aggressor.

[10]   Deterrence with conventional weapons is considerably more difficult, because aggressors can better estimate their capability to inflict punishment. Even though Britain and France had more tanks than Germany in 1940, because Hitler knew he could compensate with a lightning campaign against France, he was not deterred from attacking and decisively defeated Allied forces there. Similarly, America's naval strength in the Pacific in 1941 did not deter the Japanese attack on Pearl Harbor, and the combined armed forces of Egypt and Syria did not deter the Israeli attack in 1967, because Israel and Japan gambled that they could score a knockout blow with preemptive strikes. (Israel's gamble paid off; Japan's didn't.)

Credibility

[11]   Third, a state must convince the aggressor of its resolve and willingness to carry out its commitment to punish. Even if a defender has clearly stated its commitment to punish and has the capability to do so, deterrence can still fail if the challenger doubts the willingness of the defender to risk war. As a result, this commitment to punish must be persuasive to keep from sounding like a bluff. In part, the defender's success will depend upon its reputation, past behavior, and image.

[12]   Ironically, the fearsome destructive power of nuclear weapons that makes their retaliatory capability unquestioned also leads to a credibility problem. Would the defender really be willing to sacrifice millions of people in a nuclear war? For example, in June 1948, one year before the Soviet Union exploded its first nuclear bomb, the American nuclear monopoly was still not able to prevent the Soviets from blockading Berlin. Similarly, in both the 1973 Arab-Israeli and the 1982 Falklands wars nonnuclear challengers (Egypt and Syria, and Argentina) doubted the defenders' resolve to retaliate with their nuclear weapons. (As it turned out, neither Britain nor Israel had to resort to nuclear arms to turn back the aggressors.)

[13]   In many ways, crises where nuclear weapons are involved often resemble the game of "chicken." In the classic film *Rebel without a Cause*, James Dean and a rival play this game by racing their cars towards the edge of a cliff; the first to "chicken out" and swerve is the loser, but if neither swerves, both will go over the cliff. In this game, each player wants the other to swerve before he does, but both players prefer swerving away from the edge and letting the other side win to going over the cliff. The object of the game, like the object of deterrence in a confrontation between two nuclear powers, is to prevail by convincing the opposing player of your willingness to risk destruction.

[14]   The Cuban missile crisis is often presented as a game of chicken, where the Soviets were the first to blink. If neither side was willing to retreat or "swerve," the outcome would have been war between the nuclear-armed superpowers. This might have occurred if the Soviets had attempted to proceed with their plan of placing more missiles on Cuba and the United States had launched an air strike on Cuba or invaded the island.

[15]   To summarize, deterrence can fail because a challenger doubts the defender's commitment, capability, or credibility to punish the aggressor. However, deterrence theory recognizes instances in which the defender clearly signals its commitment to credibly defend its interests, but the challenger then calculates that the benefit or prize exceeds the punishment. In such a case, it is still rational for the challenger to choose to attack. In 1914, Austria-Hungary probably knew that an attack on Serbia would mean war with Russia, but it declared war on Serbia anyway because it believed it would win. If the government in Vienna had known that its empire would be destroyed as a result, it would not have attacked. Deterrence always involves risk and uncertainty. Like Clint Eastwood in the film *Dirty Harry*, defenders point their weapons and ask, "Do you feel lucky?" If the aggressor feels lucky despite the defender's commitment, capability, and credibility, deterrence will fail.

Source: (1995). *World politics in a new era* (pp. 506–514). Fort Worth, TX: Harcourt Brace College Publishers.

Targeting Grammar: Complements with *to* + Verb and Verb + *-ing*

Many verbs are followed by a *verb complement,* or a phrase that completes, elaborates on, or modifies the meaning of the main verb. These complements are usually of two types:

- an infinitive (*to* + verb) phrase
  Britain failed **to issue** any verbal warning to Argentina.
- a gerund (verb + *-ing*) phrase
  Hitler was not deterred **from attacking** the Allied forces in Britain and France.

Note: Many verbs in academic texts require a preposition. This is a signal that a gerund phrase will follow.

In writing, it is often difficult to decide which verb complement follows the main verb you have chosen, especially if you are unsure whether a preposition must follow the verb. The main verb is an important clue to what type of complement (*to* + verb or verb + *-ing*) will follow. A useful strategy is to use an English learner's dictionary to look up the main verb. The following entries show the type of information available.

Dictionary Entries

dissuade v. [T] to persuade somebody not to do something; dissuade sb from doing sth *a campaign to dissuade young people from smoking*—compare PERSUADE— discussion

enable v. [T] 1. to give someone the ability or opportunity to do something; enable sb to do sth *Money from her aunt enabled Jan to buy the house.* 2. *formal* to make something possible: *a policy designed to enable the introduction of flexible working hours*

Here is a list of common academic verbs followed by verb phrase complements that are used in the reading "Deterrence."

VERB + *TO*-VERB	VERB + VERB-*ING*
to attempt *to* **prevent**	to refuse *to* **reveal**
to enable (someone/something) *to* **maximize**	to seek *to* **prevent**
to fail *to* **issue**	to deter (someone/something) *from* **seizing**
to intend *to* **send**	to dissuade (someone/something) *from* **attacking**
to manage *to* **escape**	to prevent (someone/something) *from* **attacking**
to persuade (someone/something) *to* **keep**	to revolve *around* **convincing**

TASK 7: Select words from the columns to make sentences about the historical examples used by Professor Spiegel in "Deterrence." Each sentence should contain a main verb and the corresponding verb complement (including a preposition where needed). If the main verb requires an object (*someone* or *something*), include one in your sentence. Consult a dictionary if necessary. An example has been done for you.

SUBJECT	MAIN VERB	VERB COMPLEMENT
Egypt	to attempt	to attack/attacking
Germany	to enable	to dissuade/dissuading
France	to fail	to retaliate/retaliating
Cuba	to persuade	to prevent/preventing
Jewish rebels	to refuse	to seize/seizing
Hungarians	to dissuade	to issue/issuing
Britain	to prevent	to defend/defending
Argentina	to deter	to sacrifice/sacrificing

1. *Egypt did not prevent Israel from attacking in 1967.* _____

2. _____

3. _____

4. _____

5. _____

6. _____

7. _____

8. _____

TASK 8: Professor Spiegel provides many historical examples to illustrate the "three Cs" of deterrence. For each example, identify the condition (commitment, capability, or credibility) that it illustrates. Then, in your own words, state the result of the action and the generalization Professor Spiegel makes from the example. Use verb complements as needed.

EXAMPLE	CONDITION	GENERALIZATION/RESULT
The Austro-Hungarian attack on Serbia in 1914	credibility	An aggressor calculates the costs and benefits of a particular military action and decides that the benefits outweigh the costs. In this case, however, Austria-Hungary failed to accurately assess the potential costs of waging war on Serbia.
Britain's failure to clearly support France and Russia against the Triple Alliance before World War I		
Britain's failure to warn Argentina against invading the Falkland Islands		
Israel's 1967 attack on Egypt and Syria		
Egypt's blockade of the Strait of Tiran		
Japan's attack on Pearl Harbor in the face of U.S. naval strength in the Pacific		
Moscow's harsh action against the 1956 Hungarian revolt		
The Roman punishment of rebels in Masada in 70 A.D.		
The Soviet blockade of Berlin in June 1948		
U.S. strategy during the Cuban Missile Crisis in 1962		

Understanding through Listening 2

VIDEO

Lecture: Power in International Relations
Segment 3: The Two Components of Credible Deterrence

Professor: Steven Spiegel
Course: Political Science 20: World Politics
Text: *World Politics in a New Era* by Steven L. Spiegel

In this segment of the lecture, Professor Spiegel reduces the six premises underlying strategic deterrence to two conditions. Note that the conditions mentioned in this segment differ in important ways from the three Cs explained in "Deterrence."

TASK 9: Review the reading "Deterrence." In the left-hand column, write the three conditions of a successful deterrent threat that Professor Spiegel explains in this reading. Then watch the lecture and write the two conditions for deterrence that he outlines. Leave the "Paraphrase" and "Example" sections blank.

READING PASSAGE	LECTURE SEGMENT
Condition 1:	Condition 1:
	Paraphrase:
Condition 2:	Example:
	Condition 2:
Condition 3:	Paraphrase:
	Example:

TASK 10: Watch the lecture again. In the same chart, write paraphrases of the two conditions Professor Spiegel explains. Then note the most helpful examples given by Professor Spiegel and explain why they are helpful.

TASK 11: In the contrast between the reading and the lecture, we see that Professor Spiegel has changed his theory about conditions for successful deterrence. Why do you think he made this change? (*Hint:* The book was published before the lecture was given.) Discuss with a partner.

UNDERSTANDING THROUGH READING 2

This short excerpt explains the problems associated with the lack of mutual deterrence in today's post–cold war era. Taking an American perspective, the author compares the sources of power pre– and post–cold war.

TASK 12: As you read the text the first time, mark it in the following ways:

- Put a ⇐ in the left-hand margin next to paragraphs that discuss only the past (i.e., the cold war era).

- Put a ⇒ in the left-hand margin next to paragraphs that discuss only the present (i.e., the post–cold war era).

- Put a ⇔ in the left-hand margin next to paragraphs that discuss both the present and the past eras.

TEMPTATIONS OF A SUPERPOWER

Ronald Steel

[1]   During the Cold War we had a vocation; now we have none. Once we had a powerful enemy; now it is gone. Once we had obedient allies; now we have trade rivals. Once we used to know how to define our place in the world and what our interests were; now we have no idea. Once we fretted about what critics called our arrogance of power. Now we wonder whether we are too timid and cautious.

[2]   The world we knew has collapsed around us. Nations that were once meek and disciplined are now violent and chaotic. Peoples who once lived together with apparent contentment now go for each other's throats. Until the Cold War was over we did not appreciate that the conflict, for all its inequities and dangers, imposed a kind of order on the world. Now even that is gone.

[3]   The whole meaning of the superpower tango is that it is a duet. Superpowers "contain," challenge, intimidate, and even threaten to fight one another. They speak the same language and respond to the same buttons when pushed. They assemble alliances, rattle sabers, and periodically meet at "summits" to keep things from getting out of hand.

[4]   The Cold War was easy to figure out. We signed up allies by the dozens, propped up friendly tyrants, bought off greedy neutrals, fought wars in remote unlikely places for abstract causes, and patrolled the frontiers of what we staked out as the "free world." Every arena was critical, every problem, by definition, a crisis.

[5]   But the old rules have been turned upside down. Instead of "containing" the Russians, we now subsidize them. The Third World, where we fought and financed wars we considered crucial, is now a political sinkhole. And the nations we used to consider Cold War allies are now merely rapacious trading partners.

[6]   The Cold War, despite its ideological overlay, was a classic conflict among states. We and the Soviets vied for king of the mountain. Today the most violent disputes lie outside the state system: in ethnic, religious, and tribal feuds. Many of these—like the wars in the Balkans, the Caucasus, and Central Africa—date back long before the Cold War, and even before this century.

[7]   Today the competition has moved elsewhere: to the industrial megalith of Japan, to the nimble trading states of Southeast Asia, to the emerging colossus of China, and to the giant emporium of a uniting Europe.

[8]   These countries do not want to bury capitalism. On the contrary, they are determined to do it better than we do. While we struggle with our role of superpower, they concentrate on productivity, market penetration, wealth, and innovation: the kind of power that matters most in today's world. In this competition we are—with our chronic deficits, weak currency, massive borrowing, and immense debt—a very strange kind of superpower.

Source: (1995). *Temptations of a superpower* (pp. 1–5). Cambridge, MA: Harvard University Press.

In academic reading, it is helpful to look for signals that indicate the organizational pattern of the text. Recognizing these patterns before you read assists both comprehension and note-taking.

The following quote from "Temptations of a Superpower" illustrates a pattern of organization often found in academic texts: point-counterpoint. In a point-counterpoint text, the writer contrasts two theories or concepts to make an argument. The author contrasts two periods of time, signaling the contrast between the cold war and today with two words: *once* and *now*.

> **During the Cold War** we had a vocation; **now** we have none. **Once** we had a powerful enemy; **now** it is gone. **Once** we had obedient allies; **now** we have trade rivals. **Once** we used to know how to define our place in the world and what our interests were; **now** we have no idea. **Once** we fretted about what critics called our arrogance of power. **Now** we wonder whether we are too timid and cautious.

This first paragraph foreshadows the organization of the entire passage, which alternates between the cold war period and the present-day situation.

TASK 13: Below are summaries of Steel's points and counterpoints. In each blank, write the number of the paragraph that corresponds to the summary. An example has been done for you.

Purpose of ¶ in the Reading Passage

¶ _____ 1. An appropriate analogy for superpower relationships during the cold war

¶ __2__ 2. Description of the change in the international power structure

¶ _____ 3. Introduction of the contrasting roles of the United States during and after the cold war

¶ _____ 4. Superpower conduct during the cold war (as exemplified by the United States)

¶ _____ 5. The new way to become a superpower

¶ _____ 6. The collapse of the old rules

¶ _____ 7. The shift of competition and power to the economic arena

¶ _____ 8. The differing conflict in the cold war and today

TASK 14: With a partner or in a small group, discuss which of the two conditions for strategic deterrence mentioned in the lecture were satisfied in the cold war era, and how. Which are broken in the post–cold war era, and how? Create a chart that organizes the conditions and explanations that you have discussed.

Integrating Perspectives

APPLYING THE CONCEPTS

The following traditional Norwegian folktale illustrates effective strategies for deterring an enemy attack. In the tale, three billy-goats encounter a mean troll, or demon, who threatens to eat them if they cross his bridge. All three goats successfully prevent this enemy from killing them.

TASK 15: Read "The Three Billy-Goats Gruff." Then with a partner or in a small group, discuss the different deterrence strategies used by the three billy-goats Gruff. Which strategy comes closest to the definition of deterrence given in this chapter's readings and lectures? Why?

The Three Billy-Goats Gruff

Once on a time there were three billy-goats who were to go up to the hillside to make themselves fat, and the name of all three was "Gruff."

On the way up was a bridge over a *burn* they had to cross; and under the bridge lived a great ugly Troll, with eyes as big as saucers and a nose as long as a *poker*.

So first of all came the youngest billy-goat Gruff to cross the bridge.

"Trip, trap! trip trap!" went the bridge. "WHO'S THAT tripping over my bridge?" roared the Troll.

"Oh, it is only I, the tiniest billy-goat Gruff; and I'm going up to the hillside to make myself fat," said the billy-goat, with such a small voice.

"Now, I'm coming to *gobble* you up," said the Troll.

"Oh no, *pray don't* take me. I'm too little, that I am," said the billy-goat; "wait a bit till the second billy-goat Gruff comes, he's much bigger."

"Well *be off with you*," said the Troll.

A little while after came the second billy-goat Gruff to cross the bridge. "TRIP, TRAP! TRIP, TRAP! TRIP, TRAP!" went the bridge.

"WHO'S THAT tripping over my bridge?" roared the Troll.

"Oh, it's the second billy-goat Gruff, and I'm going up to the hillside to make myself fat," said the billy-goat, who hadn't such a small voice.

"Now, I'm coming to gobble you up," said the Troll.

"Oh no, don't take me; wait a little till the big billy-goat Gruff comes, he's much bigger."

"Very well, be off with you," said the Troll.

But just then up came the big billy-goat Gruff.

"TRIP, TRAP! TRIP, TRAP! TRIP, TRAP!" went the bridge, for the billy-goat was so heavy that the bridge creaked and groaned under him.

"WHO'S THAT tramping over my bridge?" roared the Troll.

"IT'S I! THE BIG BILLY-GOAT GRUFF," said the billy-goat, who had an ugly hoarse voice of his own.

"Now, I'm coming to gobble you up," roared the Troll.

> "Well, come along! I've got two spears,
> And I'll poke your eyeballs out at your ears;
> I've got besides two curling-stones,
> And I'll crush you to bits, body and bones."

That was what the big billy-goat said; and so he flew at the Troll and poked his eyes out with his horns, and crushed him to bits, body and bones, and tossed him out into the burn, and after that he went up to the hillside. There the billy-goats got so fat they were *scarce* able to walk home again; and if the fat hasn't fallen off of them, why they're still fat; and so—

> Snip, snap, snout,
> This tale's told out.

Source: Stith Thompson, (Ed.) (1968). *One hundred favorite folktales* (pp. 1–2). Bloomington, IN: Indiana University Press.

Once on a time - variation of *Once upon a time,* the traditional opening sentence in English language folktales; *burn* - Scottish term for *river; poker* - long iron rod for stirring a fire; *gobble* - eat; *pray don't* - please don't; *be off with you* - go away; *scarce* - old form of *hardly*

ANALYZING THROUGH DISCUSSION

Niccolò Machiavelli, Italian author of *The Prince* who lived from 1469 to 1527, argues the following:

A prince, therefore, should have no care or thought but for war and for the regulation and training it requires, and should apply himself exclusively to this as his peculiar province; for war is the sole art looked for in one who rules.

Source: (1992). *The prince* (N. H. Thomson, trans.) (p. 37). New York: Dover. (Original work published in 1513.)

TASK 16: Divide the class into two groups and debate whether the view of strategic deterrence expressed by Machiavelli applies to the post–cold war world. Each group should draw on the readings in this chapter or the previous chapter to develop an argument. Then each group should present a rationale to the opposing team.

EVALUATING THROUGH WRITING

The chart that follows is taken from top secret U.S. government documents. It shows the increase in U.S. nuclear capability and the changing deterrent purposes that these weapons were to serve. These statistics reflect the U.S. government's criteria for defining a credible deterrent threat.

TASK 17: Review the readings and lecture segments in this chapter to find the criteria that make a deterrent threat credible. Which of those criteria appear to have governed U.S. nuclear war plans from 1945 to 1980? Fill in the last column of the chart.

SUMMARY CHART OF NUCLEAR WAR PLANS

DATE	NUCLEAR WEAPONS STOCKPILES	ATTACK PLAN	DESIRED OUTCOME	CRITERIA THAT MAKE THE DETERRENT THREAT CREDIBLE
December 1945	2	20 to 30 bombs on 20 targets (e.g., cities)	to launch a possible surprise attack	
1949	250	300 bombs on 200 targets	possible victory in the face of a hypothetical attack by the USSR in 1957	
1957	5,450	3,261 targets	USSR destroyed	
December 1960	18,500	3,423 targets	USSR destroyed	
1974	29,000	25,000 targets	to fight a war with a country possessing a large nuclear arsenal	
1980	25,000	40,000 targets	to fight a war with a country possessing a large nuclear arsenal	

Source: Michio Kaku and Daniel Axelrod (1987). *To win a nuclear war: The Pentagon's secret war plans* (pp. x–xi). Boston: South End Press.

TASK 18: Write a paragraph that explains your choice of criteria in Task 17. Use the concepts from the chapter and the statistics in the chart to develop your ideas.

EXPANSION:
INDIVIDUAL LEADERSHIP IN WORLD POLITICS

Power in world politics is determined, to a large extent, by the personality and governing style of a country's leader. What makes a strong leader? The sources in this chapter suggest that history makes leaders—they are products of the times in which they live. Further, in formulating their policy goals, good leaders respond to the desires and needs of their followers.

Exploring the Concepts

EXPLORING THROUGH VISUAL IMAGES

Napoleon Bonaparte (1769–1821), emperor of the French, is one of the most renowned leaders in history. During his powerful reign, he enlarged the French empire and waged war against many surrounding countries including Austria, Britain, Prussia, Russia, and Sweden. Napoleon invaded Russia in 1812 with a 500,000-man army. This army laid siege to Moscow, but a harsh winter and lack of food supplies forced Napoleon and his army to retreat.

TASK 1: The cartoon seems to portray Napoleon and his army returning from Moscow. With a partner or in a small group, discuss what the cartoon suggests about leaders and followers. What qualities of leaders and followers does this cartoon imply?

EXPLORING BACKGROUND KNOWLEDGE

TASK 2: Put a √ in the "Agree" or the "Disagree" column to show your opinion about the statements. Discuss your answers with a partner or in a small group.

STATEMENTS ABOUT LEADERSHIP	AGREE	DISAGREE
Leaders often disguise their true goals in order to attract followers.	_____	_____
Leadership is always a struggle, often a feud.	_____	_____
A leader is a superior person to whom followers submit.	_____	_____
A leader does not pronounce his will to the people but carries out what is decided by the people.	_____	_____
Followers should sacrifice their needs and desires to the vision of their leader.	_____	_____
A leader, in order to be worthy of being followed, must have a focus and a clear sense of priorities.	_____	_____
Both leaders and followers "have a say" in determining their course of action.	_____	_____
Historical circumstances make leaders great.	_____	_____

EXPLORING THROUGH DISCUSSION

To be influential, world leaders can possess a variety of different leadership qualities. The list of words that follows reflects the range of such qualities.

Targeting Vocabulary: Describing Leadership Qualities

TASK 3: Place a + or − next to the words depending on whether they have positive or negative connotations. If you believe a word can have both in different contexts, put a +/− next to the word. Consult a dictionary if necessary. The first one has been done for you.

_+/−_ ambitious	_____ decisive	_____ idealistic
_____ arrogant	_____ diabolical	_____ insightful
_____ brutal	_____ dictatorial	_____ intelligent
_____ charismatic	_____ distrustful	_____ power-hungry
_____ committed	_____ egotistical	_____ pragmatic
_____ confrontational	_____ evenhanded	_____ self-confident
_____ crafty	_____ goal-oriented	_____ suspicious
_____ cynical	_____ hard-nosed	_____ visionary

TASK 4: Based on the following famous quotations from world leaders, select two or three adjectives from the list in Task 3 that best represent the quality of the person who is quoted. Discuss your choices with a partner.

QUOTATION   **LEADERSHIP QUALITIES**

a. Let us never negotiate out of fear, but let us never fear to negotiate.   _____
_____

> John F. Kennedy (1917–1963), U. S. Democratic president. Inaugural Address,   _____
> January 20, 1961.

b. I am not invested with dictatorial powers. If I were, I should be quite   _____
ready to dictate.
_____

> Sir Winston Churchill (1874–1965), British statesman, writer. Speech, August 7, 1925,   _____
> to House of Commons, as Chancellor of the Exchequer.

c. I began revolution with 82 men. If I had [to] do it again, I'd do it with   _____
10 or 15 and absolute faith. It does not matter how small you are if you
have faith and a plan of action.   _____

> Fidel Castro (b. 1926), Cuban revolutionary, premier. *New York Times* (April 22, 1959).   _____

d. The art of leadership consists in consolidating the attention of the people   _____
against a single adversary and taking care that nothing will split up that
attention. The leader of genius must have the ability to make different   _____
opponents appear as if they belonged to one category.
_____

> Adolf Hitler (1889–1945), German dictator. *Mein Kampf,* vol. 1, ch. 3 (1925).

e. If you live among wolves you have to act like a wolf.   _____

> Nikita Khrushchev (1894–1971), Soviet premier. Quoted in *Observer*   _____
> (London, September 26, 1971).

_____

f. The people, and the people alone, are the motive force in the making of   _____
world history.
_____

> Mao Zedong (1893–1976), founder of the People's Republic of China. "On Coalition   _____
> Government," April 24, 1945 (published in *Selected works,* vol. 3).

Source: (1993) *The Columbia dictionary of quotations.* New York: Columbia University Press

TASK 5: With a partner, select five adjectives that describe an ideal world leader. Share your responses with the rest of the class.

EXPLORING THROUGH WRITING

TASK 6: Many believe that effective leaders must "practice what they preach." Select one of the world leaders pictured below. Decide whether this leader practices what he or she preaches and whether this affects his or her leadership. If necessary, research information about the leader. Then write a journal entry explaining your opinion.

Nelson Mandela
President of South Africa

Bill Clinton
President of the United States

Benazir Bhutto
Pakistani political leader

Charles, Prince of Wales
Heir Apparent to the Throne of
Great Britain

Working with Sources

UNDERSTANDING THROUGH READING 1

In the following reading, Howard Gardner attributes the success of leaders to the stories they tell and the ways in which these stories influence their followers.

TASK 7: Scan Gardner's text to find the five types of leaders he identifies. Then, as you read the excerpt, locate his definitions of these five types and underline them.

A COGNITIVE APPROACH TO LEADERSHIP

Howard Gardner

[1] At the end of November 1943, three men, already figures of historical significance, met in Tehran, the capital of Iran. Now that the tide of the Second World War had finally turned in favor of the Allies, Prime Minister Winston Churchill of Great Britain, President Franklin D. Roosevelt of the United States, and Premier Josef Stalin of the Union of Soviet Socialist Republics sat down together for the first time to address a number of crucial issues. During the four-day meeting that came to be called the Eureka Summit, they and their representatives tackled such topics as the opening of a second Western front against the Germans; the policies to be pursued with respect to Poland, France, Turkey, and China; the treatment of Germany's leaders after the conclusion of the war; and the prosecution of the war against Japan, the other major Axis enemy. In addition to reaching various military and diplomatic decisions, the trio of leaders became better acquainted and placed the Alliance on a firmer footing.

[2] At the time of the Eureka Summit, Albert Einstein was living quietly in Princeton, New Jersey, continuing to work, as he had been for over four decades, on fundamental questions about the nature of physical reality. In the early years of the century, Einstein had almost single-handedly brought about a revolution in physics, first with his special theory of relativity in 1905, and then with his general theory of relativity a decade later. When initially propounded, these theories had seemed primarily of scholarly interest, as Einstein was rethinking the nature of space, time, gravity, and other fundamental forces of the universe. But various implications of his work proved to be of the utmost practical consequence, as Einstein himself

came to realize. In a 1939 letter to President Roosevelt, he called attention to the possibility that extremely powerful bombs might be constructed if one could set off nuclear chain reactions in a mass of uranium: Einstein's message proved a crucial factor in the authorization of work on nuclear weapons. By the end of 1943, work in Los Alamos, New Mexico, on the development of an atomic bomb had advanced to a crucial point; this work would have been inconceivable in the absence of Einstein's revolutionary insights about the relationship between matter and energy.

[3] When we think of leaders, we usually envision the political or military giants of an era—Alexander the Great, Napoléon Bonaparte, Abraham Lincoln, or the generals of the Civil War. The familiar photograph of Stalin, Roosevelt, and Churchill seated alongside one another on a verandah in Tehran epitomizes this common conception of what leaders look like, even as the agenda at the Eureka Summit reflected the kinds of strategic preoccupations that we attribute to those in leadership positions.

[4] At first blush, few individuals could seem more remote from this conception than Einstein, who worked on issues so abstruse that, even today, few individuals understand them completely. In addition, he preferred to ponder issues in the laboratory of his own imagination, and then perhaps discuss them with one or two close associates. During the First World War, Einstein had been a pacifist; only because of Hitler's rise, and against his strong personal inclinations, had Einstein become drawn into political issues on the eve of the Second World War. When he was approached about becoming the first president of Israel, the armchair thinker was both amused and alarmed by the idea, and immediately declined—to the relief, it is said, of both parties.

[5] In light of the deep differences between the Eureka Summit leaders, on the one hand, and Einstein, on the other, one may well ask whether it makes sense

to contemplate these individuals in the same breath (or in the same prose passage). After all, one readily applies the name *leader* to Roosevelt or Churchill; to call Einstein a leader seems a stretch, unless one adds a descriptor such as a "leading physicist."

[6]   In this book, I argue that we can understand the achievements of such figures as Churchill and Einstein better if, first, we recognize the ways in which they were similar and, second and more importantly, we survey strategic intermediate points between these such prototypical figures. To anticipate my argument very briefly, I see both Churchill and Einstein as leaders—as individuals who significantly influence the thoughts, behaviors, and/or feelings of others. Churchill exerted his influence in a direct way, through the stories he communicated to various audiences; hence, I term him a *direct* leader. Einstein exerted his influence in an *indirect* way, through the ideas he developed and the ways that those ideas were captured in some kind of a theory or treatise; hence, he qualifies as an *indirect* leader.

Relating and Embodying Stories

[7]   Leaders achieve their effectiveness chiefly through the stories they relate. Here, I use the term *relate* rather than *tell* because presenting a story in words is but one way to communicate. Leaders in the arts characteristically inspire others by the ways they use their chosen media of artistic expression, be they the phrases of a sonata or the gestures of a dance; scientists lead through the manipulation of the symbol systems favored in their domains, be they the mathematical equations of theoretical physicists or the anatomical models of neurophysiologists. In addition to communicating stories, leaders *embody* those stories. That is, without necessarily relating their stories in so many words or in a string of selected symbols, leaders . . . convey their stories by the kinds of lives they themselves lead and, through example, seek to inspire in their followers.

[8]   The ways in which direct leaders conduct their lives—their embodiments—must be clearly perceptible to those whom they hope to influence. If a military leader like Stalin calls on his troops to be courageous, it matters whether he comports himself bravely. Similarly, if a religious leader like Pope John calls on Catholics to act generously toward those of other religious and ideological persuasions, his actual behavior toward Protestant pastors or Communist workers becomes significant. People who do not practice what they preach are hypocrites, and hypocrisy mutes the effectiveness of their stories.

[9]   In contrast, the personal lives of indirect leaders are not germane to their influence; strictly speaking, it did not matter to fellow scientists whether Einstein loved his wives, tormented his children, or never spoke to others. Nonetheless, the embodiments of an indirect leader are important. What matters to fellow physicists are the particular *approaches* to science embodied in Einstein's work. Just as his successors have been influenced by the conclusions that he drew, they have also been affected by the ways that he posed questions and the ways that he formulated, approached, and solved problems. By the same token, the conceptions and methods created by Igor Stravinsky and Martha Graham have affected succeeding generations of creative composers and dancers, respectively. If such creators had achieved their products through illegitimate means—for example, through fudging of data or through plagiarism—their leadership status would have been challenged.

[10]   It proves useful to align leaders in terms of the innovativeness of their stories. The *ordinary* leader, by definition the most common one, simply relates the traditional story of his or her group as effectively as possible. An ordinary political leader like Gerald Ford or the French president Georges Pompidou or an ordinary business leader like Roger Smith of General Motors does not seek to stretch the consciousness of his contemporary audience. We can learn about the commonplace stories of a group by examining the words and the lives of ordinary leaders; we are unlikely to be able to anticipate the ways in which that group will evolve in the future. In this book I have not focused on ordinary leaders.

[11]   The *innovative* leader takes a story that has been latent in the population, or among the members of his or her chosen domain, and brings new attention or a fresh twist to that story. In recent world history, neither Thatcher nor de Gaulle nor Ronald Reagan created wholly novel stories. Rather, it was their particular genius to have identified stories or themes that already existed in the culture but had become muted or neglected over the years. In the arts, individuals who style themselves as neoclassicists, neoromantics, or even neomodernists are also attempting to revive themes and forms that have fallen into disuse. In trying to capture the glory or the innocence of an earlier era, in the face of rival contemporary currents and counterstories, these innovative leaders may succeed in reorienting their times.

[12]   By far the rarest individual is the *visionary* leader. Not content to relate a current story or to reactivate a story drawn from a remote or recent past,

this individual actually creates a new story, one not known to most individuals before, and achieves at least a measure of success in conveying this story effectively to others. The great religious leaders of the past—Moses, Confucius, Jesus, Buddha, Mohammed—certainly qualify as visionary; on a more modest scale, I view individuals like Gandhi and [French economist and diplomat Jean] Monnet as visionary leaders for our time.

The Story as Central

[13]   The ultimate impact of the leader depends most significantly on the particular story that he or she relates or embodies, and the receptions to that story on the part of audiences (or collaborators or followers).

[14]   The audience is not simply a blank slate, however, waiting for the first, or for the best, story to be etched on its virginal tablet. Rather, audience members come equipped with many stories that have already been told and retold in their homes, their societies, and their domains. The stories of the leader—be they traditional or novel—must compete with many other extant stories; and if the new stories are to succeed, they must transplant, suppress, complement, or in some measure outweigh the earlier stories, as well as contemporary oppositional "counterstories."

[15]   I deliberately use the terms *story* and *narrative* rather than *message* or *theme.* In speaking of stories, I want to call attention to the fact that leaders present a *dynamic* perspective to their followers: not just a headline or snapshot, but a drama that unfolds over time, in which they—leader and followers—are the principal characters or heroes. Together, they have embarked on a journey in pursuit of certain goals, and along the way and into the future, they can expect to encounter certain obstacles or resistances that must be overcome. Leaders and audiences traffic in many stories, but the most basic story has to do with issues of *identity.* And so it is the leader who succeeds in conveying a new version of a given group's story who is likely to be effective. Effectiveness here involves fit—the story needs to make sense to audience members at this particular historical moment, in terms of where they have been and where they would like to go. Consider the capsule version of Eleanor Roosevelt's story—that a woman who was at once ordinary in appearance and extraordinary in background and resources could improve the lot of disadvantaged people. Such a story was appropriate at mid-century; the same story might have seemed unrealistic fifty years earlier and patronizing a half-century later.

[16]   As one comes to focus more closely on individual examples of leadership—traditional or visionary, direct or indirect, inclusionary or exclusionary, successful or ineffectual—one must consider not only the particular stories that are already "in the air" but also the niche that the leader's set of stories ultimately occupies. By the same token, the particular embodiment in the life of the leader stands in competition with a myriad of earlier images and stereotypes that already stock the consciousness of audience members. Through her daily mode of existence, Roosevelt had to refute the notions that only men can lead, that persons of privilege are suspect, and that only persons of extraordinary appearance and talents can inspire a revolution. To prevail, stories need enough background, detail, and texture so that an audience member can travel comfortably within their contours; only when these accompanying features are already well known can the leader count on an audience to "fill in the text."

Source: Emma Laskin, collaborator. (1995). *Leading minds: An anatomy of leadership* (pp. 1-6, 9-11, 14-15). New York: Basic Books.

WHAT IS CLASSIFICATION?

Classification involves dividing a concept into several parts or groups, each of which has at least one distinguishing feature. Classification is the product of the writer's critical analysis of the concept. For example, in the reading, Gardner divides leaders into two types—*direct* and *indirect:*

> Churchill exerted his influence in a direct way, through the stories he communicated to various audiences; hence, I term him a **direct** leader.

> Einstein exerted his influence in an **indirect** way, through the ideas he developed and the ways that those ideas were captured in some kind of a theory or treatise; hence, he qualifies as an **indirect** leader.

WHAT PURPOSE DOES CLASSIFICATION SERVE?

Classification has several uses.

- It allows us to contrast things that may seem very similar and to compare things that may seem quite different.
- It helps clarify our thinking about a given concept.
- It helps us arrive at more precise or useful definitions of a term or concept.
- It helps to distinguish aspects of our personal experience, observation, or research when we apply them to real-life examples.

HOW CAN YOU RECOGNIZE CLASSIFICATION IN A TEXT?

- Writers often introduce classification using phrases such as the following:

  There are two basic types of leaders. . .

  Leaders can be seen as falling into two basic categories. . .

- Writers may signal classification through the use of italics:

  By far the rarest individual is the *visionary* leader.

  I deliberately use the terms *story* and *narrative* rather than *message* or *theme.*

- Classifications may be accompanied by a definition, either brief or extended.

  The *innovative* leader **takes a story that has been latent in the population, or among the members of his or her chosen domain, and brings new attention or a fresh twist to that story.**

The writer may introduce a classification briefly at the beginning of the text and then elaborate on it later in the text. For example, Gardner first introduces the classification of leaders as *direct* and *indirect* in paragraph 6. However, it is not until paragraphs 7, 8, and 9 that he gives a full explanation of these two types of leaders.

Task 8: For each of the following types of leaders described by Gardner, provide a definition in your own words. Then name an individual who exemplifies this type and explain why. The first one has been done for you.

Type of Leader	Definition	Example/Explanation
Direct	Direct leaders influence their followers by their words and actions. These are usually political leaders who directly change something in the lives of their followers.	During World War II, the president of France, Charles de Gaulle, constantly reminded French citizens, who lived under German occupation, that they were free and should resist the occupying forces. This led to the creation of the French Resistance Movement and ultimately to France's liberation.
Indirect		
Ordinary		
Innovative		
Visionary		

Task 9: Throughout "A Cognitive Approach to Leadership," Gardner emphasizes the importance of the stories that leaders relate to their followers. These statements summarize his basic ideas:

- Leaders achieve their effectiveness chiefly through the stories they relate.
- Leaders must *embody* the stories they relate.
- To be successful, a story must outweigh all other existing stories.
- Leaders and audiences traffic in many stories, but the most basic story has to do with issues of *identity.*
- Stories must make sense to the audience at the particular historical moment in which they are told.

In pairs or small groups, choose two of the statements. Locate where Gardner explains these ideas in the text and be prepared to present your understanding of them to your classmates.

Task 10: Gardner differentiates between political leaders such as de Gaulle and Churchill and scientific and artistic leaders such as Einstein and Stravinsky. According to Gardner, both kinds relate a story to their followers, but in different ways. In pairs or in a small group, choose two leaders, one political and one artistic or scientific. Discuss the differences in how these two leaders communicated their stories.

 ## Targeting Grammar: Punctuation

In "A Cognitive Approach to Leadership," you will notice that Gardner's style is complex and his sentences tend to be long. To help readers process these long sentences, he uses a variety of punctuation marks.

SEMICOLON (;)
You can use a semicolon to indicate that the first independent clause is closely linked in thought to a second independent clause.

> By the end of 1943, work in Los Alamos, New Mexico, on the development of an atomic bomb had advanced to a crucial point; this work would have been inconceivable in the absence of Einstein's revolutionary insights about the relationship between matter and energy.

> After all, one readily applies the name *leader* to Roosevelt or Churchill; to call Einstein a leader seems a stretch, unless one adds a descriptor such as a "leading physicist."

COLON (:)
A colon is most commonly used at the end of a sentence, where it means *to illustrate, for example, that is, namely,* and *in fact.*

> In a 1939 letter to President Roosevelt, he called attention to the possibility that extremely powerful bombs might be constructed if one could set off nuclear chain reactions in a mass of uranium: Einstein's message proved a crucial factor in the authorization of work on nuclear weapons.

> In speaking of stories, I want to call attention to the fact that leaders present a *dynamic* perspective to their followers: not just a headline or snapshot, but a drama that unfolds over time. . . .

COMMA (,)

A comma is used to join two sentences connected by a coordinating conjunction, such as *and, but, yet, for, so, or,* and *nor.*

> People who do not practice what they preach are hypocrites, and hypocrisy mutes the effectiveness of their stories.

> Leaders and audiences traffic in many stories, but the most basic story has to do with issues of *identity.*

DASH (—)

Dashes are often used in the middle or at the end of sentences. They interrupt or add information. Here are some ways that Gardner uses dashes.

- to give an example

  If such creators had achieved their products through illegitimate means—for example, through fudging of data or through plagiarism—their leadership status would have been challenged.

- to present additional information, almost as an afterthought

  When he was approached about becoming the first president of Israel, the armchair thinker was both amused and alarmed by the idea, and immediately declined—to the relief, it is said, of both parties.

- to introduce a list

  When we think of leaders, we usually envision the political or military giants of an era—Alexander the Great, Napoléon Bonaparte, Abraham Lincoln, or the generals of the Civil War.

- to elaborate on an abstract idea or to define a specific term

  Effectiveness here involves fit—the story needs to make sense to audience members at this particular historical moment, in terms of where they have been and where they would like to go.

- to introduce an important term

  The ways in which direct leaders conduct their lives—their embodiments—must be clearly perceptible to those whom they hope to influence.

Many composition textbooks consider the dash to be too informal for use in academic writing. Although Gardner's style is formal, his book is destined for a general audience, which may explain his frequent use of the dash.

TASK 11: Add punctuation to these sentences. Use colons, semicolons, dashes, or commas. More than one form of punctuation may be appropriate for some sentences. The first one has been done for you.

1. Gandhi's innovative approach to the resolution of conflict *satyagraha* or nonviolent resistance rarely prevailed in India after his assassination yet it has inspired political activists and dissidents throughout the world.

   Gandhi's innovative approach to the resolution of conflict—satyagraha or nonviolent resistance—rarely prevailed in India after his assassination, yet it has inspired political activists and dissidents throughout the world.

2. A leader of a nation may lead indirectly for example de Gaulle's writings represented an important contribution to the French people.

3. The world may continue to change rapidly but we can expect to be confronted by the same types of leaders in the future.

4. The leaders' view of their constituencies was typically inclusive they sought to draw more people into their circle.

5. Most psychological studies of leadership have focused on the personality of the leader his or her personal needs and early life experiences.

6. Some readers will ponder the categories of direct and indirect leaders critically yet others may find these categories useful.

7. A leader within a domain may lead his audience members directly for example by assuming the presidency of a professional organization.

8. Some of the leaders-to-be I studied were clearly popular among their peers from an early age many others had childhoods that were marked by loneliness and isolation.

☺ Targeting Vocabulary: Using Expressive Verbs

Skilled writers consciously select vocabulary with an eye toward variety and meaning. One thing they pay particular attention to is verb choice, using vivid or expressive verbs and avoiding overused verbs.

The government ~~had~~ a policy that ~~supported~~ human rights.

The government **pursued** a policy that **upheld** human rights.

Oppenheimer's efforts to ~~stop~~ the production of nuclear bombs ~~were~~ useless.

Oppenheimer's efforts to **arrest** the production of nuclear bombs **proved** useless.

George C. Marshall ~~is~~ the type of person who tirelessly ~~works~~ for his country.

George C. Marshall **epitomizes** the type of person who tirelessly **labors** for his country.

TASK 12: The underlined verbs in the sentences are weak or overused. Replace them with more vivid verbs, selected from the list. Note that in some cases you will need to replace a two-word verb with a single verb. Use a dictionary if necessary. Rewrite the sentences on a separate piece of paper. The first one has been done for you.

anticipate	convey	identify	prove	reflect
attribute	envision	ponder	pursue	refute
conduct	epitomize	pose	recognize	

1. At the Eureka Summit, Roosevelt, Stalin, and Churchill <u>worked on</u> important post–war issues.

   At the Eureka Summit, Roosevelt, Stalin, and Churchill tackled important post-war issues.

2. When considering leaders, we usually <u>think of</u> the political or military giants of history.

3. We can understand Churchill and Einstein better if we <u>see</u> the ways in which they are similar.

4. Leaders <u>tell</u> their stories by the kinds of lives they themselves lead.

5. The ways in which direct leaders <u>live</u> their lives must be clearly perceptible to their followers.

6. Einstein's successors have been strongly influenced by the ways that he <u>asked</u> questions.

7. We are unlikely to be able to <u>guess</u> the ways in which groups will change in the future.

8. Thatcher, de Gaulle, and Reagan were effective leaders because they <u>found</u> stories or themes that already existed in the culture.

UNDERSTANDING THROUGH READING 2

According to Professor Spiegel, every world leader has a style of leadership that influences his or her actions and decisions. The next passage describes the two key elements of leadership style: an individual leader's ends and the means he or she uses to attain these ends.

TASK 13: As you read the portraits of Nasser and Khrushchev, mark the text to identify each leader's ends and means.

THE INDIVIDUAL LEVEL OF ANALYSIS

Steven L. Spiegel

[1]   Many analysts believe that leaders have a major impact on foreign policy-making. This impact is most vivid in the actions of all-powerful dictators in totalitarian states. Joseph Stalin, for instance, almost single-handedly changed the political, military, and economic landscape of his country. Further, he did so by acting erratically and brutally. The impact of democratic leaders may not seem as dramatic as that of dictators, but many analysts agree that they do exert a significant influence over policy-making. Assessing the impact of leaders is difficult, for it entails a close look at the behavior makeup of the individual and of the conditions within which he or she must act.

[2]   Consider President Ronald Reagan's 1983 remark that the Soviet Union was "the focus of evil in the modern world." How should this remark be interpreted? Was Reagan merely couching the bipolar global rivalry between the United States and the USSR in moral terms in order to mobilize public support for his defense policy? Was he prompted by the crusading spirit in American political culture? Was he expressing a heartfelt personal conviction? In theory, factors operating at the systemic, state, and individual levels each exert identifiable influences on a nation's actions in the world arena, but in practice the three levels of analysis can be difficult to separate when a state's foreign policy is expressed through a leader's words and actions. Individual-level perspectives on world politics cannot present an infallible means of determining *how much* individuals matter relative to the international system and domestic politics, but they can offer organized means of looking at *how* human factors affect international relations. They examine how such factors as human nature, psychology, emotional temperament, attitudes, perceptions, and beliefs direct decision makers to choose one foreign-policy option from the available repertoire.

Personal Experience and Leadership Style

[3]   The frequency with which historical analogies are used to make inferences about current problems underscores the importance of leaders' backgrounds and experiences in affecting foreign policy decisions. Those who can remember the past are not necessarily condemned to repeat it, but everyone relies to some degree on powerful or relevant life experiences in interpreting complex situations and making difficult choices. Consequently, it is often argued that the beliefs and leadership styles of national leaders are shaped in important ways by their previous perceptions of, and experiences in, personal relationships, politics, executive or management roles, and foreign policy-making.

[4]   Leadership style consists of an individual's considerations of ends (for example, one's desired role in the foreign policy-making process; one's country's role in global affairs) and means (for example, the methods one uses to define and play out those roles; one's approach and organization—whether one delegates authority or not).

Nasser, Pan-Arabist

[5]   On July 23, 1952, a group of young military officers, part of the clandestine Free Officers Society, overthrew King Farouk of Egypt. Among this group was Egypt's first long-term president, Gamal Abdul Nasser, in office from 1954 to 1970. Nasser, the son of an Alexandria postal clerk, got his break in 1937 when the Royal Military Academy allowed young men without palace or aristocratic connections to enter the officer corps. For many from lower-class families, the academy was an opportunity to rise to a modest rank based on merit. Yet, dissatisfaction among the junior officers with their superiors and the unsuccessful attempt to prevent the establishment of Israel in 1948 created a hotbed of political activism.

[6]   Although Nasser rose from the ranks of the lower middle class and instituted many programs that benefited them, there is evidence of dualism in his personal beliefs. While appealing to the masses, he also distrusted them, destroying all political parties except the state party, and severely curtailing freedom of the press. While supporting the notion of a democratic Egypt, Nasser believed that Egypt was still in a pre-democratic stage and required authoritarian rule. He therefore employed a large corps of domestic spies to monitor the behavior of both friend and foe. As one author notes, Nasser could be "dictatorial or deferential, charismatic or suspicious, ingenuous or crafty."

[7]   For many in the Arab world, Nasser stood for defiance of the West. In 1954 he forced the British to withdraw their army of 80,000 from the Suez Canal Zone; in 1955 he acquired Soviet arms; in 1956 he recognized Communist China and in the same year nationalized the British-controlled Suez Canal Company.

[8]   Nasser's successes—or more accurately, his survival—contributed to the emergence of **Nasserism,** a personality cult that made the Egyptian leader seem bigger than life. He became identified with a new revolutionary nationalism and effectively promoted **Pan-Arabism,** a movement to unify the Arab world into a single state. Toward this end, from 1958 to 1961, Egypt and Syria unified to form the United Arab Republic, with Nasser at the helm. Yet, while many viewed Nasser as a champion of the Arab cause, Western states and conservative Arab monarchies in Jordan and the Gulf region perceived Nasser's bullying as an ambitious attempt to extend Egyptian influence throughout the region. When Nasser died of a heart attack in 1970, he was widely praised as a hero, though his dream of Pan-Arabism had fallen far short of its goal. Regardless of the final verdict on Nasser, it is clear that he played the critical role in shaping Egyptian foreign policy during nearly twenty tumultuous years.

Nikita Khrushchev and the Politics of Bombast

[9]   Nikita Sergeyevich Khrushchev, Ukrainian by birth, was outgoing, demonstrative, and confrontational. During his tenure from 1958 to 1964, he rarely shied away from taking risks, either in domestic politics or foreign policy. Khrushchev loved a good argument and was fond of making dramatic gestures. Under his leadership, the USSR temporarily took the lead in the "space race" by orbiting Sputnik and launching the first human voyages into space.

[10]   Khrushchev's bombastic pronouncements, grandiose claims, and bluffs often caused alarm in the

Western world. He once boasted, for example, that communism would "bury" the West with superior production, and during the Suez Crisis in 1956 his government threatened Britain and France with nuclear devastation. Khrushchev delighted in what politicians in later years would call "photo opportunities." He took full advantage of public appearances to unleash barrages of Cold War rhetoric (accenting a speech at the UN by banging his shoe on the rostrum) or to promote an image of himself as a warm personality who empathized with the man and woman on the street.

[11]   Khrushchev's combative stance with respect to the West was reflected in the frequent East-West crises that erupted during his tenure in office. His bombastic pronouncements during the Suez, Taiwan Straits, Berlin and Cuban crises symbolized the sharpness of the Cold War's ideological conflict. Yet, his passionate speeches did not prevent him from developing a respectful relationship with Eisenhower during his 1959 visit to the United States. Reflecting Khrushchev's mercurial style, the new relationship with Eisenhower was in turn ruined by the U-2 crisis the following year. At the same time, Khrushchev's conflict with a fellow Communist, China's Mao Zedong, was often played out on a personal level, and the poor relationship between Khrushchev and Mao certainly did nothing to lessen the growing rift between Moscow and Beijing in the late 1950s and early 1960s. Ultimately, Khrushchev's risky moves at home and abroad (such as cutting the Soviet conventional defense budget in favor of nuclear weapons, pumping resources into the "virgin lands" agricultural development fiasco, and precipitating a frightening nuclear crisis by attempting to place missiles in Cuba) alienated too many of his colleagues in the Soviet Communist party, and he was removed from power in 1964.

Source: (1995). *World politics in a new era* (pp. 691–726). Fort Worth, TX: Harcourt Brace College Publishers.

TASK 14: With a partner or in a small group, compare the leadership styles of Khrushchev and Nasser. Answer the following questions:

- Were their styles largely similar or different?
- Were their styles effective?
- Why are these leaders so memorable?

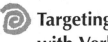 Targeting Vocabulary: Expressions with Verb + Noun + Preposition

Verbs often collocate, or combine with other parts of speech, to create new expressions. One common kind of expression consists of a verb + a noun phrase + a preposition. Adding the noun phrase and preposition changes the meaning of the original verb. Learning some of these set expressions can help to enrich your vocabulary and make your writing more fluent. As you learn these phrases, pay close attention to the noun phrase (including article and determiner usage) and to the preposition that follows the noun.

Here are some examples of such phrases from the readings in this chapter.

Followers do not **submit their will** easily **to** a leader.
                      (verb)   (noun)   (prep.)

Talking about the nobility of leaders **raises suspicion about** the weakness of followers.
                                      (verb)   (noun)   (prep.)

By giving me independence and decision-making power, my father hoped to **break down my resistance to** his authority.
(verb)   (noun)   (prep.)

TASK 15: Each of the following expressions occurs in "The Individual Level of Analysis." Match each verb with its associated noun phrase and preposition to create a common English expression. Write these expressions in the space provided. Consult a dictionary or the reading if necessary. The first one has been done for you.

VERB	NOUN PHRASE	PREPOSITION	EXPRESSION
1. assess	the rift	about	1. assess the importance of
2. change	the importance	between	2.
3. delegate	resources	for	3.
4. express	a role	in	4.
5. lessen	support	into	5.
6. make	the impact	of	6.
7. mobilize	the landscape	on	7.
8. play	a conviction	to	8.
9. promote	an inference		9.
10. pump	authority		10.
11. underscore	an image		11.

TASK 16: Choose five famous leaders, past or present, and write a sentence about the leadership style of each, using the expressions in Task 15. An example has been done for you.

1. *General William Tecumseh Sherman changed the landscape of modern warfare by waging guerrilla warfare on innocent civilians.*

2. _____

3. _____

4. _____

5. _____

6. _____

@ Targeting Grammar: Coordinating with Parallel Structures

Long sentences containing many ideas are common in academic writing. Two common problems with long sentences are that

- they can be complex and, therefore, difficult for readers to process
- writers have difficulty making them clear and understandable

One way to manage long, complex sentences is to construct them using parallel grammatical structures.

Parallel grammatical elements are coordinated using *and, but,* and *or* and must exhibit the same grammatical structure. Here are some examples:

Stalin changed the **political, military,** and **economic** landscape of his country.
(adjective) (adjective)   (adjective)

Stalin achieved this by acting **erratically** and **brutally.**
(adverb)   (adverb)

This requires looking at the behavior **of the individual** and **of the prevailing conditions.**
(prepositional phrase)   (prepositional phrase)

We cannot determine **how much individuals matter to the system,** but we can
(relative clause)

examine **how individuals affect international relations.**
(relative clause)

Nasser distrusted the masses, **destroying political parties** and **curtailing freedom of**
(verb phrase)   (verb phrase)

the press.

Khrushchev made many risky moves such as **increasing production of nuclear**
(gerund phrase)

weapons, pumping resources into a failed agricultural project, and **precipitating**
(gerund phrase)   (gerund phrase)

the Cuban missile crisis.

TASK 17: The following sentences about leadership contain coordinated elements that are not parallel. On a separate piece of paper, rewrite the sentences so that all coordinated elements are parallel.

1. To determine how individual leaders influence foreign policy, scholars examine such factors as human psychology, emotional, and attitudes and beliefs.

2. All leaders rely on relevant life experiences in interpreting complex situations and to make difficult choices.

3. Followers do not submit to the person of the leader but joining him or her in pursuit of the goal.

4. Factors that influence a leader's foreign policy objectives include when he comes to power, what world position his country occupies, and communicating with other world leaders.

5. Unfortunately, leaders who gain a place in history often do so because they are erratically and brutal, not because they are even-handedly or visionary.

6. It is foolish to think that a leader's skills can be applied to all occasions, that they can be taught outside a historical context, or one can learn them as a "secret" of control in every situation.

Understanding through Listening

> **Lecture:** Power in International Relations
> **Segment 4:** Factors Governing Individual Leadership
>
> **Professor:** Steven Spiegel
> **Course:** Political Science 20: World Politics
> **Text:** *World Politics in a New Era* by Steven L. Spiegel

VIDEO

Professor Spiegel explains two factors that affect leaders' decisions and leadership style: the analogy between a current situation and a past event, and the formative life experiences of the individual leader. He connects each point to several key examples.

TASK 18: Before watching the lecture, match the following individuals with their role in international politics and put the corresponding letter in the space provided. An example has been done for you.

	LEADERS	ROLE IN INTERNATIONAL POLITICS
_____	1. Bill Clinton	a. Congresswoman
_____	2. Robert Dole	b. U.S. president from 1968 to 1974
__j__	3. Michael Dukakis	c. Propaganda minister for Nazi Germany
_____	4. Joseph Goebbels	d. Secretary of state under Richard Nixon
_____	5. Adolf Hitler	e. Military leader of the Bosnian Serbs
_____	6. Saddam Hussein	f. U.S. president beginning in 1992
_____	7. Barbara Kennelly	g. Former prime minister of Israel
_____	8. Henry Kissinger	h. Leader of Nazi Germany
_____	9. Ratko Mladic	i. Former leader of the U.S. Senate and candidate for U.S. president in 1996
_____	10. Richard Nixon	j. Candidate for U.S. president in 1988; former governor of Massachusetts
_____	11. Yitzak Shamir	k. Leader of Iraq

TASK 19: Watch the lecture and match the information that Professor Spiegel gives with the appropriate person.

	LEADERS	RELEVANT INFORMATION
_____	1. Bill Clinton	a. condemned the U.S. policy of secretly supplying arms to Central America
_____	2. Michael Dukakis	b. equated ethnic cleansing in Bosnia with the horrors of the World War II Holocaust
_____	3. George Bush	c. lived through World War II
_____	4. Barbara Kennelly	d. saw Saddam Hussein as another Hitler
_____	5. Ratko Mladic	e. fled Warsaw on the day that Goebbels visited it in 1935
_____	6. Robert Dole	f. was affected by Vietnam
_____	7. Yitzak Shamir	g. noted that his own son was the first in many generations to know his father

Task 20: Choose four examples in Task 19. Determine which of the two main points (i.e., the two factors that affect leaders' decisions and leadership style) in Professor Spiegel's lecture these examples illustrate. With a partner or in a group, discuss the relationship between the example and the main point.

Integrating Perspectives

APPLYING THE CONCEPTS

In the following quotation, Joseph Stalin states that one factor alone determines leadership.

> You will find that men make history. But not in the way that your fancy suggests. Men make history rather in their reactions to the definite circumstances in which they find themselves placed. Every generation has a new set of circumstances to face. In general it can be said that great men are of value only in so far as they are able to deal with the circumstances of their environment. Otherwise they are Don Quixotes. According to Marx himself, one should never contrast men and circumstances. As far as my opinion goes, it is history that makes men.
>
> Source: Interview with Emil Ludwig in *Leaders of Europe, 1934* in Christopher Silvester (1993). *The Norton book of interviews: An anthology from 1859 to the present day* (p. 317). New York: W. W. Norton & Co.

Don Quixote - character from Spanish literature who had great dreams but never achieved them.

Task 21: Think of two current world leaders that you believe will be remembered in history. How did history "make" these world leaders? Discuss with a partner.

EVALUATING THROUGH LITERATURE

Task 22: Read this modern folktale about leadership to find out how the leader gained power.

The Owl Who Was God

James Thurber

[1]   Once upon a starless midnight there was an owl who sat on the branch of an oak tree. Two *ground moles* tried to slip quietly by, unnoticed. "You!" said the owl. "Who?" they quavered, in fear and astonishment, for they could not believe it was possible for anyone to see them in that thick darkness. "You two!" said the owl. The moles hurried away and told the other creatures of the field and forest that the owl was the greatest and wisest of all animals because he could see in the dark and because he could answer any question. "I'll see about that," said the secretary bird, and he called on the owl one night when it was again very dark. "How many claws am I holding up?" said the secretary bird. "Two," said the owl, and that was right. "Can you give me another expression for 'that is to say' or 'namely'?" asked the secretary bird. "*To wit,*" said the owl. "Why does the lover call on his love?" asked the secretary bird. "*To woo,*" said the owl.

[2]   The secretary bird hastened back to the other creatures and reported that the owl was indeed the greatest and wisest animal in the world because he could see in the dark and because he could answer any question. "Can he see in the daytime, too?" asked the red fox. "Yes," echoed a dormouse and a French poodle. "Can he see in the daytime, too?" All the other creatures

laughed loudly at this silly question, and they set upon the red fox and his friends and drove them out of the region. Then they sent a messenger to the owl and asked him to be their leader.

[3]   When the owl appeared among the animals it was high noon and the sun was shining brightly. He walked very slowly, which gave him an appearance of great dignity, and he peered about him with large, staring eyes, which gave him an air of tremendous importance. "He's God!" screamed a Plymouth Rock hen. And the others took up the cry. "He's God!" So they followed him wherever he went and when he began to bump into things they began to bump into things, too. Finally he came to a concrete highway and he started up the middle of it and all the other creatures followed him. Presently a hawk, who was acting as outrider, observed a truck coming toward them at fifty miles an hour, and he reported to the secretary bird and the secretary bird reported to the owl. "There's danger ahead," said the secretary bird. "To wit?" said the owl. The secretary bird told him. "Aren't you afraid?" he asked. "Who?" said the owl calmly, for he could not see the truck. "He's God!" cried all the creatures again, and they were still crying "He's God!" when the truck hit them and ran them down. Some of the animals were merely injured, but most of them, including the owl, were killed.

[4]   *Moral: You can fool too many of the people too much of the time.*

Source: (1990). *Fables for our time and famous poems illustrated* (pp. 33–34). New York: Harper & Row.

---

a ground mole - a small rodent that lives in holes underground; *to wit* - that is to say, namely (old use); *to woo* - to romance someone; *outrider* - a guide; *You can fool too many of the people too much of the time* - variation of "You can fool all of the people some of the time, some of the people all of the time, but you can't fool all of the people all of the time," Abraham Lincoln.

TASK 23: With a partner or in a small group, list some pieces of advice that you would give to the surviving animals about selecting their next leader. Base your advice on what you have learned about leadership in this unit. Compare your list with your classmates' lists.

TASK 24: Review the statements about leadership in Task 2 of this chapter. Write the statement that best represents the animals' attitude toward leadership that caused them to blindly follow the owl.

EVALUATING THROUGH WRITING

In this unit you have examined three main issues related to power in international relations: influence, deterrence, and individual leadership. The sources in the unit have presented analyses of these issues in terms of factors that contribute to or underlie them.

TASK 25: Choose one of the following topics and write an essay. Before you write, study the Academic Strategy that follows.

1. In Thurber's fable "The Owl Who Was God," the animals blindly follow the owl although his leadership brings nothing but injury and death. Choose a historical leader whom people have blindly followed. Using the sources in this unit, identify and discuss the single most important factor or the factors that contributed to this leader's influence.

2. Choose a leader who has in some way impressed you or influenced you. He or she does not have to be a political leader. Using the sources in this unit, identify and discuss the factors that have contributed to this individual's leadership.

3. "Temptations of a Superpower" on page 125 argues that superpower countries can no longer use deterrence as a primary means of exerting global power. Analyze the most important factors that have made deterrence an ineffective foreign policy strategy. Draw on any relevant sources in this unit related to influence and deterrence. You may also want to refer to examples from current world politics.

4. The moral of Thurber's modern folktale is *You can fool too many of the people too much of the time*. Analyze the most important factors that make this an untrue statement. Use the sources in the unit to develop your analysis. You may also want to refer to examples from your own experience or current world politics.

ACADEMIC STRATEGY:

ANALYZING A TOPIC BY EXAMINING CONTRIBUTING FACTORS

An effective way of analyzing a topic in academic writing is to examine factors that contribute to or underlie it. You can develop ideas for a paper analyzing contributing factors following this method:

- Decide your point of view about the topic by considering examples (e.g., historical leaders or events, examples from the readings).

    The topic is to analyze whether the following statement is true: "You can fool too many people too much of the time." World leaders such as Idi Amin, Adolf Hitler, Joseph Stalin, and Jean-Bedel Bokassa seem to suggest that this statement is true.

- Review the readings to find connections with the topic.

    This topic relates to the following sources: Professor Spiegel's lecture and reading on deterrence, the readings on influence, including "Power as Control over the Actions of Others" and "Soft Power."

- Identify and list any factors that seem pertinent to your topic.

    Some factors that seem pertinent are the three "Cs" (credibility, capability, and commitment) and the idea from "A Cognitive Approach to Leadership" that a leader's story must "make sense to audience members at this particular historical moment."

- Rank these factors from least to most important. Be prepared to give reasons for your ranking.

    From the example of Hitler and other despotic leaders, the factor of commitment (from the three "Cs") seems to be most important. Germany was willing to commit all of its military resources to pursuing its goal of gaining territory. Hitler told a story about the identity of the German people—that they were a great race and deserved to rule Europe. Because this story fit their conception of themselves, they responded to his leadership.

- Explain the relationship between the topic and the factor(s) that contribute to it, illustrating this relationship with examples to clarify your analysis.

    Hitler is one of the best historical examples of a leader who "fooled too many people too much of the time." He fooled his followers by presenting a compelling story about German identity—misguided as it was. In the example of Hitler, we see that followers can be swayed to support a leader, good or bad, who gives them an identity that they want to believe. His story could fool them because it came at the right historical moment—directly following their crushing defeat in World War I.

INSIGHTS FROM ASTRONOMY

4

INTRODUCTION:

ARE WE ALONE?

People have always been fascinated by outer space. In fact, many countries have committed resources to travel to outer space. At the same time, people have always wondered if life exists on other planets and if other beings have ever visited Earth. Some people believe that mysterious lights in the sky and other unexplained objects are evidence that extra-terrestrials have indeed traveled to our planet. These sightings are called unidentified flying objects, or UFOs.

Exploring the Concepts

EXPLORING THROUGH VISUAL IMAGES

We often use humor toward things we don't understand or things that threaten us. For example, UFOs are often the subject of humorous writing and cartoons.

51

TASK 1: This cartoon portrays one person's view of a meeting between humans and a being from another planet, or an extraterrestrial. We usually find cartoons funny because they reveal some truth about human behavior and attitudes. With your classmates, write a brief explanation of what this cartoon reveals about our attitudes toward and stereotypes of extraterrestrials.

THE FAR SIDE   By GARY LARSON

"Yes, yes, already, Warren! . . . There IS film in the camera!"

Exploring through Background Knowledge

In addition to UFOs, many other events and phenomena are mysterious and unexplained.

TASK 2: List examples of events or phenomena that remain a mystery. Find examples of phenomena that cannot be explained by existing knowledge. Compare your list with another classmate's list. An example has been done for you.

1. how Stonehenge in England was built _____

2. _____

3. _____

4. _____

TASK 3: When you see the word *UFO*, what do you think of or associate with it? Fill in the lines near the cube with whatever comes to mind about UFOs. On a separate piece of paper, choose one aspect of UFOs and expand it into a paragraph.

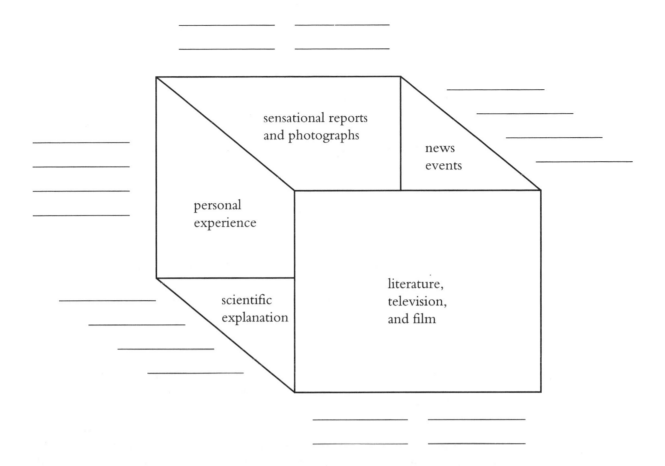

TASK 4: Below is a brief description of a UFO from an encyclopedia. Read it and formulate four questions you have about UFOs. Share these with your classmates. An example has been done for you.

---

unidentified flying object (UFO) *or* **flying saucer**, an object or light phenomenon reportedly seen in the sky whose appearance, trajectory, and general dynamic and luminescent behavior do not suggest a logical, conventional explanation. Although many alleged sightings have been interpreted as reflections of the sun's rays from airplanes, as weather balloons, or as various meteorological phenomena, some sightings remain unexplained by investigators in terms of known phenomena.

Source: (1991). *The concise Columbia encyclopedia.* New York: Columbia University Press.

Question 1: <u>When was the first UFO sighting reported?</u>

Question 2: _____

Question 3: _____

Question 4: _____

TASK 5: Write a journal entry about UFOs that addresses these questions:

1. How do you feel about UFOs?

2. Do you think they are possible?

3. If so, what would the implications of visits from extraterrestrials be for humans?

Use the cubing exercise you did in Task 3 to help get you started.

Working with Sources

UNDERSTANDING THROUGH READING

In the following essay, the authors attempt to answer the question "Are UFOs for real?" by presenting various theories to explain the existence of UFOs.

TASK 6: Read this selection to find out why it is so difficult to determine whether UFOs exist.

ARE UFOS FOR REAL?

Barry E. Zimmerman and David J. Zimmerman

[1]   The modern UFO (unidentified flying object) era officially began in 1947. A man named Kenneth Arnold was flying an airplane in the state of Washington when he saw nine disc-shaped objects flying at a fantastic speed. For some reason the newspapers picked up the story and gave it a good deal of press.

[2]   Since then there have been well over 100,000 UFO sightings recorded worldwide. In 1987 a Gallup poll revealed that almost half of all Americans believed UFOs were real and one out of eleven claimed to have seen one. If this percentage is accurate, it means that over 25 million people believe they have seen a UFO—an experience referred to as a close encounter of the *first kind.* Clearly, there is something out there. Determining exactly what that something is, however, has proven rather elusive.

[3]   The extraterrestrial theory of UFOs is by far the most popular. Scientists have calculated that, based upon the number of suns in the universe and the probable number of planets revolving around them, life almost assuredly exists on many other worlds. So why shouldn't they visit Earth once in a while? Distance, for one thing. Earth is most likely so incredibly far from any planet that might conceivably contain intelligent life that it would take thousands of years for its inhabitants

to reach us, even traveling at nearly the speed of light. (Presently, our spaceships can attain speeds of about one ten-thousandth the speed of light.)

[4]   But have no fear: If aliens cannot visit us from other worlds, maybe they can be living right on Earth—or in Earth. Another theory of UFOs, popular in the 1950s and 1960s, was the *Hollow Earth* theory. It proposed the existence of a secret civilization that lived inside our hollow planet. Two openings, one at each pole, allowed their flying saucers to enter and exit. By the early 1970s, however, seismographic data and the behavior of artificial satellite orbits showed that Earth was indeed solid and could not sustain a subterranean people.

[5]   Whether we conjure up UFOs from outer space or from within Earth or from deep below the sea (yet a third theory), the scientific world is very reluctant to accept such explanations in the absence of hard evidence. (A visitation in which evidence is left behind is known as a close encounter of the *second kind.*)

[6]   Scientists are waiting for some piece of indisputable physical evidence that an encounter has taken place—a piece of the UFO, the body of an alien. To date, we do not have such proof, although many ufologists are convinced the air force has retrieved and is hiding exactly this sort of thing. What we do have is a ton of circumstantial evidence. Slag and other bits of molten metal allegedly thrown off by UFOs have been collected and studied. Analysis, however, is never

conclusive. Although certain unusual alloys of aluminum, magnesium, and iron have turned up, nothing has been found that could not have been manufactured on Earth or deposited by a meteor.

[7]   Power outages and the malfunctioning of automobiles and televisions generally show a much higher incidence at the time and place of UFO sightings. Where UFOs have allegedly landed or hovered close to the ground, there are circular scorched or baked areas that cannot satisfactorily be explained as having been caused by lightning or fireballs. High levels of radiation often accompany these scorchings. In one particular alleged contact with extraterrestrials, the space people were health-food enthusiasts. A specimen of the food they cultivated, a potato grown on the moon, was analyzed and found to have five times more protein than potatoes grown here on Earth.

[8]   Whatever theory or theories one subscribes to concerning the existence of UFOs, problems arise when creatures are seen emerging from these spacecraft. And emerge they do. UFO occupants come in every size and shape. Although little green men are a favorite, we also have encountered a Mothman, a Vegetable Man, and "a fire-breathing monster ten feet tall with a bright-green body and a blood-red face." Perhaps the oddest creature was sighted in Lima, Peru, in 1957. A man saw what he described as "two amoebalike creatures that looked like rough-textured bananas" outside a spaceship. They explained to the flabbergasted human that they were sexless and proved the point by promptly dividing in half.

[9]   Sightings of living entities are called close encounters of the *third kind*. When the extraterrestrials want to get to know you better, it is a close encounter of the *fourth kind*—contact and interaction. Most CE4s involve abductions of humans by aliens, and they are by far the most fascinating as well as the most terrifying encounters.

[10]   If these visitations are not hoaxes—and the sheer volume of cases suggests they are not—then what the heck is happening? In *Communion*, Whitley Streiber offers several possible hypotheses. Some sound as if they came straight out of the twilight zone. If nothing else, they are fascinating.

[11]   According to Streiber the visitors could be

1. from another planet or planets.

2. earthlings who have come back from the future. This might explain their interest in helping us.

3. the adult form of the human species. Perhaps death is a time of metamorphosis, in which we, the larvae, transform into mature human beings.

4. beings from another space-time altogether—from a different dimension or universe traveling through what physicists call wormholes.

5. from within us. They could be spiritual projections of ourselves or the collective unconscious of our species. Many *abductees* experience the feeling of leaving their physical bodies behind during the abduction. This sort of separation of the spirit from the body (astral projection) is also reported during near-death experiences.

6. elaborate hallucinations. The brain is an electrical device. As such, it produces a faint electromagnetic field in the extra-low-frequency range of 1-30 hertz. Earth itself generates an extra-low-frequency electromagnetic field. Perhaps there are natural phenomena that trigger these wild imaginings in the brain.

[12]   One thing is certain: the more we investigate these extraordinary events the less we truly understand. Perhaps the problem is that there has been no serious attempt made by the scientific community to examine the UFO phenomenon. And world governments—the U.S. government in particular—seem to be more concerned with coverups than truthful disclosure. Tabloids make a mockery of the whole thing by purporting to show aliens shaking hands with presidents and presidential candidates. Perhaps the time has come to take this matter seriously.

Source: (1993). *Why nothing can travel faster than light . . . and other explorations in nature's curiosity shop.* pp. 105–113. Chicago: Contemporary Books.

TASK 7: Read each statement and locate the paragraph(s) in which the idea is contained. Write the paragraph number(s) on the line provided. The first one has been done for you.

¶ __6__ 1. Before scientists can believe that UFOs exist, they need hard physical evidence.

¶ _____ 2. When UFO sightings occur, there are often unusual phenomena that accompany them.

¶ _____ 3. Many people report that they have seen what they believe to be a UFO.

¶_____ 4. Given what astronomers have taught us about the existence of other planets that can support life, it is not inconceivable that extraterrestrials could exist.

¶_____ 5. Several people have reported meeting space aliens or even being taken away in a spaceship.

¶_____ 6. The authors imply that scientists have not taken UFO sightings seriously.

¶_____ 7. There are so many reported sightings that we cannot easily dismiss them.

¶_____ 8. One speculation is that extraterrestrials come from another space or time.

Targeting Grammar: Integrating Partial Quotations into a Sentence

Writers often choose to incorporate, or "weave," parts of quotations into their own sentences. This is especially true for elements of the source text that the writer finds particularly vivid or colorful, or which are especially well phrased. Examine the following example from Zimmerman and Zimmerman's article:

> Although little green men are a favorite, we also have encountered a Mothman, a Vegetable Man, and **"a fire-breathing monster ten feet tall with a bright-green body and a blood-red face."**

> A man saw what he described as **"two amoebalike creatures that looked like rough-textured bananas"** outside a spaceship.

Partial quotations must fit into the structure of the whole sentence. For example, if the quoted element is a noun or noun phrase, it must fit into a position in the new sentence where a noun or noun phrase would belong (e.g., the subject or object). Notice how in the first example above, the quoted element is a noun phrase that follows two other noun phrases and is connected by the conjunction *and*. In the second example, the quoted element begins with a noun phrase that follows the conjunction *as*. The same principle holds true when incorporating quotes that begin with other grammatical structures, such as adjective phrases, adverbs, prepositional phrases, etc.—the quote must fit into the structure of the sentence.

TASK 8: Fill in each blank with the portion of the original quotation that grammatically fits the sentence. The first one has been done for you.

1. Original text: "A man named Kenneth Arnold was flying an airplane in the state of Washington when he saw nine disc-shaped objects flying at a fantastic speed."

   Partial quotation: Reportedly, Kenneth Arnold witnessed "<u>nine disc-shaped objects flying at a fantastic speed,</u>" making him the first known human ever to sight a UFO.

2. Original text: "In 1987 a Gallup poll revealed that almost half of all Americans believed UFOs were real."

   Partial quotation: Despite the lack of concrete evidence, statistics indicated that "_____" believe in the existence of UFOs.

3. Original text: "But have no fear. If aliens cannot visit us from other worlds, maybe they can be living right on Earth—or in Earth."

   Partial quotation: One theory of UFOs contends that aliens may exist
   "_____."

4. Original text: "To date we do not have [indisputable physical evidence]. What we do have is a ton of circumstantial evidence."

   Partial quotation: According to the authors, despite the lack of convincing physical proof as to the existence of UFOs, there is "_____."

5. Original text: "A man saw what he described as 'two amoebalike creatures . . .' outside a spaceship. They explained to the flabbergasted human that they were sexless and proved the point by promptly dividing in half."

   Partial quotation: A 1957 sighting in Lima, Peru, involved two "_____ _____" who purported to be "_____" and who demonstrated this quality "_____."

TASK 9: As we saw in the cartoon in Task 1, UFOs are often the subject of humor. Jokes and funny stories about UFOs abound. With a partner or in a small group, describe a humorous UFO incident that you know of. If you can't think of one, imagine that you saw a UFO and describe it to amuse your listener(s).

Targeting Vocabulary: Key Terms

The words below are taken from the themes and ideas in this chapter.

cosmic	interstellar travel	space
extraterrestrials	investigation	speculation
galaxy	mystery	theory
hoax	plausibility	universe
hypothesis	prediction	unknown

TASK 10: Consider how these words might be related to each other. Arrange them into three or four groups based on relationships you see. Be prepared to explain your groupings.

GROUP 1	GROUP 2	GROUP 3	GROUP 4
_____	_____	_____	_____
_____	_____	_____	_____
_____	_____	_____	_____
_____	_____	_____	_____
_____	_____	_____	_____

TASK 11: The following pairs of words are related either as *synonyms*, words with similar meanings, or *antonyms*, words with contrasting meanings. Decide what the relationship is between the paired words and mark your choice in the appropriate column. Look up any unfamiliar words in a dictionary. The first one has been done for you.

WORD PAIR	SYNONYM	ANTONYM
1. conclude, terminate	X	
2. skeptical, gullible		
3. puzzle, conundrum		
4. credible, plausible		
5. adequate, insufficient		
6. hypothesize, theorize		
7. predictable, uncertain		
8. viewpoint, perspective		
9. valid, untenable		
10. intuition, experimentation		

TASK 12: In your notebook, write a definition for each word in Tasks 10 and 11.

UNDERSTANDING THROUGH LITERATURE

The following is a true story about a UFO sighting.

TASK 13: Read the excerpt and decide if you believe this really happened.

SKY BEINGS
AND THE GATHERING OF EAGLES

Brad Steiger and Sherry Hansen-Steiger

[1]   Jon Terrance Diegel remembers vividly the night in 1954 when, after a college dance in Orange County, California, he and his date decided to crawl out on the large rocks that enter the ocean near Balboa.

[2]   "It must have been about one-thirty in the morning," Jon said, "and we sat watching the lights of the little boats that were fishing in the canal. It was an extremely picturesque and romantic scene, and we decided to continue all the way on the rocks to the very end of the jetty."

[3]   "We were about halfway there when I looked up at the sky because I heard something that sounded kind of like the wind," Jon recalled. "Coming from the land side and going toward the ocean was a craft that was every bit as large as a 747 jet or larger. But, of course, we had no jet aircraft like that then. The commercial airlines still used propeller planes. This thing picked up speed as it went, and it was over the horizon in about twelve seconds. It didn't make any mechanical-type sounds. There was only the sound of the wind moving past it."

[4]   Searching his memory further, Jon recalled that the UFO definitely had "portholes, which were lighted." He could discern no wings or tail on the craft.

[5]   "It was long, so I'd have to say that it was cigar-shaped. It was very low and only about fifty yards away. Needless to say, it scared the beans out of us, and we went home immediately!"

Source: (1992). *Montezuma's serpent* (pp. 174–175). New York: Paragon House.

TASK 14: Discuss the following questions in groups:

1. Do you believe such accounts as the one in "Sky Beings and the Gathering of Eagles"? Why or why not?

2. Have you ever heard or read about encounters with aliens or UFO sightings? If so, relate the story to your classmates.

3. Is there a possible scientific explanation for this sighting?

4. Even if these accounts are not true, why do such stories keep emerging?

TASK 15: Write an original sentence incorporating the underlined portion of each sentence below as a partial quotation. The first one has been done for you.

1. We were about halfway there when I looked up at the sky because I heard something that sounded <u>kind of like the wind.</u>

   <u>John and his date were convinced that they had enountered a UFO when they</u>
   <u>heard a noise "kind of like the wind."</u>

2. Needless to say, it <u>scared the beans out of</u> us, and we went home immediately.

   _____

   _____

3. It was long, so I'd have to say that it was <u>cigar-shaped</u>.

   _____

   _____

4. Coming from the land side and going toward the ocean was a craft that was <u>every bit as large as a 747 jet or larger.</u>

   _____

   _____

5. This thing picked up speed as it went, and it was <u>over the horizon in about twelve seconds.</u>

   _____

   _____

 Targeting Vocabulary: Word Families

TASK 16: The verbs in the left-hand column below are often used to discuss scientific methods. Each of these verbs has a corresponding noun form. Using a dictionary, find the noun form and write it in the column on the right. The first one has been done for you.

VERB FORM	NOUN FORM	VERB FORM	NOUN FORM
1. assume	_assumption_	9. hypothesize	_____
2. conclude	_____	10. judge	_____
3. confirm	_____	11. observe	_____
4. contradict	_____	12. predict	_____
5. estimate	_____	13. rely	_____
6. evaluate	_____	14. reproduce	_____
7. exclude	_____	15. speculate	_____
8. explain	_____	16. verify	_____

TASK 17: Use the nouns that you wrote in Task 16 to complete the following sentences. More than one noun could fit each blank, and some will require plural forms. The first blank has been completed for you.

1. After scientists form <u>hypotheses</u> based on their _____, they seek

   _____ of their theories by conducting experiments.

2. The _____ of researchers on other scientists to test their

   hypotheses is another feature of the scientific method. This additional supporting

   evidence helps them to draw _____.

3. Do extraterrestrials inhabit other galaxies? For now their existence is just

   _____. But the _____ of many is that they

   do indeed exist.

4. What _____ would you make about future space exploration?

UNDERSTANDING THROUGH LISTENING

VIDEO

> **Lecture:** UFOs
> **Segment 1:** A Personal Experience with UFOs
>
> **Professor:** Robert Hurt
> **Course:** Astronomy 3: Introduction to Astronomy
> **Text:** *The Search for Life in the Universe* by Donald Goldsmith and Tobias Owen

In Segment 1 of his lecture, Professor Hurt, an astronomer, tells about his own UFO sighting.

TASK 18: After you watch the lecture, discuss the following questions in groups.

1. How is Professor Hurt's account of his UFO sighting different from the one that you read about in "Sky Beings and the Gathering of Eagles"?

2. What information does Professor Hurt use to conclude that he did not sight a UFO?

3. What point does Professor Hurt want to make by telling about his UFO sighting?

TASK 19: Select six students from the class to be guest panelists on a television talk show and one student to be the talk show host. The topic for the day's program is investigating UFOs. The panelists should assume the following roles:

- Whitley Streiber, author of the book *Communion* about alien encounters
- Barry Zimmerman, co-author of "Are UFOs for Real?"
- Jon Terrance Diegel and his date
- Professor Hurt, UCLA
- Natasha Miransky, a woman from Topeka, Kansas, who recently saw a UFO. (She was driving home near dusk when she saw a sequence of lights shooting across the sky. As she followed the lights, the pattern kept changing.)

The rest of the class will be the studio audience, who are welcome to add comments or ask questions of any of the panelists. The talk show host can start the discussion by asking Jon or his date and Natasha to relate their UFO sightings; the other panelists and the audience should then give their reactions or ask questions. You may want to review "Are UFOs for Real?" and "Sky Beings and the Gathering of Eagles" and watch the lecture again before you begin.

Integrating Perspectives

ANALYZING THROUGH VISUAL IMAGES

This unusual picture is an actual message that was sent to outer space in 1974 by the Arecibo telescope in Puerto Rico.

TASK 20: This visual message is encoded in mathematical form and should be read from top to bottom. Answer the following questions with a partner.

1. What do you think the diagram represents?

2. Can you provide an explanation for the order in which the information is presented?

3. What information did these astronomers think was essential to communicate?

TASK 21: What message would you send to life forms on other planets? Work in groups to draw a visual representation of it on a separate piece of paper. Then explain what your drawing means to the other groups.

EVALUATING THROUGH WRITING

ACADEMIC STRATEGY:

TIMED WRITING

In academic contexts such as examinations, you may need to write essays under time limits. Although writing a timed essay is not the same as writing an out-of-class essay, some steps in the process are similar. Here are some guidelines for writing under time restrictions.

- Read the question or topic for the essay carefully to make sure you understand it. Underline key direction words such as *summarize, analyze, describe,* or *define.* Also underline key words related to the topic.

- Decide roughly how much time you should spend on various steps of the writing process: reflecting on the topic, planning your essay organization, developing (writing), and editing.

- Think and plan before you write. Take time to reflect on possibilities for your response. Use any strategy for generating and organizing ideas that you have found useful, e.g., making a list of ideas, writing key words, making a brief outline, creating a cluster. If you start writing immediately without reflecting and planning, you may have trouble developing a topic or organizing ideas as you write.

- Give yourself enough time to read and edit your essay when you have finished. You may need to read the essay several times to make corrections.

TASK 22: Time yourself, allowing fifteen minutes to answer the following question on separate paper.

In this chapter, you have encountered several different ways of explaining UFO sightings: science, humor, and folk wisdom or stories. Despite the strong influence of science, humorous and folk accounts of UFO sightings still persist. Why do you think this is so?

EXPLORATION:

EVALUATING UFO SIGHTINGS

Scientists do not evaluate UFO sightings in the same way as nonscientists. When they receive reports of a sighting, scientists draw on two methods of evaluation: the scientific method and logic. This chapter includes a lecture in which the professor shows how the scientific method and logic are applied to three famous UFO sightings.

Exploring the Concepts

EXPLORING THROUGH DISCUSSION

TASK 1: Many scientists are famous because of the new theories that they devised to explain mysteries in the natural world or in the universe. Following are the theories of several famous scientists. In groups, choose *one* theory to discuss. Consider the following:

1. What mystery does each theory attempt to explain?

2. Do you know of other explanations that were given to explain these mysteries before these theories were proposed? If so, how did these theories change people's thinking about each mystery?

Theory of Gravity

Newton, Sir Isaac, 1642–1727, English mathematician and natural philosopher (physicist); considered by many the greatest scientist of all time. He was Lucasian professor of mathematics (1669–1701) at Cambridge University. Between 1664 and 1666 he discovered the law of universal gravitation. In his monumental *Philosophiae naturalis principia mathematica* [*Mathematical Principles of Natural Philosophy*] (1687), he showed how his principle of universal gravitation explained both the motions of heavenly bodies and the falling of bodies on earth. The *Principia* covers dynamics (including Newton's three laws of motion), fluid mechanics, the motions of the planets and their satellites, the motions of the comets, and the phenomena of tides. He was president of the Royal Society from 1703 until his death.

Source: (1991). *The concise Columbia encyclopedia.* New York: Columbia University Press.

gravitation (gràv´î-tâ´shen), the attractive force existing between any two particles of matter. Because this force acts throughout the universe, it is often called universal gravitation. Isaac Newton was the first to recognize that the force holding any object to the earth is the same as the force holding the moon and planets in their orbits.

Source: (1991). *The concise Columbia encyclopedia.* New York: Columbia University Press.

Laws of Planetary Motion

Ptolemaic system, historically the most influential of the geocentric cosmological theories, i.e., theories that placed the earth motionless at the center of the universe with all celestial bodies revolving around it. The system is named for the astronomer Ptolemy, who in the 2d cent. A.D. combined simple circular motions to explain the complicated wanderings of the planets. The Ptolemaic system dominated astronomy until the advent of the heliocentric Copernican system in the 16th century.

Source: (1991). *The concise Columbia encyclopedia.* New York: Columbia University Press.

Copernican system, the first modern European heliocentric theory of planetary motion; it placed the sun motionless at the center of the solar system with all the planets, including the earth, revolving around it. Copernicus developed his theory (which replaced the Ptolemaic system) in the early 16th cent. from a study of ancient astronomical records.

Source: (1991). *The concise Columbia encyclopedia.* New York: Columbia University Press.

Kepler's laws, three mathematical statements by Johannes Kepler that accurately describe the revolutions of the planets around the sun. The first law states that the shape of each planet's orbit is an ellipse with the sun at one focus. The second law states that if an imaginary line is drawn from the sun to the planet, the line will sweep out equal areas in space in equal periods of time for all points in the orbit. The third law states that the ratio of the cube of the semimajor axis of the ellipse (i.e., the average distance of the planet from the sun) to the square of the planet's period (the time it needs to complete one revolution around the sun) is the same for all the planets.

Source: (1991). *The concise Columbia encyclopedia.* New York: Columbia University Press.

Theory of Evolution

Darwin, Charles Robert, 1809–82, English naturalist. He firmly established the theory of organic evolution. His position as official naturalist aboard the H.M.S. Beagle during its world voyage (1831–36) started Darwin on a career of accumulating and assimilating data that resulted in the formulation of his concept of evolution. In 1858 he and Alfred Russel Wallace simultaneously published summaries of their independently conceived notions of natural selection; a year later Darwin set forth the structure of his theory and massive support for it in his *Origin of Species.* This was supplemented by later works, notably *The Descent of Man* (1871).

Source: (1991). *The concise Columbia encyclopedia.* New York: Columbia University Press.

Lamarck, Jean Baptiste Pierre Antoine de Monet, chevalier de, 1744–1829, French naturalist. Regarded as the founder of invertebrate paleontology, he is noted for his study and classification of invertebrates and for his evolutionary theories. Lamarck's theory of evolution, or Lamarckism, asserted that all life forms have arisen by a continual process of gradual modification throughout geological history. It was based on the theory of acquired characteristics, which held that new traits in an organism develop because of a need created by the environment and that they are transmitted to its offspring. Although the latter hypothesis was rejected as the principles of heredity were established, Lamarck's theory was an important forerunner of Charles Darwin's theory of evolution.

Source: (1991). *The concise Columbia encyclopedia.* New York: Columbia University Press.

Exploring through Writing

Task 2: Write a journal entry in which you explain all you know about the scientific method (i.e., how scientists research and arrive at conclusions about new or existing phenomena).

Working with Sources

Understanding through Reading 1

Introductory college texts explain information from a specific field to students who are new to this field. The writers of such texts assume that the readers have little background knowledge about the field's approach to the subject. However, writers do assume that readers have some information or folk wisdom about the topic. For this reason, they often structure their texts to compare and contrast their readers' folk knowledge with the field's approaches to this same subject.	**Academic Strategy:** **Comparing Existing Knowledge to New Information in Texts**

In the following excerpt from *The Search for Life in the Universe*, the authors describe the scientific method as it is applied to understanding the origins of life on Earth and the possibility of life on other planets. They assume that their readers already have some opinions about these two subjects. Therefore, they compare the reader's existing knowledge and attitudes to the way that astronomy approaches these subjects.

Task 3: As you read the excerpt, look for examples of these comparisons.

The Scientific View of the Universe

Donald Goldsmith and Tobias Owen

[1]   This book describes the universe from the moment of its birth to the present day, with an emphasis on the clues we can find to the twin mysteries of life's origin on Earth and its distribution in the universe.

[2]   Because we have no definite answers to these mysteries, we must attempt to draw conclusions from life, its fossil record on Earth, and the observations we can make of conditions on other planets. We must then speculate, as best we can, in order to judge the probability of finding life elsewhere in space. We shall see that a great difference exists between unbounded speculation and speculation that draws on what we know about the universe. Scientific speculation—

speculation that is directed by knowledge and bounded by physical laws rather than by fantasy—does not have so widespread an appeal as the more traditional forms of human conjecture, completely unfettered by science. In contemplating extraterrestrial life, science may seem mainly a drag on our imaginations, a weight that prevents our fancy from soaring free. Many people find the universe beyond the Earth so strange that they react either by never thinking about it, or by believing that anything goes: that no sort of life should be more improbable than another, or that laws of nature as yet unknown to us appear in everything from extrasensory perception to the Bermuda Triangle.

[3]   In contrast to these views, and with a track record of success, scientists hold the view that we must proceed carefully from what we understand—through multiple observations and experiments—toward our speculations about things that we do not understand. . . . The key to the scientific method is its reliance upon

testing and verification rather than upon assertion alone. If scientist A claims a detection of gravity waves, or cold fusion, or high-temperature superconductivity, then scientist B must be able to reproduce this result independently before it will be generally accepted. In fact, scientist A will usually explain how to repeat the experiment, or will suggest new experiments to test the theory. It doesn't matter how famous scientists are, how successful in life, or how impressive their previous work has been. Either the experiment works or it doesn't; either the observations are accurate or they aren't; either the theory makes a correct prediction or it doesn't. These canons of science have on occasion been violated by fraudulent or overly credulous researchers, but eventually the truth wins out, precisely because scientists place such stress on being able to repeat experiments and achieve the same result before they will accept that result as true. When we look at the world, we rely on the opinions of wise people, but only up to a point; to be completely certain, we must be able to test what they say.

[4]   On occasion, some new and startling fact seems to contradict the theories that summarize what we know about the universe. These are intensely exciting moments. In such cases, scientists remain reluctant to change their theories *until* they have become convinced that they can exclude any other explanation that would not require such a change.

Using this approach, most scientists will not, for example, regard UFO reports as evidence of extraterrestrial spacecraft until they have eliminated human error, psychological reactions, natural phenomena, or fraud as the causes of the UFO reports. On the other hand, a well-documented UFO sighting that was clearly evidence for a visit to Earth by extraterrestrials would be welcomed with keen interest by the scientific community.

[5]   The scientific view of the universe does not, of course, provide the only method to experience reality. There are many ways to tell the same story, and only a small fraction of humans attempt to maintain a scientific outlook continuously. To do so often violates human intuition, with which we maintain a system of beliefs that formed long before the scientific outlook emerged. What makes science look good as a world view is that *science works.* The model of the physical universe that scientists use can successfully explain observations and make accurate predictions of future events. Furthermore, the scientific model allows changes to occur in the framework of our understanding as new discoveries are made. The changes may provoke great debate among scientists, who nevertheless agree upon the principles through which they must alter their framework of knowledge.

Source: (1992). *The search for life in the universe* (2nd ed., pp. 10–12). Reading, MA: Addison-Wesley.

TASK 4: Complete the following chart with information from "The Scientific View of the Universe." This information will summarize how scientists investigate life on Earth and elsewhere.

EVIDENCE SCIENTISTS CONSIDER TO DRAW CONCLUSIONS ABOUT LIFE ON EARTH	METHODS OF INVESTIGATING UFO SIGHTINGS	ADVANTAGES OF THE SCIENTIFIC METHOD	DISADVANTAGES OF THE SCIENTIFIC METHOD

TASK 5: Reread "The Scientific View of the Universe" and answer the following questions with a partner.

1. The authors say that "Scientific speculation . . . does not have so widespread an appeal as the more traditional forms of human conjecture. . . . " Explain the meaning of this statement.

2. According to the authors, how do scientists approach the question of life elsewhere in the universe?

3. How do scientists react to new facts that seem to contradict current theories about the universe?

4. What procedures would scientists follow to evaluate a UFO report?

5. How does the scientific approach to life in the universe compare with the way that you have considered this issue before reading this excerpt?

Targeting Grammar: References Using *This*

When writers make reference to a previously stated idea in a text, they often use *this* (demonstrative pronoun), or *this* (demonstrative adjective) + noun phrase (i.e., a single noun or a noun plus its complements) to remind the reader of the previously referenced idea.

Here are some examples from an article you will read later in this chapter, "An Explanation for the Absence of Extraterrestrials on Earth." The idea referred to by *this* or *this* + noun phrase in the second column is indicated in bold type in the first column.

IDEA	*THIS* (+ NOUN PHRASE)
a. **Are there intelligent beings elsewhere in our Galaxy?**	a. **This** is the question which astronomers are asked by laymen.
b. **Fact A,** like all facts, **requires an explanation.**	b. Once **this** is recognized, an argument is suggested which indicates an answer to our original question.
c. Another frequently mentioned obstacle to interstellar travel is **the magnitude of the energy requirements.**	c. **This problem** might be insurmountable if only chemical fuels were available.
d. The possibility exists that the reason no extraterrestrials are here is simply because **none have yet had the time to reach us.**	d. To judge how plausible **this explanation** might be, one needs some estimate of how long it might take a civilization to reach us.

For more than one idea, writers may use *these* or *these* + noun phrase. Here are some more examples from the reading:

IDEA	*THIS* (+ NOUN PHRASE)
e. **Certain explanations claim that extraterrestrial visitors have never arrived on Earth because some physical difficulty makes space travel infeasible.**	e. We shall refer to **these** as physical explanations.
f. It was sometimes suggested that one or more of the following would make space travel unreasonably hazardous: **(a) the effects of cosmic rays; (b) the danger of collisions with meteoroids; (c) the biological effects of prolonged weightlessness; (d) unpredictable or unspecified dangers.**	f. With the success of the Apollo and Skylab missions, it appears none of **these hazards** is so great as to prohibit space travel.

As a rule, use *this* or *these* alone only if the reference will be obvious without a noun. Otherwise, add a word or phrase to make the reference clear.

TASK 6: Locate the following reference words or phrases in "The Scientific View of the Universe." The paragraph and line number are given for each. Then find the ideas being referred to and write them in the last column. Include the paragraph and line numbers. The first one has been done for you.

¶	LINE	REFERENCE	IDEA REFERRED TO
3	1	these views	Many people find the universe beyond the Earth so strange that they react either by never thinking about it, or by believing that anything goes: that no sort of life should be more improbable than another, or that laws of nature as yet unknown to us appear in everything from extrasensory perception to the Bermuda Triangle. (¶ 2, lines 16–22)
3	19	these canons of science	
4	3	these	
4	8	this approach	

TASK 7: The following sentences contain information from this unit. Rewrite the last sentence of each example, using a noun or noun phrase after *this* or *these* to replace the unclear reference form in bold type. The first one has been done for you.

1. Many UFO sightings have been identified as reflections of the sun's rays. Meteorological phenomena explain others. However, investigators have not been able to explain some of **these.**

   However, investigators have not been able to explain some of these sightings.

2. The Ptolemaic system placed the earth at the center of the universe. It was named after Ptolemy, who was a second-century astronomer. **This** explained the movement of planets.

   _____

3. Sir Isaac Newton discovered the law of gravitation sometime between 1664 and 1666. At the time he was a professor at Cambridge University. Among other things, **it** explained the motions of heavenly bodies.

   _____

4. Newton's theory that light is composed of particles was replaced by the wave theory of light. It was in the nineteenth century that the wave theory was proposed. **They** were combined in the modern quantum theory.

   _____

5. Kepler's laws describe the revolutions of the planets around the sun. **These** state facts about the shape of orbits and other mathematical relationships.

   _____

UNDERSTANDING THROUGH LISTENING

VIDEO

Lecture: UFOs
Segment 2: UFO Sightings

Professor: Robert Hurt
Course: Astronomy 3: Introduction to Astronomy
Text: *The Search for Life in the Universe* by Donald Goldsmith and Tobias Owen

In this lecture segment, Professor Hurt applies the scientific method to UFO sightings. He presents three reports of UFOs. He also discusses how the scientific method was used to explain each UFO sighting.

TASK 8: Recall what you have read about the scientific method. On a separate piece of paper, summarize this way of explaining mysteries or unknown phenomena and predict how the scientific method can be applied to UFO sightings.

TASK 9: As you watch the lecture by Professor Hurt, take notes and fill in the table.

UFO SIGHTING	DESCRIPTION OF WHAT WAS SEEN	EXPLANATION BASED ON ALREADY-KNOWN PHENOMENA
Lubbock lights		
Venus		
Physical evidence of UFO landing, Socorro, New Mexico		

Task 10: Each of the three UFO reports was later explained by technology or nature. Write a short explanation of how the scientific method was used to explain each of these three UFO sightings. Watch the lecture again, if necessary.

UFO SIGHTING	HOW THE SCIENTIFIC METHOD WAS USED TO EVALUATE WHETHER THE PHENOMENON WAS A UFO
Lubbock lights	
Venus	
Physical evidence of UFO landing, Socorro, New Mexico	

Targeting Vocabulary: Expressing Negation with Prefixes

Three prefixes, *in-, un-,* and *im-,* are commonly used to make adjectives negative.

in-	A request that is *not appropriate* is **in**appropriate.
un-	A conclusion that is *not reasonable* is **un**reasonable.
im-	An expression that is *not polite* is **im**polite.

TASK 11: Write the negative form of each adjective. Use a dictionary to check the prefixes. The first one has been done for you.

POSITIVE FORM	NEGATIVE FORM	POSITIVE FORM	NEGATIVE FORM
1. adequate	1. inadequate	6. plausible	6. _____
2. believable	2. _____	7. possible	7. _____
3. credible	3. _____	8. predictable	8. _____
4. feasible	4. _____	9. probable	9. _____
5. imaginable	5. _____	10. verifiable	10. _____

TASK 12: Use the negative form of the word in parentheses in the "Topic" column of the chart to make a comment, in the second column, about the topic. Then add a comment that explains the first comment. Try to use another negative form of an adjective. The first one has been done for you.

TOPIC	COMMENT	ADDITIONAL COMMENT
1. the chance that you will meet an extraterrestrial being (probable)	I consider that highly improbable.	I live in a densely populated area, and I think it's unbelievable that aliens would come here.
2. claims that aliens are living in the White House in Washington, D.C. (credible)		
3. many of the accounts people have given of having met extraterrestrials (verifiable)		
4. the length of time it would take to travel to another galaxy (imaginable)		
5. the amount of evidence for extraterrestrials (adequate)		

Understanding through Reading 2

This reading by Michael Hart (pages 173–178) has six parts. Part 1 is the introduction. It is one astronomer's explanation for why there are no beings from other planets visiting Earth. Hart evaluates whether extraterrestrials could visit Earth. In addition to using the scientific method to evaluate this possibility, he also uses ordinary reasoning.

Task 13: Read the following passage to identify Hart's four explanations.

An Explanation for the Absence of Extraterrestrials on Earth

Michael Hart

Part 1: Introduction

[1]   Are there intelligent beings elsewhere in our Galaxy? This is the question which astronomers are most frequently asked by laymen. The question is not a foolish one; indeed, it is perhaps the most significant of all questions in astronomy. In investigating the problem we must therefore do our best to include all relevant observational data.

[2]   Because of our training, most scientists have a tendency to disregard all information which is not the result of measurements. This is, in most matters, a sensible precaution against the intrusion of metaphysical arguments. In the present matter, however, that policy has caused many of us to disregard a clearly empirical fact of great importance, to wit: *There are no intelligent beings from outer space on Earth now.* (There may have been visitors in the past, but none of them has remained to settle or colonize here.) Since frequent reference will be made to the foregoing piece of data, in what follows we shall refer to it as "Fact A."

[3]   Fact A, like all facts, requires an explanation. Once this is recognized, an argument is suggested which indicates an answer to our original question. If, the argument goes, there were intelligent beings elsewhere in our Galaxy, then they would eventually have achieved space travel, and would have explored and colonized the Galaxy, as we have explored and colonized the Earth. However, (Fact A), they are not here; therefore they do not exist.

[4]   The author believes that the above argument is basically correct; however, in the rather loose form stated above it is clearly incomplete. After all, might there not be some other explanation of Fact A? Indeed, many other explanations of Fact A have been proposed; however, none of them appears to be adequate.

[5]   The other proposed explanations of Fact A might be grouped as follows:

[6]   (1) All explanations which claim that extraterrestrial visitors have never arrived on Earth because some physical, astronomical, biological or engineering difficulty makes space travel unfeasible. We shall refer to these as "physical explanations."

[7]   (2) Explanations based on the view that extraterrestrials have not arrived on Earth because they have chosen not to. This category is also intended to include any explanation based on their supposed lack of interest, motivation or organization, as well as political explanations. We shall refer to these as "sociological explanations."

[8]   (3) Explanations based on the possibility that advanced civilizations have arisen so recently that, although capable and willing to visit us, they have not had time to reach us yet. We shall call these "temporal explanations."

[9]   (4) Those explanations which take the view that the Earth *has* been visited by extraterrestrials, though we do not observe them here at present.

[10]   These four categories are intended to be exhaustive of the plausible alternatives to the explanations we suggest. Therefore, if the reasoning in the next four sections should prove persuasive, it would seem very likely that we are the only intelligent beings in our Galaxy.

Source: Donald Goldsmith (Ed.) (1980). *The quest for extraterrestrial life* (p. 228). Menlo Park, CA: Benjamin Cummings.

TASK 14: Skim Part 1 again. In your own words, summarize the four explanations for the argument against aliens from outer space living on Earth. Then decide whether each is or is not a plausible explanation for Fact A, based on what you might speculate from your general knowledge. The first one has been done for you.

1. Physical explanations:

    Some people believe that beings from outer space have not come to Earth either because they do not have technology sophisticated enough for space travel or because they themselves are physically or biologically limited in some way.

Are these explanations plausible?

    Yes, perhaps beings from outer space have not yet developed the technology to travel great distances in outer space. We ourselves do not have this technology yet. We cannot, for instance, travel faster than light, so we cannot visit planets that are light years away from us.

2. Sociological explanations:

    _____

    _____

    _____

Are these explanations plausible?

    _____

    _____

    _____

3. Temporal explanations:

    _____

    _____

    _____

Are these explanations plausible?

    _____

    _____

    _____

4. Extraterrestrials have been here, but we don't observe them at present:

    _____

    _____

    _____

Are these explanations plausible?

    _____

    _____

    _____

TASK 15: Divide the class into four equal groups. Each group will read and answer questions about *one* of the four subsections of the article: part 2, 3, 4, or 5. As you read, think about the questions below. Answer them in your group as one person takes notes on the discussion. That person or someone else should be prepared to present your group's responses to the class.

1. Hart explains the obstacles that visitors from other planets would have to overcome to travel to Earth or reasons that life forms on other planets would not want to travel in space. What are these obstacles or reasons?

2. According to Hart, each of these obstacles or reasons can be explained away. What weak spots does the author find in these explanations? What are some ways that the author proposes to overcome the obstacles to interstellar travel by other beings?

3. Why does Hart point out these weak spots? How does it strengthen his argument?

4. Does Hart ultimately agree with the explanation given in this section for why extraterrestrials have not visited Earth? If he does, how does he come to this agreement?

An Explanation for the Absence of Extraterrestrials on Earth (cont'd)

Part 2: Physical Explanations

[11]   After the success of Apollo 11 it seems strange to hear people claim that space travel is impossible. Still, the problems involved in interstellar travel are admittedly greater than those involved in a trip to the Moon, so it is reasonable to consider just how serious the problems are, and how they might be overcome.

[12]   The most obvious obstacle to interstellar travel is the enormity of the distances between the stars, and the consequently large travel time involved. A brief computation should make the difficulty clear: the greatest speeds [*sic*] which manned aircraft, or even spacecraft, have yet attained is only a few thousand km hr^{-1}. Yet traveling at 10 per cent of the speed of light, a one-way trip to Sirius, which is one of the nearest stars, would take 88 years. Plainly, the problem presented is not trivial; however, there are several possible means of dealing with it:

[13]   (1) If it is considered essential that those who start on the voyage should still be reasonably youthful upon arrival, this could be accomplished by having the voyagers spend most of the trip in some form of "suspended animation." For example, a suitable combination of drugs might not only put a traveler to sleep, but also slow his metabolism down by a factor of 100 or more. The same result might be effected by freezing the space voyagers near the beginning of the trip, and thawing them out shortly before arrival. It is true that we do not yet know how to freeze and revive warm-blooded animals but: (a) future biologists on

Earth (or biologists in advanced civilizations elsewhere) may learn how to do so; (b) intelligent beings arising in other solar systems are not necessarily warm-blooded.

[14]   (2) There is no reason to assume that all intelligent extraterrestrials have life spans similar to ours. (In fact, future medical advances may result in human beings having life expectancies of several millennia, or even perhaps much longer.) For a being with a life span of 3000 years a voyage of 200 years might seem not a dreary waste of most of one's life, but rather a diverting interlude.

[15]   (3) Various highly speculative methods of overcoming the problem have been proposed. For example, utilization of the relativistic time-dilation effect has been suggested (though the difficulties in this approach seem extremely great to me). Or the spaceship might be "manned" by robots, perhaps with a supplementary population of frozen zygotes which, after arrival at the destination, could be thawed out and used to produce a population of living beings.

[16]   (4) The most direct manner of handling the problem, and the one which makes the fewest demands on future scientific advances, is the straightforward one of planning each space voyage, from the beginning, as one that will take more than one generation to complete. If the spaceship is large and comfortable, and the social structure and arrangements are planned carefully, there is no reason why this need be impracticable.

[17]   Another frequently mentioned obstacle to interstellar travel is the magnitude of the energy requirements. This problem might be insurmountable if only chemical fuels were available, but if nuclear energy is used the fuel requirements do not appear to be extreme.

[18]   It can be seen that neither the time of travel nor the energy requirements create an insuperable obstacle to space travel. However, in the past, it was sometimes suggested that one or more of the following would make space travel unreasonably hazardous: (a) the effects of cosmic rays; (b) the danger of collisions with meteoroids; (c) the biological effects of prolonged weightlessness; and (d) unpredictable or unspecified dangers. With the success of the Apollo and Skylab missions it appears that none of these hazards is so great as to prohibit space travel.

Part 3: Sociological Explanations

[19]   Most proposed explanations of Fact A fall into this category. A few typical examples are:

[20]   (a) Why take the anthropomorphic view that extraterrestrials are just like us? Perhaps most advanced civilizations are primarily concerned with spiritual contemplation and have no interest in space exploration. (The Contemplation Hypothesis.)

[21]   (b) Perhaps most technologically advanced species destroy themselves in nuclear warfare not long after they discover atomic energy. (The Self-Destruction Hypothesis.)

[22]   (c) Perhaps an advanced civilization has set the Earth aside as their version of a national forest, or wildlife preserve. (The Zoo Hypothesis.)

[23]   In addition to variations on these themes (for example, extraterrestrials might be primarily concerned with artistic values rather than spiritual contemplation) many quite different explanations have been suggested. Plainly, it is not possible to consider each of these individually. There is, however, a weak spot which is common to all of these theories.

[24]   Consider, for example, the Contemplation Hypothesis. This might be a perfectly adequate explanation of why, in the year 600,000 B.C., the inhabitants of Vega III chose not to visit the Earth. However, as we well know, civilizations and cultures change. The Vegans of 599,000 B.C. could well be less interested in spiritual matters than their ancestors were, and more interested in space travel. A similar possibility would exist in 598,000 B.C., and so forth. Even if we assume that the Vegans' social and political structure is so rigid that no changes occur even over hundreds of thousands of years, or that their basic psychological makeup is such that they always remain uninterested in space travel, there is still a problem. With such an additional assumption the Contemplation Hypothesis might explain why the Vegans have never visited the Earth, but it still would not explain why the civilizations which developed on Procyon VI, Sirius II, and Altair IV have also

failed to come here. The Contemplation Hypothesis is not sufficient to explain Fact A unless we assume that it will hold for *every* race of extraterrestrials—regardless of its biological, psychological, social or political structure—and at *every* stage in their history after they achieve the ability to engage in space travel. That assumption is not plausible, however, so the Contemplation Hypothesis must be rejected as insufficient.

[25]   The same objection, however, applies to any other proposed sociological explanation. No such hypothesis is sufficient to explain Fact A unless we can show that it will apply to every race in the Galaxy, and at every time.

[26]   The foregoing objection would hold even if there *were* some established sociological theory which predicted that most technologically advanced civilizations will be spiritually oriented, or will blow themselves up, or will refrain from exploring and colonizing. In point of fact, however, there is no such theory which has been generally accepted by political scientists, or sociologists, or psychologists. Furthermore, it is safe to say that no such theory will be accepted. For any scientific theory must be based upon evidence, and the only evidence concerning the behavior of technologically advanced civilizations which political scientists, sociologists and psychologists have comes from the human species—a species which has neither blown itself up, nor confined itself exclusively to spiritual contemplation, but which has explored and colonized every portion of the globe it could. (This is *not* intended as proof that all extraterrestrials must behave as we have; it *is* intended to show that we cannot expect a scientific theory to be developed which predicts that most extraterrestrials will behave in the reverse way.)

[27]   Another objection to any sociological explanation of Fact A is methodological. Faced with a clear physical fact astronomers should attempt to find a scientific explanation for it—one based on known physical laws and subject to observational or experimental tests. No scientific procedure has ever been suggested for testing the validity of the Zoo Hypothesis, the Self-Destruction Hypothesis, or any other suggested sociological explanation of Fact A; therefore to accept any such explanation would be to abandon our scientific approach to the question.

Part 4: Temporal Explanations

[28]   Even if one rejects the physical and sociological explanations of Fact A, the possibility exists that the reason no extraterrestrials are here is simply because none have yet had the time to reach us. To judge how plausible this explanation is, one needs

some estimate of how long it might take a civilization to reach us once it had embarked upon a program of space exploration. To obtain such an estimate, let us reverse the question and ask how long it will be, assuming that we are indeed the first species in our Galaxy to achieve interstellar travel, before we visit a given planet in the Galaxy?

[29]	Assume that we eventually send expeditions to each of the 100 nearest stars. (These are all within 20 light-years of the Sun.) Each of these colonies has the potential of eventually sending out their own expeditions, and their colonies in turn can colonize, and so forth. If there were no pause between trips, the frontier of space exploration would then lie roughly on the surface of a sphere whose radius was increasing at a speed of 0.10 c. At that rate, most of our Galaxy would be traversed within 650,000 years. If we assume that the time between voyages is of the same order as the length of a single voyage, then the time needed to span the Galaxy will be roughly doubled.

[30]	We see that if there were other advanced civilizations in our Galaxy they would have had ample time to reach us, unless they commenced space exploration less than 2 million years ago. (There is no real chance of the Sun being accidentally overlooked. Even if the residents of one nearby planetary system ignored us, within a few thousand years an expedition from one of their colonies, or from some other nearby planetary system, would visit the solar system.)

[31]	Now the age of our Galaxy is ~10^{10} years. To accept the temporal explanation of Fact A we must therefore hypothesize that (a) it took roughly 5000 time-units (choosing one time-unit = 2×10^6 years) for the first species to arise in our Galaxy which had the inclination and ability to engage in interstellar travel; but (b) the second such species (i.e. us) arose less than 1 time-unit later.

[32]	Plainly, this would involve a quite remarkable coincidence. We conclude that, though the temporal explanation is theoretically possible, it should be considered highly unlikely.

Part 5: Perhaps They Have Come

[33]	There are several versions of this theory. Perhaps the most common one is the hypothesis that visitors from space arrived here in the fairly recent past (within, say, the last 5000 years) but did not settle here permanently. There are various interesting archaeological finds which proponents of this hypothesis often suggest are relics of the aliens' visit to Earth.

[34]	The weak spot of that hypothesis is that it fails to explain why the Earth was not visited earlier:

[35]	(a) If it is assumed that extraterrestrials have been able to visit us for a long time, then a sociological theory is required to explain why they all postponed the voyage to Earth for so long. However, any such sociological explanation runs into the same difficulties described earlier.

[36]	(b) On the other hand, suppose it is assumed that extraterrestrials visited us as soon as they were able to. That this occurred within 5000 years (which is only 1/400 of a time-unit) of the advent of our own space age would involve an even more remarkable coincidence than that discussed in the previous section.

[37]	Another version of the theory is that the Earth was visited from space a very long time ago, say 50 million years ago. This version involves no temporal coincidence. However, once again, a sociological theory is required to explain why, in all the intervening years, no other extraterrestrials have chosen to come to Earth, and remain. Of course, any suggested mechanism which is effective only 50 percent (or even 90 percent) of the time would be insufficient to explain Fact A. (For example, the hypothesis that *most* extraterrestrials wished only to visit, but not to colonize, is inadequate. For colonization not to have occurred requires that *every* single civilization which had the opportunity to colonize chose not to.)

[38]	A third version, which we may call "the UFO Hypothesis," is that extraterrestrials have not only arrived on Earth, but are still here. This version is not really an explanation of Fact A, but rather a denial of it. Since very few astronomers believe the UFO Hypothesis it seems unnecessary to discuss my own reasons for rejecting it.

Source: Donald Goldsmith (Ed.) (1980). *The quest for extraterrestrial life* (pp. 228–231). Menlo Park, CA: Benjamin Cummings.

TASK 16: After each group has presented its summary, work together as a class to answer the following question: Based on Hart's arguments, what conclusions can we draw about the existence of intelligent life in our galaxy beyond Earth?

TASK 17: Now read "Part 6: Conclusions and Discussion." Compare your conclusions with those Hart reached.

AN EXPLANATION FOR THE ABSENCE OF EXTRATERRESTRIALS ON EARTH (cont'd)

Part 6: Conclusions and Discussion

[39]   In recent years several astronomers have suggested that intelligent life in our Galaxy is very common. It has been argued (Shklovskii and Sagan, 1996) that (a) a high percentage of stars have planetary systems; (b) most of these systems contain an Earth-like planet; (c) life has developed on most of such planets; and (d) intelligent life has evolved on a considerable number of such planets. These optimistic conclusions have perhaps led many persons to believe that (1) our starfaring descendants are almost certain, sooner or later, to encounter other advanced cultures in our Galaxy; and (2) radio contact with other civilizations may be just around the corner.

[40]   These are very exciting prospects indeed; so much so that wishful thinking may lead us to overestimate the chances that the conjecture is correct. Unfortunately, though, the idea that thousands of advanced civilizations are scattered throughout the Galaxy is quite implausible in the light of Fact A. Though it is possible that one or two civilizations have evolved and have destroyed themselves in a nuclear war, it is implausible that every one of 10,000 alien civilizations had done so. Our descendants might eventually encounter a few advanced civilizations which never chose to engage in interstellar travel; but their number should be small, and could well be zero.

[41]   If the basic thesis of this paper is correct there are two corollary conclusions: (1) an extensive search for radio messages from other civilizations is probably a waste of time and money; and (2) in the long run, cultures descended directly from ours will probably occupy most of the habitable planets in our Galaxy.

[42]   In view of the enormous number of stars in our Galaxy, the conclusions reached in this paper may be rather surprising. It is natural to inquire how it has come about that intelligent life has evolved on Earth in advance of its appearance on other planets. Future research in such fields as biochemistry; the dynamics of planetary formation; and the formation and evolution of atmospheres, may well provide a convincing answer to this question. In the meantime, Fact A provided strong evidence that we are the first civilization in our Galaxy, even though the cause of our priority is not yet known.

Source: Donald Goldsmith (Ed.) (1980). *The quest for extraterrestrial life* (p. 231). Menlo Park, CA: Benjamin Cummings.

 Targeting Grammar: Adjective Clauses

In "An Explanation for the Absence of Extraterrestrials on Earth," Hart uses adjective clause structures to define competing explanations.

Pattern 1: All explanations **which claim that extraterrestrial visitors have never**
(adjective clause)

arrived on Earth because some physical, astronomical, biological or engineering
(adjective clause, continued)

difficulty makes space travel unfeasible. (physical explanations)
(adjective clause, continued)

NOUN PHRASE	WHICH	REPORTING VERB	THAT	CLAIM OR STATEMENT
All explanations	which	claim	that	extraterrestrial visitors have never arrived on Earth because some physical, astronomical, biological or engineering difficulty makes space travel unfeasible. (physical explanations)

Pattern 2: Explanations **based on the view that extraterrestrials have not arrived on**
(adjective clause)

Earth because they have chosen not to. (sociological explanations)
(adjective clause, continued)

NOUN	BASED ON	ABSTRACT NOUN OR NOUN PHRASE	THAT	CLAIM OR STATEMENT
Explanations	based on	the view	that	extraterrestrials have not arrived on Earth because they have chosen not to. (sociological explanations)

TASK 18: Following are hypotheses about extraterrestrials. Rewrite each hypothesis by completing the adjective clauses in the two ways they are presented in the preceding explanation. Choose reporting verbs and abstract nouns, respectively, from the list.

REPORTING VERBS		ABSTRACT NOUNS THAT EXPRESS IDEAS/OPINIONS	
argue	maintain	belief	perspective
assert	propose	concept	possibility
claim	state	idea	probability
declare	suggest	notion	view
		opinion	

1. The Contemplation Hypothesis: Advanced civilizations may be concerned with spiritual contemplation rather than space exploration.

   The Contemplation Hypothesis is an explanation which _____

   _____

   _____

   The Contemplation Hypothesis is an explanation based on _____

   _____

   _____

2. The Zoo Hypothesis: An advanced civilization may have set Earth aside as a kind of wildlife preserve.

   The Zoo Hypothesis is an explanation which _____

   _____

   _____

   The Zoo Hypothesis is an explanation based on _____

   _____

   _____

TASK 19: Scan "Part 3: Sociological Explanations" and locate the Self-Destruction Hypothesis. Next write two types of adjective clauses, as you did in Task 18, to define this hypothesis.

The Self-Destruction Hypothesis is an explanation which _____

_____

_____

The Self-Destruction Hypothesis is an explanation based on _____

_____

_____

TASK 20: In "Part 5: Perhaps They Have Come," the author describes several versions of the theory that extraterrestrials have actually been here. An incomplete summary of his discussion follows. Complete the adjective clauses with information from the reading.

One version is based on the hypothesis that visitors arrived fairly recently but (1) _____

_____ .

There is another version which (2) _____

that (3) _____ .

A third version is based (4) _____ the (5) _____ that (6) _____

_____ .

Integrating Perspectives

ANALYZING THROUGH DISCUSSION

TASK 21: Respond to the following questions in small groups.

1. Which principles discussed in "The Scientific View of the Universe" does Hart use in his article to examine the question of life on other planets?

2. What do you think Professor Hurt's response would be to Hart's argument for the absence of extraterrestrial life?

APPLYING THE CONCEPTS

TASK 22: The chart contains information taken from *The Gallup Poll Monthly*. Study the responses to the question and, in small groups, discuss any trends. What factors might explain the differences in the belief that life exists elsewhere in the universe?

Do you think there are people somewhat like ourselves living on other planets in the universe?

	YES	NO	NO OPINION
1996	39%	50%	11%
1990	46%	36%	18%
1989	41%	48%	11%
1978	51%	33%	16%
1973	46%	38%	16%

Source: (1996, March). People like us? *The Gallup Poll Monthly.*

ANALYZING THROUGH WRITING

When reading academic texts, good readers look for the *claims,* or position statements, that authors make. The critical reader not only identifies these claims, but also evaluates them by asking questions such as the following:

Is it valid?   Is it feasible?

Is it practical?   Is it ethical?

Is it sound?

ACADEMIC STRATEGY:

CRITICAL READING: EVALUATING A CLAIM

For example, when evaluating the claim "Mysterious objects in the night sky are UFOs," the critical reader would ask "Is this feasible?" and would probably arrive at the answer "It's not feasible that all mysterious objects in the night sky are UFOs; however, some of them could be." Thus, by asking the question, the reader has established some doubt about the author's claim.

Similarly, when evaluating the claim "The U.S. government has been withholding evidence since 1950 proving the existence of UFOs," the critical reader might ask "Is this feasible?" and conclude that it would be very difficult for all the people involved in government operations to keep this information a secret for such a long time. The reader could also ask "Is it ethical?" and conclude that while withholding evidence is not ethical, governments do not always act ethically. By asking these questions, the reader has established that this claim is unlikely but still within the realm of possibility.

You will be writing an argument by evaluation essay at the end of this unit. The first step in this assignment will be to evaluate the claims in the source readings.

TASK 23: For the following claim, pick two or three of the questions in the Academic Strategy box on the previous page that help you evaluate the claim. Using these questions as a guide, allow twenty minutes to write an evaluation of the claim. Use a separate piece of paper.

Claim: It is important to fund efforts to contact intelligent life in our galaxy.

Targeting Grammar: Unreal Conditionals

PURPOSE AND STRUCTURE OF CONDITIONAL STATEMENTS

Conditional statements are useful when writing an argument by evaluation. In these statements, writers

- explain facts and present opinions
- speculate about what will happen in the future
- state the criteria or conditions that would have to exist for something to occur

The condition, i.e., the situation, event, or action that has to occur for the result to follow, is stated in the dependent clause beginning with *if.* This clause may come either before or after the result (expressed in the main clause).

CONDITION: *IF*-CLAUSE	RESULT: MAIN CLAUSE
If we accepted a hypothesis that had no procedures to test its validity,	we would abandon our scientific approach.

RESULT: MAIN CLAUSE	CONDITION: *IF*-CLAUSE
We would abandon our scientific approach	if we accepted a hypothesis that had no procedures to test its validity.

UNREAL CONDITIONALS

In "An Explanation for the Absence of Extraterrestrials on Earth," the author uses several conditional statements to argue his position. Many of these are *unreal conditionals,* which state hypothetical conditions or conditions that are the opposite of what really happened. Unreal conditionals may be present tense or past tense.

PRESENT UNREAL CONDITION (past tense verb)	PRESENT RESULT (*would* + base verb)
If extraterrestrials **lived** on Earth,	we **would have** evidence that they exist.

PRESENT UNREAL CONDITION (past tense verb)	PAST RESULT (*would have* + base verb)
If extraterrestrials **existed,**	they **would have visited** us by now.

PAST UNREAL CONDITION (*had* + past participle)	PAST RESULT (modal verb + *have* + past participle)
If extraterrestrials **had visited** us a very long time ago,	we **should have had** other visitors since.

TASK 24: The following statements are taken from "An Explanation for the Absence of Extraterrestrials on Earth." Put parentheses ( ) around the condition; put brackets [ ] around the result. Underline the main verbs in each clause. The first one has been done for you.

1. (If, according to Fact A, extraterrestrials had visited Earth), [we would definitely be able to find evidence of their presence.]

2. If, the argument goes, there were intelligent beings elsewhere in our Galaxy, then they would have explored and colonized the Galaxy, as we have explored and colonized the Earth.

3. If there were no pause between trips, the frontier of space exploration would then lie roughly on the surface of a sphere whose radius was increasing at the speed of 0.10 *c*.

4. If there were other advanced civilizations in our Galaxy, they would have had ample time to reach us, unless they commenced space exploration less than two million years ago.

TASK 25: Using the information in Task 24, rewrite each sentence beginning with the result clause. You may need to simplify the sentence by omitting unnecessary information or make other changes in wording. The first one has been done for you.

1. We would definitely be able to find evidence of extraterrestrials if they had visited Earth.

2. _____

_____

3. _____

_____

4. _____

_____

TASK 26: For the sentences in Task 24, why do you think the author put the condition first?

TASK 27: With a partner, write a list of five conditions that are imaginary or contrary to fact. Exchange your conditions with another pair of students. Make up results for each of the conditions your classmates have given you. Share a few of your completed statements with the rest of the class. The first one has been done for you.

1. If Einstein had never lived, perhaps I would have discovered the theory of relativity.

2. _____

3. _____

4. _____

5. _____

EXPANSION:
OUR FASCINATION WITH EXTRATERRESTRIAL LIFE

Despite attempts through the scientific method to question or disprove most UFO sightings, many people remain fascinated with the possibility of UFOs and life in outer space. This final chapter explores some possible reasons for this persistent fascination.

Exploring the Concepts

EXPLORING THROUGH VISUAL IMAGES

TASK 1: This cartoon portrays one human impulse that accounts for our interest in life beyond Earth. With your classmates, define this human impulse and discuss how it relates to our continued fascination with life on other planets.

By permission of Johnny Hart and Creators Syndicate, Inc.

EXPLORING BACKGROUND KNOWLEDGE

TASK 2: Give three reasons why you think people continue to believe that UFOs can and do exist. Use the following vocabulary. The first one has been suggested for you.

theorize   hypothesize   speculate   conclude

Reason 1:   _People speculate about the existence of UFOs because they want to_

believe that Earth is not the only planet capable of sustaining life.

Reason 2: _____

_____

_____

_____

_____

Reason 3: _____

_____

_____

_____

_____

Working with Sources

UNDERSTANDING THROUGH LISTENING

VIDEO

Lecture: UFOs
Segment 3: Why Are We Fascinated by UFOs?

Professor: Robert Hurt
Course: Astronomy 3: Introduction to Astronomy
Text: *The Search for Life in the Universe* by Donald Goldsmith and Tobias Owen

In this segment of the lecture, Professor Hurt explains why he thinks people remain interested in UFOs despite the fact that so many sightings have been proven false.

TASK 3: Professor Hurt gives reasons for people's belief in UFOs. As you listen, place a √ next to those reasons that you hear.

_____ UFOs really do exist, but we don't have the technology to detect them yet.

_____ Humans need to find patterns for things they can't understand.

_____ Humans have always wondered about the stars.

_____ Scientific breakthroughs and technologies have taken away most mysteries.

_____ Humans fear being alone in the universe.

_____ Humans have a great capacity to lie to themselves.

_____ UFOs suggest the existence of intelligent beings who can explore and think—they are like us.

TASK 4: Watch the lecture again for the three reasons that Professor Hurt gives. He supports the reasons with examples. In the table, write each reason, the example, and an explanation of how the example illustrates the point that Professor Hurt is making.

	REASON	EXAMPLE	HOW IT HELPS EXPLAIN OUR INTEREST IN UFOS
1.			
2.			
3.			

TASK 5: Write a journal entry that answers this question: If Professor Hurt were on a national panel that gave research money for investigating unsolved problems, do you think he would grant money to people who investigate UFO sightings? Why or why not?

The debate over whether other intelligent life exists in the universe continues with this excerpt from a book about the search for other life.

TASK 6: As you read this excerpt, compare your views about cosmic loneliness and the theory of evolution to what the authors have to say about these subjects.

COSMIC LONELINESS

Donald Goldsmith and Tobias Owen

[1] For millennia, humans have generally held that an ever-watching cosmic force guides all events on Earth. During the past few hundred years, some of the human population has lost this view, believing instead that individuals have responsibility for what they do, even if a deity exists. This change in viewpoint, which scientists in particular have often led, has tended to emphasize the importance of humanity, since a greater sense of our own power over our lives has naturally produced a greater awareness of our ability to affect the world. We are now entering a new phase of this awareness, in which we are beginning to recognize our responsibilities for taking care of the planet we inhabit.

[2] This new perspective has often been accompanied by a vague sense of loneliness, the feeling that we are terribly isolated in a huge, uncaring universe. This view ignores the fact that we are part of the great cosmic web that holds the myriads of stars in our galaxy, and the countless galaxies that journey through the vast dark spaces beyond. Similarly, the unease of "cosmic loneliness" has led many people to reject the idea that our own planet was once entirely devoid of human beings, and that an immensely complex and slow process brought us to our present state. In fact the prehuman period includes more than 99.9 percent of the Earth's history, and therefore has the most to tell us about life on Earth.

[3] Modern theories of how life achieved its present condition date back to 1859. In that year, Charles Darwin proposed a theory of the evolution of species, seeking to explain how a planet without human beings came to acquire them through the transformation of species types. The immediate and widespread opposition to Darwin's theory among the general population demonstrated how much most people cherished the idea of an Earth that has always had humans living upon it, that was in fact created for that very purpose. Despite adverse public reaction, Darwin's theory received detailed confirmation as scientists uncovered the fossil history of life on Earth, extending now 3.5 billion years into the past.

[4] Today, die-hard "creationists" continue to oppose the theory of evolution, claiming that sacred texts show the theory must be wrong, or that the loose ends of the theory show its fundamental incorrectness. This desire to reject the model of evolution testifies to our reluctance to abandon the concept of humanity as centrally placed in the structure and history of the universe. The great Russian rocket pioneer Constantin Tsiolkovshy once said that "the Earth is the cradle of humanity—but one cannot live in the cradle forever." This bold thought remains an excellent reminder of the fact that our human attitudes tend to keep us from recognizing the truth about our role in the universe: We are part of the cosmos, but a fragile and extremely young part.

[5] Darwin's model for the evolution of life on Earth has been verified in a host of ways. But the existence—let alone the evolution—of life beyond the Earth remains completely speculative. Some consider speculations about extraterrestrial life complete foolishness: How can we study what we know nothing about? The answer to this question lies in the fact that we do know a great deal about the general principles of life in the universe, if life on Earth provides a reasonably typical example. In simple terms, if evolution made us the way we are, then roughly similar conditions should have led to the development of roughly similar forms of life elsewhere. Our study of the evolution of the universe therefore extends our perspective from life on Earth now, and the fossil record of bygone life, to the still more varied possibilities of life elsewhere, perhaps flourishing now, perhaps in existence only in the past, perhaps only in the future.

[6] To study how life might have evolved far from Earth, we must first study how the universe itself has evolved. Then we can look for the likeliest sites for the origin and development of life, and can see what prelife conditions arise spontaneously in astronomical situations. We can then proceed to consider life on Earth and the conditions that exist on other planets in our solar system. Our goal is to estimate the likelihood of life and of its development into technologically advanced civilizations throughout our galaxy and beyond. Could millions of civilizations exist among the stars, perhaps in contact with each other? If so, we seek to learn how we can join the galactic network and end forever our cosmic loneliness.

Source: (1992). *The search for life in the universe* (pp. 14–16). Reading, MA: Addison-Wesley.

TASK 7: For each idea, identify the paragraph in "Cosmic Loneliness" in which the idea is found and write the paragraph number in the left-hand column. Note that each paragraph may contain more than one idea. The first one has been done for you.

¶ _1_   a) Humans used to be viewed as being under the control of a larger cosmic force that had power over everything on Earth.

¶ ___   b) Though the theory of evolution has been verified, the existence of life on other planets has not.

¶ ___   c) The sense of cosmic loneliness does not take into account that humans are part of the complex universe.

¶ ___   d) Our study of evolution on Earth can assist us in speculating about life elsewhere.

¶ ___   e) As a result of the view that humans have a great effect on the world, people began to feel extremely isolated in an impersonal universe.

¶ ___   f) The sense of cosmic loneliness also ignores the fact that humans are the result of a long evolutionary process.

¶ ___   g) The view of a controlling cosmic force was replaced by the idea that humans have control of and responsibility for their place in the universe.

¶ ___   h) Those opposing Darwin's views want to hold onto the idea that humans have a central and controlling place in the universe.

¶ ___   i) Knowledge gained about the preconditions for the evolution of life on Earth can help us determine where else in the universe life is likely to exist.

¶ ___   j) Darwin's theory of evolution and subsequent research on the fossil record have promoted the view that humans are the result of species transformation.

TASK 8: Discuss these questions with your classmates.

1. Review the reasons given in "Cosmic Loneliness" and in Professor Hurt's lecture for believing in UFOs. What is the strongest reason given? Why?

2. Which principles did you apply to judge the strongest reason? On what did you base this decision?

⊚ Targeting Vocabulary: Concept Words

Academic writers often use words that express general categories or concepts, such as *factors, issues, problems,* or *theories.* These words occur frequently and are often used in introductory and summary statements.

SHADES OF MEANING

Concept words express slightly different shades of meaning and cannot be used interchangeably. To determine which concept word to use, find the concept word that best fits the idea that you are summarizing or replacing. For example, the following two concept words both describe parts of a whole; however, they have different shades of meaning and therefore cannot be used to express the same part/whole relationship.

> *aspect*   a particular part of a many-sided situation, idea, or plan
>
> *feature*   a (typical or noticeable) part or quality

Aspect can be used more generally than *feature,* which must refer to either typical or noticeable parts of a whole. For example, we can talk about an "architectural feature," like a tower, but not about an "architectural aspect." On the other hand, we can talk about the "most critical aspects of global warming" but not about the "most critical features of global warming."

GENERAL AND ABSTRACT MEANINGS

Concept words have both a general and an abstract meaning. They refer to ideas (either concrete or abstract) in a previous sentence or paragraph. When you look up these types of words in a dictionary, you will find that most of them have several meanings, often a more specific as well as a general one.

Note, for example, that the word *facet* has two definitions. Definition 2 is the concept word.

1. the flat surfaces on an outside of an object, especially a precious stone
2. part or aspect of something, e.g., *the facets of a person's life*

TASK 9: Each of the word groups on page 191 contains concept words that share a general meaning; however, each word has a different shade of meaning and can be used only in certain contexts. Divide into five groups of students; each group will work on one set of words (choose from Groups B–F). Do the following:

1. Use a dictionary to check the meanings of the words in your set and write the appropriate dictionary definition for each word.
2. Decide what similarity binds together the words in each set.
3. Determine any differences that exist in the uses of these words.

Group A has been done as an example. Do the others on a separate piece of paper.

GROUP A	GROUP B	GROUP C	GROUP D	GROUP E	GROUP F
aspect	law	explanation	dilemma	assumption	opinion
element	precept	hypothesis	issue	concept	perspective
facet	principle	rationale	paradox	idea	viewpoint
feature	rule	theory	problem	notion	
			quandary	thought	

Example: Group A
1. Aspect: a particular part of a many-sided situation, idea, or plan
   Element: a part of a whole
   Facet: any of the many parts of a subject
   Feature: a typical or noticeable part or quality of a thing
2. These words all describe parts of a whole.
3. All four words are very similar in meaning.

TASK 10: Choose one of the following words to refer to each of the concepts listed below from the readings and lectures. There may be more than one correct answer. Be prepared to defend your choice of words. The first one has been done for you.

aspect	issue
dilemma	facet
rationale	principle
rule	assumption
concept	theory

<u>theory</u> 1. evolution

_____ 2. why there are currently no extraterrestrials on Earth

_____ 3 the testing and observation that are essential in the scientific method

_____ 4. The reason there are no extraterrestrials currently on Earth is that they have chosen not to engage in space travel.

_____ 5. Michael Hart's reasoning for believing that the only explanation for Fact A is that there are no other life forms evolved enough for interstellar travel

_____ 6. cosmic loneliness

⌾ Targeting Grammar: Verb Tense Shift

Writers often use more than one verb tense in the same paragraph. For example, a paragraph may begin in the present perfect tense and shift to the present tense. Here is one example from the "Cosmic Loneliness" passage:

Darwin's model for the evolution of life on Earth **has been verified** in a host of ways.

(present perfect)

But the existence—let alone the evolution—of life beyond the Earth **remains** completely speculative.

(present)

Writers shift verb tenses for a number of reasons.

1. To state the effects of past events

   Since the advent of space exploration, we **have been able** to compare and contrast other worlds with our own. This new knowledge **gives** us valuable insight into the origins and extent of our natural resources.

   Here the writer shifts from *present perfect* to *present tense* to show the effects of space exploration on our current knowledge about our own world.

2. To support present claims with past examples

   Theories that accurately **describe** the workings of physical reality can have a significant effect on civilization. For example, the seventeenth-century scientist Isaac Newton **succeeded** in describing how the planets orbit the sun.

   The writer begins with a generalization made in the *present tense* and supports it with an example from the past, referred to in the *simple past tense*.

3. To compare past and present beliefs, attitudes, actions, or events

   For thousands of years people **have looked** up at the heavens and contemplated the universe. Like our ancestors, we **find** our thoughts turning to profound creations as we gaze at the stars.

   This is similar to example 1 above. The writer provides a comparison between our past interest in the stars (*present perfect tense*) and our present fascination with them (*present tense*).

4. To express comments or present opinions about the past

   The course of civilization **was** greatly **affected** by one realization: The universe **is** comprehensible. This first awareness **is** one of the great gifts that come to us from ancient Greece.

   The first sentence is in the *past tense* because people realized long ago that the universe can be understood. The general truth itself and the writer's opinion about it are in the *present tense*.

TASK 11: Several verb tense shifts occur in the first, second, and fourth paragraphs of "Cosmic Loneliness." In the blanks, write the verbs in the main clause of each sentence in the paragraph. Then discuss in which sentence the verb tense shift occurred and why. Paragraph 1 has been done for you.

PARAGRAPH 1

SENTENCE NUMBER	MAIN CLAUSE VERB	REASON FOR VERB TENSE SHIFT
1	have held	The verb shift occurs in sentence 4 because the author is comparing past beliefs with present ones. The first three sentences discuss changes in attitude about who or what controls the earth; the fourth sentence discusses the change in that awareness now.
2	has lost	
3	has tended	
4	are entering	

PARAGRAPH 2

SENTENCE NUMBER	MAIN CLAUSE VERB	REASON FOR VERB TENSE SHIFT
1	_____	_____
2	_____	_____
3	_____	_____
4	_____	_____

PARAGRAPH 4

SENTENCE NUMBER	MAIN CLAUSE VERB	REASON FOR VERB TENSE SHIFT
1	_____	_____
2	_____	_____
3	_____	_____
4	_____	_____
5	_____	_____

TASK 12: On separate paper, write a short paragraph discussing a change you made in your beliefs or actions. Compare what you believed or did in the past and what you believe or do now. Then identify all the main clause verbs and their tenses. If you have shifted verb tense, decide which reason for changing tense applies.

Integrating Perspectives

EVALUATING THROUGH LITERATURE

Fiction has long been a rich medium for stories about extraterrestrial life. The following story raises some interesting philosophical questions about human response to the possibility of such life.

TASK 13: As you read "R.S.V.P.—A Story," try to formulate the philosophical questions the author embeds in the story. What is your response to these questions?

R.S.V.P.—A STORY

Robert Nozick

[1]   The Project began with high hopes, excitement even. Though people later came to think it just dumb, founded on a mistake so obvious that those who started it deserved its consequences, no one raised objections until well after the project was operating. True, everyone said it would be a long venture, probably not producing results for many generations. But at the beginning the newspapers carried frequent reports on its progress ("Nothing yet"). Practical jokers would call saying, "Is this the Interstellar Communications Project? Well I'm a BEM you'd be interested in talking to," or "I have a collect call for the Interstellar Communications Projects from the constellation of Sagittarius. Will you accept the charges?" It was in the public eye, looked fondly upon.

[2]   Much thought had been given to deciding what listening devices to use and what sorts of signals to study intensively. What would be the most likely wavelengths for messages to come on? Would the messages be something like TV signals rather than consecutive prose? How would one tell that a signal would be sent by intelligent beings rather than produced by some natural process? Investigating this last problem produced the Theological Project as a side-effect, for proponents of the argument from design, one traditional argument for the existence of God, had long wrestled with the same difficulties: couldn't any pattern, however intricate and wonderful, have been produced by some unknown mechanism? How could one be sure that an intelligence was behind it? Some foolproof test was needed, especially since, with a sufficiently complex manual of translation, any glop coming across could be decoded into an interesting message. Sending a return message and receiving a reply would take many years, perhaps generations, and it wouldn't do to have everyone on earth jumping for joy and holding their breath if they were just talking to the interstellar equivalent of the bedpost. The solution lay in abstract mathematical patterns,

not realized (so far as anyone knew) in any actual casual mechanism and which (it was thought) couldn't be so realized. For example, there's no known casual process that generates the sequence of prime numbers in order; no process that is, that wasn't expressly set up by an intelligent being for that purpose. There doesn't seem to be any *physical* significance to precisely that sequence, to a sequence which leaves out only the non-primes, and it's difficult to imagine some scientific law containing variable ranging only over primes. Finding that a message began with a group of prime-numbered pulses, in order, would be a sure sign that an intelligence was its course. (Of course, something might be the product of an intelligent being even though it didn't exhibit such an abstract pattern. But a being wishing to be known to others would do well to include a pattern.) With alacrity the theologians jumped on this idea, gaining their first National Foundation Grant. Among themselves they called their project "Hunting for God," and the idea (about which other theologians had their reservations) was to look at the fundamental lineaments and structures of the universe, the clustering of galaxies, relationships among elementary particles, fundamental physical constants and their relationships, etc., searching for some abstract noncasual pattern. Were such a pattern found, one could conclude that a designing intelligence lay behind it. Of course it had to be decided precisely which abstract patterns would count, and which features of the universe were fundamental enough. Discovering prime-numbered heaps of sand on some heretofore uninhabited island wouldn't do the trick, since one would expect to find something like that somewhere or other; what the significance would be of finding such patterns in cortical functioning or in the structure of DNA was a matter of dispute, with those viewing man as no more fundamental than the heaps of sand accusing their opponents of anthropocentrism. Theologians establishing the Reverend Thomas Bayes Society became expert in forming complex and intricate probability calculations and in debating delicate issues about assigning a priori probabilities. The results of the "Hunting for

God" project being well known, no more need be said here.

[3]   The initial excitement aroused by the Interstellar Communications Project was connected with a vague hope that other beings would enlighten people about the meaning and purpose of life, or with the hope that at least people would learn they weren't alone. (No one explained why the "we" group wouldn't just expand, leaving people plus the others still quite alone.) After the project was set up, the best scientists went on to other more challenging tasks, leaving the rest to wait and listen. They listened and they examined and they computed and they waited. No qualifying abstract pattern was detected, nor was any message that looked intelligent even minus a pattern. Since newsmen do not find a uniform diet of "no progress" reinforcing, the project was reduced, in order to fill the auditorium for their third annual press conference, to inviting reporters from college newspapers, Sisterhood bulletins, and the like. Up gets this woman to ask why they should expect to hear anything; after all, they were only just listening and not doing any sending, why wouldn't everyone be doing the same?; maybe everyone else was just listening also and no one was sending messages.

[4]   It is difficult to believe that the project had reached this point without anyone's having thought about why or whether extraterrestrial beings would want to try to make their presence known to others. Even though during the Congressional debate on the subject, in all the newspaper columns and editorials, no one suggested setting up a transmitting station, no questioner asked whether other beings would do so. Little thought is required to realize that it would be dangerous simply to start sending out messages announcing one's existence. You don't know who or what is out there, who might come calling to enslave you, or eat you, or exhibit you, or experiment with you, or toy with you. Prudence dictates, at a minimum, listening in for a while to find out if other parties are safe and friendly, before making your presence known. Though if the other parties are at all clever, they would send reassuring messages whatever their intentions. They most certainly would not beam out on TV signals showing themselves killing and eating various intelligently behaving foreigners. And if they are really clever, then (by hypothesis) they'll succeed in deceiving anyone not adhering to a policy of staying silent no matter what. Such considerations were neither explicitly formulated nor publicly expounded, but it must have been some feeling about the foolhardiness of broadcasting first (how else could one account for it?) that led to the notable but not-then-noted absence of proposals to establish broadcasting stations in addition to the listening posts.

[5]   Once again the project was a topic of conversation. "Of course," everyone said, "it's ridiculous to expect anyone to broadcast: it's too dangerous. No interplanetary, interstellar, intergalactic civilization, however far advanced, will broadcast. For they don't know that an even more advanced and hostile civilization isn't lurking at the other end of their communications beam." Interest in flying-saucer reports diminished considerably when the conclusion was drawn that the sending out of observation ships presents hazards similar to those of broadcasting messages, since the process of a ship's returning information to its source can be tracked. (Even if a ship were designed to give information to its makers by not transmitting any physical signal, or even returning to its base, there must be some contingencies under which it would do so, since nothing can be learned from a detection device that gives the same response no matter what it detects.) It was said that if its planning committee had included some psychologists or game-theorists or even kids from street gangs in addition to the scientists and engineers, the project never would have gotten started in the first place. The legislature wouldn't openly admit its blunder by ending the project completely. Instead they cut off funds. They did not authorize the broadcasting of messages. The members of the staff had various reasons for staying with the project ranging, one mordantly remarked, from masochism to catatonia. All in all, they found their jobs agreeable. Like night clerks in completely empty resort hotels, they read and thought and coped comfortably with the lack of outside stimulation. In that manner the project continued, serenely, for another eight years, with only a few comedians desperate for material giving it any mention at all; until the receipt of the first message.

[6]   Studious observation of reversals in public opinion and their accompanying commentaries has never been known to enhance anyone's respect for the public's intellectual integrity. (As for its intelligence, this would be a late date, indeed, to proclaim the news that the public adopts a view only after it is already known to be false or inadequate, or to note the general inability to distinguish between the first-person present tense of the verb "to believe" and the verb "to know.") People just refuse to admit that they have changed their minds, that they have made a mistake. So the very same people who said at first, "How exciting, I wonder when the messages will begin arriving," and who later said, "How silly to listen for a message; it's too dangerous for anyone," now said, after the receipt of the first message, "Of course a civilization will broadcast, even though it's dangerous, if it's even more dangerous for it not to broadcast."

[7]   The first message picked up and decoded was a call for help. They were threatened by a coming supernova outburst of their star. No spaceships could escape the wide parameter of destruction in time, and in any case they could not evacuate all of their population. Could anyone advise them about what to do, how to

harness their star to prevent the outburst? Their astronomical observations had shown them that occasionally such outbursts didn't take place as predicted, and since they could discover no alternative explanation for this anomaly, they thought it possible that some civilizations had mastered a technique of inhibiting them. If no one told them how to do it, or came to their aid, they were doomed.

[8] Over the next year and a half they beamed out their literature, their history, their accumulated wisdom, their jokes, their sage's sayings, their scientific theories, their hopes. Mankind was engulfed in this concentrated effulgence of a whole civilization, enthralled, purified, and ennobled. To many they became a model, an inspiration. Their products were treasured and they were loved. Did they view this outpouring as a gift to others, an inducement for others to help, a distillation for its own sake of the essence of themselves? No person knew or was prone to speculate as each, silently with them, awaited their tragedy. Never before had persons been so jointly elevated as in experiencing these beings.

[9] At the end of a year and a half came a renewed call for aid; and in addition a call for some response, even from those lacking technical knowledge to help with the supernova. They wanted, they said, to know their messages had been received and understood, to know that what they held most important and dear would be preserved. They wanted to know as they died, that others knew of them, that what they had done would continue, that it would not be as if they had never existed at all.

[10] Only to the misanthropic can the ensuing debate have brought pleasure, the debate that raged among persons, and within some.

[11] "It might be a trick, don't reply, it's too dangerous."

[12] "Beings capable of *that* civilization couldn't be up to trickery."

[13] "Perhaps they are quoting another civilization they've conquered, or an earlier phase of their own; Nazis could and would quote Goethe."

[14] "Even if they're not tricking us, perhaps some other aggressive civilization will overhear our message to them."

[15] "How can we let them perish without responding?"

[16] "If we could help them escape their fate then certainly we should send a message telling them what to do, even though this would mean running serious risks. But we can't help them, and we shouldn't run risks merely in order to bid them a sentimental farewell."

[17] "We can save them from believing, as they die, that they are sinking into oblivion."

[18] "Why the irrational desire to leave a trace behind? What can that add to what they've already accomplished? If eventually the last living being in the universe dies, will that mean that the lives of all the rest have been meaningless? (Or is it vanishing without trace while others still remain on that is objectionable?)"

[19] "How shall we face our children if we don't respond?"

[20] "Will we have grandchildren to face if we do respond?"

[21] No government sent a message. The United Nations issued a proclamation beginning with a lot of "whereas's" but containing near the close a gathering of "inasmuch's" so it didn't proclaim its proclamation of regret very loudly. But it did issue an order, in its stated role as guardian of the interests of the earth as a whole, that no one endanger the others by replying. Some disobeyed, using makeshift transmitters, but these were seized quickly, and their signals were too weak to reach their destination intact through the interstellar noise.

[22] Thus began the grim watch and countdown. Watching for their rescue, listening for some word to them from elsewhere. Waiting for their doom. The time, for which their astronomers and earth's also had predicted the supernova outburst, arrived. Some persons paused, some prayed, some wept. All waited, still.

[23] The existence of a finite limit to the velocity of causal signals had been of some interest to physicists. Epistemologists had worried their little heads over the question of whether what is seen must be simultaneous with the seeing of it, or whether people can see far into the past. Now came the turn of the rest. The fate of that distant planet was already settled, one way or the other, but knowledge of it was not. So the wait continued.

[24] For another year and a quarter, remembering their debates, mulling over their actions and inactions, contemplating the universe, and themselves, and the others, people waited. Poetically just things could have happened. A message could have arrived saying it was humanity that had been tested, it was the sun that was due to outburst, and since the earth's people hadn't ventured to render others aid or comfort, others would not help them. Or, they could have been rescued. (How greatly relieved people then would have felt about themselves. Yet why should someone else's later acts so alter one's feelings about one's own?) But the universe, it would appear, is not a poem. No messages to them were detected. Light from the outbursting of their star reached earth as their broadcasts (should they have terminated them a year and a quarter before the end?), as their hopes and their fears and their courage and their living glow ended.

[25]   Some people used to think it would be terrible to discover that human beings were the only intelligent beings in the universe, because this would lead to feelings of loneliness on a cosmic scale. Others used to think that discovering intelligent beings elsewhere would remove their own last trace of uniqueness and make them feel insignificant. No one, it seems, had ever speculated on how it would feel to allow another civilization to vanish feeling lonely, insignificant, abandoned. No one had described the horrendousness of realizing that the surrounding civilizations are like one's own; of realizing that each neighbor remaining in the universe, each of the only other ones there are, is a mute cold wall. Limitless emitlessness. Lacking even the comfort of deserving better, facing an inhabited void.

Source: Edward Regis, Jr. (Ed.) (1985). *Extraterrestrials: Science and alien intelligence* (pp. 267–273). Cambridge: Cambridge University Press.

TASK 14: Answer the following questions about "R.S.V.P.—A Story" in small groups.

1. Describe the Interstellar Communications Project. What were its goals? Who was involved with the project?
2. What was the danger involved in sending messages to outer space rather than receiving them?
3. How did the attitude of the public change toward the project as time went on? Why?
4. Why did the civilization in need of help send so much information about itself over a long time span?
5. Consider the various arguments for and against responding to the call for help. Which ones did you agree with most and why?

EVALUATING THROUGH WRITING 1

"R.S.V.P.—A Story" raises questions about how we on Earth would respond to communication from other civilizations and, in particular, what we should do if we received a request to prevent another civilization from being annihilated by a catastrophic event.

TASK 15: In small groups, summarize orally the main events of the story. Then on separate paper, write a one-paragraph summary. Exchange your summary with another group and compare information.

TASK 16: Make a list of the potential problems posed to Earth by visitors from other planets and compare your list with those of your classmates.

APPLYING THE CONCEPTS

TASK 17: Working in small groups, create a set of principles that people on Earth could use to deal with other civilizations that ask for help. Consider the following:

1. When should humans ignore requests?
2. Under what circumstances, if any, should humans respond to requests for help?
3. How should humans respond to them?

Write these principles as a list and be prepared to explain your reasons for them to other class members. Then compare and evaluate your lists of problems and principles with others in the class. How are they similar? How do they differ? Would you add anything to your list of problems or revise any of your principles?

EVALUATING THROUGH WRITING 2

ACADEMIC STRATEGY:

ARGUMENT BY EVALUATION

In one of the most frequent kinds of argument, we evaluate something. Some of the things we evaluate and the criteria we use to evaluate them include whether

- an idea or concept is valid
- a proposal is feasible, practical, or ethical
- a course of action is feasible, practical, or ethical
- someone's conclusions are sound or valid
- a policy is practical, ethical, or sound

The guidelines, or "basics," for an evaluative argument are as follows:

Summary: Summarize the concept, proposal, course of action, policy, or conclusions. This information can be obtained from lecture notes, course readings, or library research.

Criteria: Define the criteria used to evaluate the concept, proposal, or course of action. To do this, answer the following questions:

- How do people judge the idea, proposal, or course of action that you are evaluating?
- List the standards or principles that you will use to evaluate or judge. Ask questions such as *Is it sound (good, bad, ethical, immoral, valid, feasible, practical, etc.)?*
- Explain the specified criteria. For instance, *What constitutes a feasible proposal, an ethical course of action, a valid idea?*

The argument: Explain why the concept, proposal, or course of action does or does not meet the criteria you have established for evaluating it.

TASK 18: Choose one of the following topics and write an essay in which you argue by evaluating. Before writing, complete Task 19.

1. Imagine that you are a member of a panel of scientists asked to review reported UFO sightings. This review will be used to decide whether such sightings should be systematically investigated. Using the scientific method, evaluate the validity of three of the UFO sightings described in this unit's readings and lectures.

2. Both Professor Hurt in his lecture segments and the authors of "Cosmic Loneliness" attempt to explain why we are fascinated with extraterrestrials and UFOs. Choose the explanation that you think best accounts for our fascination with outer space. Argue the validity of this explanation.

3. "R.S.V.P.—A Story" illustrates how we might respond if we received a request to prevent another civilization from being annihilated by a catastrophic event. Write an essay in which you evaluate whether the course of action that the people in this story decided to take was ethical. Consider both the short-term and long-term consequences of their decision.

4. "R.S.V.P.—A Story" is not so far from reality. Currently, some governments spend money to contact civilizations in outer space. Argue whether this is an ethical and/or practical use of money.

TASK 19: Create your thesis statement using the following diagram. Circle the appropriate words based on the topic you have chosen in Task 18 and provide the reasons.

This	course of action explanation phenomenon	is (not)	valid ethical feasible practical	because . . .

Reason 1: _____

_____

_____

Reason 2: _____

_____

_____

Reason 3: _____

_____

_____

INSIGHTS 2 SKILLS-AT-A-GLANCE

	UNIT 1			UNIT 2			UNIT 3			UNIT 4		
	INTRODUCTION	EXPLORATION	EXPANSION	INTRODUCTION	EXPLORATION	EXPANSION	INTRODUCTION	EXPLORATION	EXPANSION	INTRODUCTION	EXPLORATION	EXPANSION
VOCABULARY	• Key terms • Guessing meaning through context	• Informal versus formal language • Abstract nouns with prepositions	• Shades of meaning	• Describing contacts with people • Key terms	• Colloquial language • Describing emotions and reactions	• Expressing tendencies	• Key terms • Collocations	• Key vocabulary	• Describing leadership qualities • Using expressive verbs • Expressions with verb + noun + preposition	• Key terms • Word families	• Expressing negation with prefixes	• Concept words
GRAMMAR	• Timeless conditionals • Expressing possession and relation in *of*-phrases	• Complete versus reduced relative clauses • Passives in explanations	• Complex structures as sentence subjects • *-ing* participial phrases with *by*	• Introducing explanations with *it* constructions	• Using modal verbs to describe possibility in the past	• Adverbials expressing concession	• Repetition of structures • General versus specific article use	• Complements with *to* + verb and verb + *-ing*	• Punctuation • Coordinating with parallel structures	• Integrating partial quotations into a sentence	• References using *this* • Adjective clauses • Unreal conditionals	• Verb tense shift
ACADEMIC STRATEGY	• Finding and noting important ideas from examples in lectures	• Recognizing signals of key information in lectures	• Using a thesaurus • Developing ideas for an analytical essay	• Asking clarification questions in a lecture or discussion section	• Paraphrasing	• Reading a research report • Taking readers' knowledge into account	• Finding central propositions in an academic text	• Double-entry lecture notes • Recognizing point-counterpoint text organization	• Recognizing classification • Analyzing a topic by examining contributing factors	• Timed writing	• Comparing existing knowledge to new information in texts • Critical reading: evaluating a claim	• Argument by evaluation

Text Credits

"Genetically Programmed Behavior," "Genetically Determined Behavior," and "Behavioral Ecology": Excerpts from *Life: The Science of Biology*, 4th ed., by W. K. Purves, G. H. Orians, and H. C. Heller, Sinauer, 1995. Reprinted with permission.

"Learned Behavior": Excerpt from *Biology: The Unity and Diversity of Life*, 5th ed., by C. Starr and R. Taggart, Wadsworth, 1989. Reprinted with permission.

Excerpts from *Cry of the Kalahari* copyright © 1984 by Mark J. and Delia D. Owens. Reprinted by permission of Houghton Mifflin Co. All rights reserved.

"Jujuy" from *The Whispering Land* by Gerald Durrell, copyright © 1961 renewed 1989 by Gerald Durrell. Used by permission of Viking Penguin, a division of Penguin Books USA. Reprinted by permission of Curtis Brown, Ltd. Copyright by Gerald Durrell, renewed.

Chart on Proximate/Ultimate Causes of Animal Behavior adapted from *Animal Behavior: An Evolutionary Approach* by J. Alcock, Sinauer, 1993. Reprinted with permission.

Excerpt from *Pilgrim at Tinker Creek* by Annie Dillard © 1974 by Annie Dillard. Reprinted by permission of HarperCollins Publishers, Inc.

"Why Male Ground Squirrels Disperse" by K. E. Holekamp and P. W. Sherman from *Exploring Animal Behavior* by P. W. Sherman and J. Alcock, Eds., Sinauer, 1993. Reprinted with permission.

Description from "Social Organization in Jackals" by P. D. Moehlman from *Exploring Animal Behavior* by P. W. Sherman and J. Alcock, Eds., Sinauer, 1993. Reprinted with permission.

Description from "Avian Siblicide" by D. W. Mock, H. Drummond, and C. H. Stinson from *Exploring Animal Behavior* by P. W. Sherman and J. Alcock, Eds., Sinauer, 1993. Reprinted with permission.

"Altruism" from *Late Night Thoughts on Listening to Mahler's Ninth Symphony* by Lewis Thomas. Copyright ©1983 by Lewis Thomas. Used by permission of Viking Penguin, a division of Penguin Books USA Inc.

From *Never Cry Wolf* by Farley Mowat. Copyright © 1963, 1973 by Farley Mowat. By permission of Little, Brown and Company.

"Civil Inattention": Reprinted with the permission of The Free Press, a division of Simon & Schuster. From *Behavior in Public Places* by Erving Goffman. Copyright © 1963 by The Free Press.

Excerpts from "Bystander 'Apathy'" by Bibb Latané and John M. Darley from *Urbanman: The Psychology of Urban Survival*, by J. Helmer and N.A. Eddington (Eds.). Permission from Bibb Latané and John M. Darley (Princeton University Psychology Department).

"Witness to Child Abuse" by Joanna Simms. Copyright © 1989 Gruner & Jar USA Publishing. Reprinted from *Parents Magazine*, May 1989 by permission.

Dear Abby: *Los Angeles Times*, Friday August 4, 1995, Universal Press.

"A Doctor's Dilemma": From *Newsweek*, June 12, © 1995, Newsweek, Inc. All rights reserved. Reprinted by permission.

"Stranger Intervention into Child Punishment in Public Places" by P. W. Davis, *Social Problems 38*(2), 227-246.

"When You See a Parent Lose It, What Do You Do?" by L. Smith, *Los Angeles Times*, Wednesday, August 2, 1995.

"Wilshire Bus" by Hisaye Yamamoto, from *Seventeen Syllables and Other Stories* © 1988 by Hisaye Yamamoto DeSoto. Reprinted by permission of the author and of Kitchen Table: Women of Color Press, P.O. Box 40-4920 Brooklyn, NY 11240-4920.

From *Sherman's March* by Cynthia Bass. Copyright © 1994 by Cynthia Bass. Reprinted by permission of Villard Books, a division of Random House, Inc.

"Soft Power": Reprinted with permission of *Foreign Policy* 80 (Fall 1990) Copyright © 1990 by the Carnegie Endowment for International Peace.

"The Warrior Culture": Reprinted by permission of Farrar, Straus & Giroux, Inc. Excerpt from *The Snarling Citizen* by Barbara Ehrenreich. Copyright © 1995 by Barbara Ehrenreich.

"Deterrence" and "The Individual Level of Analysis": Excerpts from *World Politics in a New Era*, by Steven L. Spiegel, copyright © 1995 by Harcourt Brace & Company, reprinted by permission of the publisher.

Entries for *dissuade* and *enable*: From the *Longman Dictionary of Contemporary English*. Reprinted by permission of Addison Wesley Longman, Ltd.

Photo Credits

page 2: Spider web—© John Gerlach/DRK Photo; Frigate bird—H.C. Heller, Biology Department, Sanford University; Cheetah—EARTH SCENES © Ana Laura Gonzalez; Squirrel—© Stock Boston

page 54: Elevator photo: © Michael A. Dwyer/Stock Boston

page 64: Facial expressions: woman—© Deborah Kahn/Stock Boston; young man—© Stu Rosner/Stock Boston; young woman—Gale Zucker/Stock Boston; man—Gale Zucker/Stock Boston

page 78: Stranger on street: The Image Works. Copyright © Charles Gatewook.

page 98: General Sherman: National Portrait Gallery, Smithsonian Institution/Art Resource, NY.

page 133: Mandela and Clinton—© Yousuf Karsh/Woodfin Camp and Associates; Bhutto—© Charyln Zlotnik/Woodfin Camp and Associates; Prince Charles—© Bob Daemmrich/Stock Boston

Art Credits

page 18: "Far Side" cartoon, Gary Larson Chronicle Features.

page 34: Illustration by Rudolf Freund and Guy Tudor from "The Evolution of Behavior in Gulls" by N. Tinbergen, October 1960. Copyright © by Scientific American. All rights reserved.

page 60: Non Sequitur by Wiley, "Urban Compassion" cartoon. Copyright © Washington Post Writers Group. Reprinted with permission.

page 62: Callahan "Help Us!" cartoon. Reprinted with permission of Levin Represents.

page 89: Baby Blues cartoon by Rick Kirkman and Jerry Scott. King Features.

page 95: "We Are the World, We Are the World" cartoon by Conrad, Los Angeles Times.

page 111: "Uncle Sam Around the World" by Paul Conrad. Copyright, 1996, *Los Angeles Times.* Reprinted by permission.

page 113: "Reagun" cartoon by Conrad, Los Angeles Times.

page 130: "Napoleon" cartoon by Gerard Scarfe.

page 152: "Far Side" cartoon, Gary Larson Chronicle Features.

page 161: Illustration from "The Search for Extraterrestrial Intelligence" by Carl Sagan and Frank Drake, May 1975. Copyright © by Scientific American. All rights reserved.

page 185: B.C. cartoon. By permission of Johnny Hart and Creators Syndicate, Inc.